FUTUREOFFICE

NEXT-GENERATION WORKPLACE DESIGN

RIBA Publishing

NICOLA GILLEN

© AECOM Ltd, 2019

Published by RIBA Publishing, 66 Portland Place, London, W1B 1NT

ISBN 9781859468456

The rights of Nicola Gillen and AECOM to be identified as the Authors of this Work has been asserted in accordance with the Copyright, Designs and Patents Act 1988 sections 77 and 78.

British Library Cataloguing-in-Publication Data
A catalogue record for this book is available from the British Library.

Commissioning Editor: Ginny Mills
Project Editor: Daniel Culver
Production: Richard Blackburn
Designed by PH Media
Typeset by Academic + Technical Typesetting, Bristol
Printed and bound by Page Bros, Great Britain
Cover image credit: WeWork

While every effort has been made to check the accuracy and quality of the information given in this publication, neither the Author nor the Publisher accept any responsibility for the subsequent use of this information, for any errors or omissions that it may contain, or for any misunderstandings arising from it.

www.ribapublishing.com

CONTENTS

Led by Nicola Gillen, the production of this book has been a true team effort, drawing on the latest thinking, research and exemplar case studies from across the world.

We would like to thank our authors, professional colleagues at AECOM, clients, partners and leading voices within the workplace sector for giving their time and expertise so generously, and supporting our commitment to drive debate and progress as we create the workplaces of the future. In particular, thank you to Bruce Daisley for his support in writing our foreword, and a special thanks to Frank Duffy and the wider DEGW legacy, whose past work and insight shaped the origins of this book.

Key contributions were made by Shevira Bissessor, Glenn Fyvie, June Koh, Dieter Kursietis, John Lewis, Emily Loquidis, Ben Martin, Professor Jeremy Myerson and the WORKTECH Academy, Antony Oliver, Andy Payne, Stephanie Rees, Professor Flora Samuel, Illan Santos, Doug Shaw, David Thornley, Amelia Tucker Mear, Dr Joanna Yarker from Kingston Business School, Clara Weber from Zurich University of Applied Sciences, Ricky Wells, Lauren Williams and Stephen Wong Chun Seng.

We are extremely grateful to the individuals and organisations who shared their workplace experiences and stories, helping to bring our book alive with groundbreaking real-life examples. This includes Accenture, Ascendas-Singbridge, Airbnb, Allford Hall Monaghan Morris, Allied Works Architecture, Archer Architects, Julian Breinersdorfer Architecture, Deloitte Netherlands, Delta Development Group, Derwent London, DIRTT Environmental Solutions, Factory Berlin, GlaxoSmithKline (GSK), the Government Property Agency, Grigoriou Interiors, Bridget Hardy (Independent Expert), HASSELL, HMRC, Hopkins Architects, Huckletree, Leesman, Lendlease, MetLife, National Grid, Nine Yard Club, Ocubis, OVG Real Estate, Pixar, PLP Architecture, Rogers Stirk Harbour + Partners, Rolls-Royce plc, Sky, Sogeprom, Squire and Partners, Sydney Opera House, The Boston Consulting Group (BCG), The Estée Lauder Companies, Uniqlo, University of East London, Vitsœ, WeWork and WWF.

Permission to reproduce extracts from the 2016 edition of BSI's Guide to BIM Level 2 is granted by BSI Standards Limited (BSI). No other use of this material is permitted. Please note that this edition of the guide is no longer current and has been withdrawn from publication. For further information, please visit the official BIM Level 2 website: http://bim-level2.org/en/guidance/

We also want to thank BSRIA, the European Commission and the Workplace Consulting Organisation (WCO) for allowing us to feature extracts from their work.

Finally, our thanks go to the editorial team, Celia Back, Dimitra Dantsiou, Liz Earwaker, Sara Halliday, Natalie Killian, Laura Le Maire, Paul Margree, Nina Patel, Fay Sweet, Carolyn Whitehead and Jackie Whitelaw, as well as Ginny Mills, our commissioning editor, peer reviewers and the team at the RIBA – whose hard work helped to make the book possible.

ACKNOWLEDGEMENTS

Whether we'll learn to regret this in the future, the way we think about work today is still interwoven with ideas of places. It is not to say that we can't recognise that work has become a thing we do rather than simply a place we go to, but we still draw such energy from going to a workplace that it becomes what we think about first. Even mindful of rising trends of remote working, our jobs remain cognitively entwined with our workplaces.

Working life has seen immense change in the last decade — the arrival of email on smartphones has by some accounts seen the average working day increase by two hours (from seven and a half hours a day to nine and a half hours a day).[1] Half of all people who check emails out of work hours are showing signs of stress.[2] And, unless we resolve that stress, modern working is likely to continue to feel unsustainable.

Much of the way we appraise modern work is filled with guilt. Are we personally working hard enough? Are others working smarter than us? Will our most dazzling talents want to leave to work for that firm with slides and firemen's poles in the centre of their office? With so much to take in, it is no surprise that we have ended up being persuaded by the superficial impact of the most brightly exciting things, rather than the evidence behind the most quietly important ones.

But increasingly new technology has permitted us to start following data and evidence, removing some of the noise from our analysis. Using the latest sociometric badges, Ethan Bernstein and Stephen Turban, both from different Harvard faculties, spent time studying the impact a certain form of open-plan offices had on the workers of a Fortune 500 company.[3] We are familiar with aesthetically impactful workspaces being statements of intent. One of the unexpected consequences of images of the vast open savannahs of tech firms was that managers around the world wanted to mimic them. Bernstein and Turban wanted to understand how real-life working culture would change as a result of the open-plan office typology.

Following the office refit, they found that employees spent 73 per cent less time talking face-to-face and emails went up by two thirds. The firm thought they were buying open collaboration, but the way that colleagues coped with constant interruptions was to move to digital dialogue. It is important to note that the project studied does not seem to have included any staff consultation or behaviour change management, both of which are essential to a successful project of this nature. The 'open plan' approach, which is a concept created more than 100 years ago (as set out in Chapter 1 of this book) has also evolved with modern-day developments providing a greater variety of spaces, including quiet areas. In a time when work is rapidly transforming, how we construct our offices has a defining role to play. When 42 per cent of British workers say they lack a close friend at work, it is inspiring to challenge ourselves to question whether the office of the future couldn't help solve that.[4] Or whether, if left alone, our workplaces might make it worse.

That is why this book is so timely and so keenly needed. Throughout its zesty and thought-provoking pages, there is a clear message that, if we are going to succeed in the future, we need to equip and adapt. Equipping workers with the tools for the job – whether laptops, quiet spaces or wifi everywhere – and allowing the solutions we create to be able to be adapted as the future continues to dazzle us with unexpected turns.

The world's leading expert on workplace culture, Adam Grant, told me that he was optimistic for the future, because we are leaving behind the era of opinion and entering the era of evidence. As we set about trying to contemplate what the future of work looks like, let this stimulating, substantiated volume be your inspiration.

Bruce Daisley
Vice-President – Europe, Middle East and Africa, Twitter, and author of
The Joy of Work

FOREWORD

Nicola Gillen

Kelly Bacon

Mike Burton

David Cheshire

Dimitra Dantsiou

Gavin Davies

Charlotte Hermans

Hilary Jeffery

Martin Kellett

Simon Lerwill

Sandra M. Parét

Dale Sinclair

Carolyn Whitehead

Ant Wilson

Nicola Gillen

Nicola is a global practice lead for workplace strategy, and workplace market sector lead in Europe, the Middle East and Africa (EMEA). She is an architect with a business degree. Her team includes architects, designers, psychologists and sociologists focused on workplace strategy, design and change management. Nicola specialises in the relationship between behaviour and the built environment. Clients include Rolls-Royce, BMS, BP, Sky, The Estée Lauder Companies, Palace of Westminster and Museum of London. Now based in London, Nicola has worked across Europe, North America and Asia. She drives thought leadership around the future of work, regularly publishing and speaking at conferences.

Kelly Bacon

Kelly leads a workplace practice in the United States. Her degrees in business, sociology and predictive analytics enable her to provide societal context for organisational change. Kelly has deep expertise in applying behavioural research methods and diverse design strategies in corporate environments to drive impactful and sustainable transformation. Kelly is dedicated to multiple areas of research – human–computer interaction, occupier wellbeing and cognitive ergonomics. She recognises that a corporate environment is an ecosystem, and takes a holistic view in her approach to evidence-based workplace strategies.

Mike Burton

Mike is a Chartered Engineer and Fellow of CIBSE, with more than 25 years of experience in building services, and has designed many award-winning international offices for both developers and occupiers. Mike is currently working on new landmark offices in London and Dubai, addressing the needs of the future occupiers. Mike has been a British Council for Offices (BCO) judge and adviser for the Guardian Sustainability Awards. Mike has provided technical advice on many industry research and design guides looking at the future of the workplace, including the BCO Guide to Specification and Guide to Fit Out, and the CIBSE Guide.

David Cheshire

David specialises in sustainability in the built environment. David has more than 20 years' experience acting as a sustainability champion on construction projects, and is a Chartered Environmentalist and BREEAM Accredited Professional. He has written best-practice industry guidance, including CIBSE's Sustainability Guide. David is the author of *Building Revolutions*, a book for the RIBA on applying circular economy thinking to the built environment. The hierarchy proposed in David's book is referenced in the latest London Plan consultation.

Dimitra Dantsiou

Dimitra is a workplace strategy consultant and architect, with an MPhil in environmental design and a PhD in architecture. Her research and design background, along with her interest in wellbeing and healthy workplaces, drive her evidence-based workplace strategy approach. Dimitra has strong experience in post-occupancy evaluation studies in commercial and residential buildings within the UK and overseas. She has also researched comfort and energy-use practices, and the effect of feedback as a medium for change at the workplace.

AUTHOR BIOGRAPHIES

AUTHOR BIOGRAPHIES

Gavin Davies
Gavin is a programme director for digital transformation within construction. He obtained a PhD in building ventilation, and has worked in research and development, building engineering physics and design for manufacturing and assembly for a number of leading engineering and construction services companies. He is now responsible for the development of new digital tools, supporting solutions networks and driving adoption of new solutions and processes on to projects.

Charlotte Hermans
Charlotte is an organisational psychologist with a background in workplace strategy and change management. Driven by a strong interest in the intersection between people and space, her primary professional ambition is to understand, promote and leverage the human element in the design of healthy workplaces that support wellbeing and facilitate positive organisational change. Charlotte is an advocate of evidence-based practice and seeks to underpin strategic workplace advice with a blend of real-time data, academic theory and a human-centred, psychological perspective.

Hilary Jeffery
Hilary is an organisational strategy consultant and change director, with a BSc in psychology. Hilary has 12 years' experience of working with clients to drive culture change within their organisation, using the workplace as a catalyst. With a strong research and evidence-based approach to change, Hilary has led projects for a wide range of clients including National Grid and Rolls-Royce. Hilary is currently working in human resources, leading a team focused on leadership development, culture change and talent management.

Martin Kellett
Martin is an experienced cost manager for the office fit-out and commercial sector. Martin has more than 25 years' experience as a cost manager, working for major clients both in the UK and mainland Europe. Martin's project experience includes all aspects of pre- and post-contract cost management across projects and sectors. Martin's particular areas of expertise include early-stage cost modelling and data analysis. He is a qualified RICS APC assessor.

Simon Lerwill
Simon is an expert in specification consulting, specialising in the delivery of specification documentation on behalf of architects and designers that safeguards the design intent and reduces the risk of contractual claims. A Chartered Architectural Technologist, Simon has more than 30 years' experience in the industry. With an interest in digital project delivery, Simon is keen to facilitate a process-led approach to ensure efficient delivery of robust project information tailored to suit the UK and international markets.

Sandra M. Parét

Sandra is an architect and interior designer with expertise that relies on understanding clients' business challenges and focusing on developing design solutions to meet those challenges. She fosters seamless collaboration across architecture, design, engineering and consulting disciplines on every engagement. An innovator in the area of efficient project delivery, Sandra aims to redefine the way companies work with design firms by establishing project delivery efficiencies and consistencies through team composition and ideal delivery approaches that are customised and scalable to achieve real-estate objectives.

Dale Sinclair

Dale has a Master's degree in architecture and is responsible for the technical delivery of projects. Described as a pragmatic futurist, he is passionate about using new digital tools to transform design and construction. He has written a number of design management books, authored the BIM Overlay to the RIBA Outline Plan of Work 2007, and edited the RIBA Plan of Work 2013, alongside producing supporting guides. His book, *Leading the Team: An Architect's Guide to Design Management*, reinvigorates and redefines the lead designer role for the digital age.

Carolyn Whitehead

Carolyn is an environmental psychologist with 30 years' experience. A key focus of her work has been the use of quantitative methods to investigate the relationship between people and place. She has contributed to publications by CIRIA, the Health and Safety Executive and the BRE, looking at various aspects of health in buildings. She worked on the recent BCO report, *Office Occupancy: Density and Utilisation*, and is a co-author of the book *The Distributed Workplace*. She has ten years' experience in systems analysis and software applications development.

Ant Wilson

Ant Wilson is recognised as one of the most influential sustainable building services engineers in the UK, and has considerable experience in low- and zero-carbon systems, facade engineering and green measurement tools. He was awarded an MBE for services to building and engineering, and has won a number of industry-leading awards including the BESA Gold Award in 2017, and an IMechE outstanding contribution to construction and building services in 2009. He is a Fellow of the Royal Academy of Engineering, CIBSE and the Energy Institute.

AUTHOR BIOGRAPHIES

In many ways, the workplace has come full circle over the past 300 years: from the local communities where people worked, lived, learned and grew food together, to today's vibrant mixed-use city quarters with offices, homes, restaurants, gyms and spaces for relaxation or play.

But the office and people's ways of working have changed significantly in between – and continue to disrupt the world of work at pace.

Much of the change we expect to see tomorrow is already happening today. The next generation of worker wants greater job satisfaction and more control over how, where and when they work. They also want spaces that allow them to collaborate, share ideas and innovate.

The belief that people are a company's most important and expensive resource is now widespread across organisations.[1] It makes sense, therefore, that we are seeing a growing trend among organisations to put workers and their needs at the front and centre of office design.

The next generation of worker is also more digitally savvy than ever before. Total connectivity, boundless data, virtual communication tools and increasing automation are not only changing how work is done, but are also completely transforming how offices are designed, constructed and operated through smarter, faster and more automated processes. As our work is increasingly virtual, so office design becomes focused on creating a community base that enables technological change and blends functionality, aesthetics and insights from psychology.

This book is intended as a practical design guide for architects, associated professionals, clients and occupiers, and those studying to join the industry. To assist them in their work, it delves into the past and gazes into the future to understand more about how to design the offices of tomorrow, and how to put the needs of people at the centre of it all. Set out over 11 chapters, it is written by workspace experts who draw on their first-hand experience, alongside industry insight and real-life workplace and office design projects from across the world, to identify lessons for the future.

The book addresses four core themes: buildings, technology, people and delivery.

Starting with buildings, Chapter 1 looks at how commercial office design typologies have changed drastically since the 18th century, and remain varied. It takes us from the rows of clerical desks in East India House and the towering northern mills of the Industrial Revolution, through to today's iconic office towers and the emergence of mixed-use developments and concepts including agile working practices and co-working spaces.[2] This chapter identifies the core challenge at the centre of office design: how to balance people's evolving needs with the demands of technology, place, profit and purpose to create workplaces that truly work.

Building on this, Chapter 2 argues that the sheer volume and array of raw materials needed to construct offices, the high levels of construction waste, the rise in popularity of shorter leases and the global drive for sustainability are all increasing the demand for office buildings

INTRODUCTION

xiii

that can be adapted easily and that last. Today, new approaches to office design and construction are emerging, shifting from the linear to the circular, encouraging refurbishment over demolition, and requiring designers to think about the whole life of the building to keep resources in use as long as possible. Chapter 2 explores this new circular economy model alongside innovative resource- and time-efficient approaches such as modular design and construction, to see how buildings could be designed for adaptability and to reduce the demand for new materials.

With the world of real estate embarking on the next big stride forward in applying digital tools to building design and operation, Chapter 3 analyses how tech solutions, such as building information modelling (BIM) and sensors, can encourage greater collaboration between the developer, consultant and contractor, leading to smarter, more efficient buildings. But, as the chapter posits, this is just the start, with a huge amount of untapped value still to be secured across the project life cycle through the analysis and use of big data.

Turning away from the people who create and run our office workplaces, Chapter 4 looks to the people who use them; it discusses the impact of technological innovation and the virtual world on people's working lives, and how we can make the most of the new tools that are emerging within the office environment. It focuses on three main areas – collaboration, mobility and voice – to gain a clearer picture of how workplaces can and, potentially, will use new technology to help workers get the job done.

Increasingly, the success or failure of any office space is judged by how well it responds to the expectations and needs of the people who use it. With research showing strong links between occupant wellbeing and increased staff engagement, productivity and even enhanced brand perception, Chapter 5 explores how to design offices that promote the wellness of people who work in them. It sets out a new holistic approach to wellbeing at work that looks at the interrelationships between the physical, psychological, intellectual, spiritual, material and social factors that contribute to a person's wellbeing, and highlights how much is to be gained by applying these ideas to both new and existing offices.

If they are to meet occupants' needs effectively, it is critical that architects and designers have a full understanding of how people will use a workspace right from the start of a project. In practice, however, it is not always that easy to achieve. As Chapter 6 details, this is where investing in research-led design, and using more people-focused post-occupancy evaluations through approaches like the UK-based Soft Landings initiative, can help greatly. The benefits we are already seeing from monitoring and measuring a building's performance long after the keys have been handed over, and from creating and maintaining lasting relationships between designer, occupant and operator, suggest it is time for the industry to redefine 'project end'.

Research shows that investing in the physical environment, when supported by effective change management, can lead to higher productivity, occupant satisfaction and wellbeing. But to realise the power of design and the physical environment as a tool for change, you need to create the right conditions. Chapter 7 considers what those conditions should be, and how to realise them. This includes the need for organisations to start investing more in considered change management strategies. Design teams will increasingly be required to strike a balance between change and project management when delivering schemes. The authors are clear that good communication and support from senior management is crucial to any successful change management process. For them, it is equally important to make sure workers feel engaged – part of both the change that is taking place and the new environment being created.

Shifting to delivery, developers' and occupants' wish lists are growing longer and more detailed by the day, with sustainability gradually moving towards the top. Driven by tenants' desire to reduce running costs, and positive climate change schemes such as the Paris climate change agreement – non-domestic buildings account for 17 per cent of UK carbon emissions – offices are increasingly being designed to meet strict emissions targets.[3] But, alongside ambitions to achieve low emissions, delivering occupant wellbeing, achieving a high quality of design, and meeting health and safety requirements also remain important. Chapter 8 sets out what can we learn for the future from existing low-energy building design projects. Here, our experts look at embodied energy, the future of electric power, and graphene in office buildings among other trends, as well as offering practical advice about specifications.

As activity-based and agile working practices become the norm, organisations are coming under pressure to adapt and repurpose their spaces, while also doing more with less. Chapter 9 assesses the role that procurement can play in balancing design requirements and users' needs with long-term value. To reduce both capital and operating costs through procurement, the key will be to build longer-term flexibility into initial designs, and for architects to share these details early on with procurement teams.

We are already designing offices more intelligently than ever before, and Chapter 10 examines which trends are most likely to inform future office design. With a shift from 2D to 3D and from craft to automation, lead designers need to better balance design and delivery, and get used to a faster and more collaborative design process. Ultimately, good design will depend on the industry's ability to reimagine the role of the architect in a digital world.

Finally, as Chapter 11 reasons, we can best understand what the future office will be like by both looking to the past and at the shape of changes we are already seeing today, and by collectively sharing lessons learned, ideas and experiences.

This book seeks to spark debate around the future of work and how the future office will need to be designed to truly support people and drive productivity, while keeping design, construction and operation costs down. The intention is that it will become a valuable resource for those committed to creating sustainable workspaces that promote collaboration, innovation and wellbeing.

INTRODUCTION

BUILDINGS

PART I

A PLACE IN TIME – OFFICE TYPOLOGIES

**Nicola Gillen and
Dimitra Dantsiou**

1

CHAPTER

Traditional thinking states that, in the 1800s – as industrialisation gathered pace in the USA, UK and the rest of Europe – so too did the need to manage work activity and production. Clerks' rooms became rows of desks with identically suited workers, whose administrative efficiency mirrored the manufacturing processes they oversaw.

This archetype for the commercial office endured for a century, until the advent of fast, efficient IT transformed people's attitudes and approaches to work and led to the creation of new office typologies. The new offices followed an open-plan arrangement, and working practices prioritised collaboration over task-based concentration. At the same time, an army of freelancers and entrepreneurs pioneered ways of working outside of corporate structures.

If we look closer, however, the reality behind this narrative is more complex. Admittedly, the traditional image of the office with workers sitting at rows of desks is familiar, because it has been so dominant. It is also true that there has been a growth in location-independent working, inside and outside corporate life, in recent years.

But a number of other models of workplace organisation existed prior to the Industrial Revolution. For example, the vibrant coffee houses of 18th-century London supported people in the gathering and exchanging of knowledge. Elsewhere industrialists, such as Robert Owen at New Lanark Mill in Scotland, stressed the importance of the community in which work, housing and education combined to create a healthy, productive workforce.

These ideas bring humanity back into the design process. They, and others like them, have gained increased traction in recent decades. Workers are no longer seen as cogs in an administrative machine – they are autonomous human beings, whose skills and experience bring fresh ideas and new ways of doing things. As a result, any history of the office should do more than simply map layouts – it should articulate how people have become the focus of design for planners, architects and chief executives alike.

THE EARLY OFFICE

What was the first office? Ever since the start of writing and commerce, from medieval scriptoria to warehouse work tables in Renaissance Europe, people have needed spaces in which to collect and manage information – with several different approaches to workplace design emerging.

The company

One influential blueprint for the first corporate office was the London headquarters of the British East India Company (Theodore Jacobsen; 1729), which between 1699 and 1774 accounted for 13 to 15 per cent of all Britain's imports (see Figure 1.1).[1] Around 200 clerks, known as 'writers', were arranged in rows of seats in East India House's Great Court Room in the City of London, copying and filing the huge numbers of documents that kept this corporate behemoth running.[2] As Robins and others argue, the command and control bureaucracy put in place by the East India Company defined corporate life long after the company had ceased operations.[3]

Coffee and knowledge

London's coffee houses – where business, gossip and politics mingled in a hectic free-for-all – stood in stark contrast to the company's rigid and centralised hierarchy. By 1739, there were 551 coffee houses in London, with information the main commodity being traded.[4] The London Stock Exchange started in Jonathan's Coffee House (named after its founder, Jonathan Miles) in Exchange Alley in the City of London in 1680, and the insurer Lloyd's of London took its name from the house in Tower Street where its founders issued their first shipping list and insurance registers in the 1680s.[5,6] As Weller and Bawden point out, these coffee houses were the archetypal knowledge network, governed by a self-organising principle and a self-selecting population.[7]

Figure 1.2: New Lanark Mills (Clyde Valley, Scotland; David Dale; 1786)

Workforce welfare

In the 19th century, industrialisation brought with it overcrowding and the spread of slums and tenements, as people moved into cities looking for work. Although this squalor was not of great interest to most factory and mill owners, others thought differently. For David Dale and Robert Owen, owners of the New Lanark cotton mill on the banks of Scotland's River Clyde, as shown in Figure 1.2, the welfare of the workforce was an important part of the industrial process. There had been dormitories for workers onsite since the mill had started production in 1786. When Owen took over in 1799, he also commissioned more housing and a school ('The Institute').[8]

Similarly, George Cadbury's Quaker beliefs in fairness and parity informed his plans to build 'a factory in a garden' at Bournville near Birmingham in 1879, combining affordable housing and open spaces, designed by William Alexander Harvey, next to the factory.[9] Two decades later, in 1898, Ebenezer Howard developed his garden city concept (see Figure 1.3), where living, working and nature would be harmoniously bound in small and well-connected satellite cities.[10] Crucially, as Frampton has argued, garden cities weren't just about pleasant surroundings,

Figure 1.1: East India House (London, UK; Theodore Jacobsen; 1729)

but also Howard's idea – still radical, even now – of shared ownership of the town, with communal land and buildings.[11]

Today, elements of these approaches are re-emerging in the latest thinking around 'city quarter' developments. This includes mixed-use neighbourhoods, and the choice of some developers to stay and manage both the spaces and the services they provide for those who live and work there. Some developments have introduced service charges that not only fund the upkeep of communal areas, but also events and new roles such as community liaison officers or concierges to manage the interface between locals and building owners.

THE OFFICE AS MACHINE

By the start of the 20th century, the office had become a hub for administration and management. Innovations such as the railways and the telegraph meant that offices no longer had to be situated next to the factories they served. Governance of the processes of production and those tasked with overseeing them were often heavily influenced by the ideas of management expert F.W. Taylor, whose 1911 book *Principles of Scientific Management* saw logic and efficiency as the key to productivity, and whose methods were adopted by generations of industrialists in the USA and beyond.[12]

The rise of logic and efficiency

In early 20th-century offices, workers were part of a scientifically managed organisational machine. Typewriters, electric lights and telephones meant that people could stay at work for longer and get more done while they were there. Open-plan spaces were busy, noisy and hot, as clerks and administrators played their part in the quest for optimum productivity. Executives usually inhabited plush private offices on the floors above them.

These buildings looked to embody the aspirations and achievements of the organisations they housed. Frank Lloyd Wright's Larkin Administration Building (Buffalo, USA; 1906), with its striking geometric form constructed in red sandstone over six storeys, is an expression of power and solidity (see Figure 1.4). The Sears, Roebuck and Company Administration Building in Chicago, also completed in 1906 and designed by Nimmons & Fellows, displays a similar low-rise heft. While many of these buildings maintained a utilitarian interior in keeping with Taylorist principles, the seeds of what would become workplace wellbeing were being sown in others. The Larkin Administration Building was one of the first to be fitted with air-conditioning, and walls and furniture were designed with noise-absorbing properties.

By the time Lloyd Wright came to design the head office for Johnson's Wax (Wisconsin, USA; 1939) three decades later, inside and outside combined to form a pioneering vision of a modern workplace. The elegant curves of its exterior, rendered in 'Cherokee red' brickwork, exemplified the Art Moderne style, a variant of Art Deco that appeared in the USA during the 1930s and 1940s.[13] The streamlined exterior was complemented by large inside spaces, as shown in Figure 1.5, supported by mushroom-shaped structural columns and Pyrex skylights. The organic, forest-like forms aimed to give workers a sense of pride in their company and thus increase productivity. Although it is celebrated as a Lloyd Wright masterpiece, it is important to note that, within this space, managers still sat on an upper level. The building also had no outside views to distract workers from their 'to do' list.[14] The office was still a machine – albeit one of striking design.

It was at this point that the focus of design moved to the process of production. The management principle

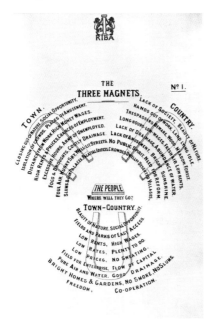

Figure 1.3: The Three Magnets (Ebenezer Howard; 1898)

Figure 1.4: Larkin Building (Buffalo, USA; Frank Lloyd Wright; 1906)

7

Figure 1.5: Johnson Wax/SC Johnson and Son Administration Building (Racine, USA; Frank Lloyd Wright; 1939)

Figure 1.6: Chrysler Building and Chanin Building, (New York, USA; William Van Alen; 1930)

of command and control dictated that people needed to be seen in order to be managed. This idea still dominates in some modern offices, despite the paradigm shift in technology and culture.

TOWERS OF POWER

While Taylorism made workers inside the office building as efficient as a production line, rising land values in cities prompted planners to look for ways to increase the density of constrained business districts. Elisha Otis's invention of the elevator in the 1850s made it possible to expand vertically. The emergence of steel as a viable building material in the 1880s, and the adoption of clever structural engineering techniques from Chicago and New York's suspension bridges around the same time, set the scene for the age of the skyscraper.

Reaching up

Chicago was an early testing ground. As Condit writes, following the 1871 Chicago Great Fire that destroyed more than

18,000 of the city's buildings, architects including Daniel Burnham, William Le Baron Jenney and John Root created a portfolio of buildings characterised by steel frames and distinctive window grids that allowed daylight to flood in while offering natural ventilation.[15]

The 1920s skyscraper boom saw towers rising across American cities. However, it wasn't until the end of the decade, with the country teetering on the edge of the Great Depression, that the Art Deco majesty of the Chrysler Building (New York, USA; William Van Alen; 1930), one of the most recognisable and architecturally distinguished examples of the form, came into existence (see Figure 1.6).

Looking outward

For the most part, the Depression slowed the development and evolution of skyscrapers. But, as Bennett and Steinkamp highlight, after the Second World War, as the American economy regained confidence, so did its architecture – taking a more outward-facing stance, influenced by America's postwar role as a

global superpower and by the functionalist thinking of European architects including Le Corbusier, Walter Gropius and Ludwig Mies van der Rohe.[16]

This International Style eschewed ornament in favour of engineering excellence and architectural harmony, with glass and steel boxes predominating. Uniformity was a deliberate choice, but Mies van der Rohe's Seagram Building (New York, USA; 1958) stands out for the quality of its materials and painstaking attention to detail (see Figure 1.7), not least in its bronze and glass facade, luxurious interiors and granite plaza that connects the building to the city.[17]

Despite their impressive appearance, these Bauhaus-inspired machines for working were little more than Taylorism writ large. It would take more progressive thinking from Europe to bring people back to the forefront of the design process.

The use of such buildings as corporate symbols of power was an enduring idea throughout the 1980s and early 1990s, appealing particularly to sectors such

Figure 1.7: Seagram Building (New York, USA; Ludwig Mies van der Rohe; 1958)

as banking. This can be seen in financial centres around the world: in Frankfurt, Hong Kong, New York, and at Canary Wharf in London. But, as work has become more mobile and now follows people, so occupiers are finding they need less space and different kinds of spaces. The future direction for towers is likely, therefore, to be more mixed-use – for example, providing more communal and community space.

BUILDING A COMMUNITY

In Germany, at the same time that the Seagram Building was seducing observers in the US, Eberhard and Wolfgang Schnelle devised an office typology based around human interaction. The Schnelle brothers created the Bürolandschaft (office landscape), which broke up the rows of desks that had previously dominated into smaller sections using curved screens and potted plants. Layouts used irregular, 'organic' circulation patterns. Instead of positioning management on upper floors, all levels of staff were encouraged to sit together.

Fostering a new approach, communication and collaboration were as important as administrative repetition.

In the UK, the concept of Bürolandschaft was introduced in the 1960s by Frank Duffy, one of the founders of the design and workplace strategy practice DEGW. He studied the relationship between organisational structure and office layouts (see Figure 1.8), and led the debate on new ways of working and their relationship to the city.[18]

The open-plan Building Design Partnership offices in Preston, UK (1968) were an early example of the Bürolandschaft principles in practice (as shown in Figure 1.9). What was then seen as an innovative managerial and social experiment over time became the beginning of a collaborative and multidisciplinary workplace culture.

Human-centred design

Where Bürolandschaft focused its human-centred design on the individual office floor, Dutch architect Herman

Figure 1.8: The level of autonomy and interaction are defined by work process and supported by technology (DEGW; 1993)[19]

Hertzberger took aim at the whole building. His Centraal Beheer Insurance Building (1972) in Amsterdam was made up of a series of 56 blocks in four quadrants, creating functional workspaces replicated throughout the building. The design was adaptable, and took team working as a governing principle to create an office building that was a social space as well as a commercial one.[20]

Figure 1.9: Office for Building Design Partnership (Preston, UK; Building Design Partnership; 1968)

Now, more than 45 years later, the building is set to be redeveloped, aligning with Hertzberger's original intent that buildings like this should be allowed to adapt as times change: 'The building has never been intended to be an untouchable artwork but meant to be a structure to bear different contents as long as the structure itself would vindicate.'[21]

It is important to note that the environmental quality of a space like this – daylight provision, thermal comfort, etc. – matters just as much as its openness. Spaces such as the Centraal Beheer Insurance Building were about flattening hierarchy and designing for smaller team units. Germany and Scandinavian countries have had worker welfare regulations relating to access to daylight since the 1950s; for example, people must sit within seven metres of natural light. This has resulted in the narrow floorplate typology typical in these countries.

In the United States, too, people-centred design began to assert itself, spurred in part by an individualist approach informed by theories such as William H. Whyte's 'The Organization Man', which called for creativity and entrepreneurialism in corporate life.[22] Designer Robert Propst's 'Action Furniture' concept, launched in the mid-1960s, is a good example. Aiming to give office workers privacy while still providing interaction, Propst's vision was of a dynamic office where different activities could be carried out at the same time.[23]

Inevitably, mass adoption caused the flexibility of the Action Furniture approach to fossilise into a single physical form: the cubicle. By 1998, 40 million employees in North America worked in cubicles and, as Saval and others have argued, a system that aimed to liberate workers had become just another way to maximise the efficiency of the floorplan.[24]

Thus, not all of the experiments in postwar office design succeeded. Ideas that put people first often came up

against the eternal drive for corporate efficiency. Even so, the Schnelle brothers, Hertzberger and Propst had succeeded in adding a human dimension to the design process. The open-plan spaces they pioneered can now be seen in offices on every continent. Workers were no longer viewed as machines, but as people with social and spatial needs.

A WORLD IN YOUR ATRIUM

In the 1990s, offices emerged as symbols of corporate power. Gradually, instead of faceless money-making entities, corporations became brands, adopting consumer-focused language to present a softer, more nuanced face to the world. Workforces also became more diverse, reflecting wider societal changes and the growing awareness that employing people with different skills and backgrounds can benefit an organisation. A continued focus on the bottom line also highlighted the costs of recruitment, with companies adding gyms and cafes to their buildings to keep employees happy and motivated.

The groundscraper

As work and life became more intertwined, the modernist skyscraper's relationship to the city appeared increasingly disconnected. Norwegian architect Niels Torp unpicked this aloof disengagement with his 'groundscraper' designs for the Scandinavian Airlines (SAS) headquarters (1987) at Frösundavik, near Stockholm in Sweden. Torp brought the city into the building, creating a mini town of seven low-rise structures. An internal street was a critical element, providing space for 2,000 staff to mingle as they travelled between the offices, restaurants, shops and sports facilities onsite. As shown in Figure 1.10, Torp's Waterside complex for British Airways (BA) at Hillingdon, on the outskirts of London, adopted the same

typology – internal street and all – with its profusion of open spaces and breakout areas reflecting BA's shift to agile, collaborative working.

The next generation of coffee houses

With SAS Frösundavik and BA Waterside, those lateral lines echoed the coffee house culture 300 years earlier. Clerks and writers were replaced by knowledge workers whose creativity and insight added value to the information generated by the organisation's processes and systems. Back in the city, laptops, wifi and mobile phones drove a whole new coffee house renaissance. This time it was freelancers, contractors and other

Figure 1.10: British Airways Waterside (Hillingdon, UK; Niels Torp with RHWL Architects; 1998)

itinerant workers who fuelled their eternal race towards the next deadline with endless caffeine hits.

Attempts to reconnect the skyscraper to the city brought public space and mixed-use development into locations that had, up until then, had a uniquely commercial intent. City quarters gave architects a fresh way to conceptualise town and tower, even as New Lanark and Bournville's utopian visions stalked their plazas and corridors. The Broadgate development in London, by Stanhope (completed in 1995), spread tall towers across a 13-hectare site above and beside the major transport hub of Liverpool Street mainline and Underground stations. Shops, cafes, bars and restaurants helped workers ease the stresses and strains of corporate life, and there was even an ice rink installed for the winter.

WITHIN THE CITY

New Lanark and Bournville were also the start of a dialogue between the workplace and local communities or places of production that continues to this day. This is a departure from the narrative that has disengaged offices from the cities they occupy, when they could be in a synergistic dance. Commerce depends on the labour, transport infrastructure and services that cities provide and, in turn, feeds back resources into the urban fabric in terms of consumer spending and business growth.

This point is echoed in the location of The Boston Consulting Group's (BCG) New York office (Gensler; 2017), which occupies six upper-level floors of 10 Hudson Yards, part of the largest development project in the city since the Rockefeller Center (see Figure 1.11).[25]

BCG designed the space to optimise the 'collision coefficient' (see Figure 1.12) – using the latest technologies combined with a wealth of communal meeting areas on each floor, including kitchen and dining areas,

Figure 1.11: BCG's employees in New York have access to a range of communal spaces in which to work and meet (New York, USA; Gensler; 2017)

Figure 1.12: BCG designed their new office to encourage greater interaction between staff (the collision coefficient) (New York, USA; Gensler; 2017)

Figure 1.13: Uniqlo City (Tokyo, Japan; Allied Works Architecture; 2017)

and the Highline Cafe – to encourage greater interaction between staff. Outside, a whole new Manhattan neighbourhood is being created around them, expanding New York's Midtown business district right to the Hudson River, with homes, shops, offices and restaurants alongside parks and public spaces.[26]

Taking the energy and order of urban districts as its inspiration, the new global headquarters and primary creative studio for Fast Retailing, the parent company to labels including Uniqlo, Theory and Helmut Lang, was timed with the relocation of the company's staff and logistics operations to Tokyo's Ariake District. Core to the office design is a meandering central street which passes through and links a sequence of plazas or squares. Covering more than 1.8 hectares on a single, continuous floorplate, it accommodates around 1,200 employees (Allied Works Architecture; 2017).

The urban logic extends into the development of diverse 'neighbourhoods' and shared resources centred around specific product lines or releases, as well as critical roles in the production process: product development, marketing and store development. These are interwoven with places of learning and regeneration, including a roof garden and restaurant, print library and coffee bar, media hub, gallery, meeting hall, and informal lounges embedded within the work lofts (see Figure 1.13). Like the city itself, the experience of these workspaces is fluid, connected and ever-changing.

Collectively, the design was seen by CEO Tadashi Yanai and President of Global Creative John C. Jay as a critical investment in a rapidly evolving industry that will better integrate their global operations, attract and retain talent, and

give their staff a wide range of tools and amenities that will enable them to do their best work.

Yet cities can also be a distraction – some companies, particularly research or learning institutions, prefer the option of locating their workforce away from the hubbub. This also offers the opportunity to provide a different approach, with more space and more expansive green landscapes.

BEYOND THE CITY

Taking inspiration from university campuses, business parks aimed to create this sense of pastoral concentration. The first modern example opened in 1955 in Mountain Brook, Alabama, USA (Warren H. Manning), and others soon followed its safe, low-rise uniformity, in stark contrast to congested American cities of the postwar period. The combination of lower suburban land values, affordable cars and cost-effective floorplates (it is cheaper to expand horizontally than vertically) proved difficult to resist, and the rest of the world soon caught on.

This opportunity to standardise in purpose-built business parks offers efficiencies that continue to appeal to some corporate occupiers today; a number of the world's most successful tech firms see this as the ideal space in which to dream up the next world-changing idea. In 2015, Facebook opened a 40,000m², Frank Gehry-designed campus in Menlo Park, outside San Francisco, USA. The Googleplex (Clive Wilkinson Architects; 2005) is 28.8 million square metres of buildings and green space in Mountain View, California, to which Google employees commute from nearby San Francisco via low-emission, wifi-enabled shuttle buses.

Opened to employees in early 2017, Apple Park in Cupertino, California is the latest example, with the dazzling UFO curves of its Foster + Partners' main building standing in contrast with the rest of the site and making it seem more like a traditional corporate nerve centre than a business park for the 21st century. These businesses rely on the rapid-firing brains of their people for the disruptive innovations that drive their stock price skyward. Their campuses mirror their flat organisational structures and collaborative atmospheres.

FULL CIRCLE

The current office landscape is a varied ecosystem of typologies. Gleaming towers, whose advanced construction and minimal environmental impact are in glaring contrast to the old-fashioned organisational cultures at work beyond the lobby, coexist with out-of-town campuses full of rule-breaking tech geniuses. Redeveloped city quarters reverse post-industrial decline with their vibrant mixture of work, leisure and culture.

Inspiring creativity

Hybrids exist within these typologies. Increasing numbers of organisations are adopting agile working policies, replacing rows of desktop PCs with wifi, shared desks and a range of spaces for informal breakouts, formal meetings and quiet concentration. Media organisations rework their spaces so that the imaginations of their journalists, copywriters, art directors and digital gurus can run free. Advertising powerhouse Chiat\Day (now TBWA\Chiat\Day) swapped the postmodern ostentation of its Venice Beach 'Binoculars Building' headquarters (Frank Gehry; 2001) for an 11,000m² 'advertising city' complex in Playa Del Ray, Los Angeles. Behind its innocuous exterior, this warehouse redevelopment formed a series of work neighbourhoods (including tents for project rooms), with basketball courts, billboards, and an interior central park and main street to create a sense of working in a vibrant creative community (Clive Wilkinson Architects; 1998).

Shared spaces

Today's coffee shops are full of laptop jockeys, although it's hard to tell whether these are freelancers or full-timers making the most of flexible working policies to enjoy a latte and a muffin as they finalise the latest management report.

For entrepreneurs who have outgrown a tiny table and expensive mochaccino, or for start-ups that need more room from day one, the flexibility offered by shared workspaces is becoming increasingly attractive. The co-working model is not exactly new, and remains popular. For example, in the 1990s, Enjoy-Work attempted to steer a traditional, facilities management-heavy business park towards a funkier, more service-orientated style.[27]

Co-working combines small office spaces in central city locations with services like broadband, printing and security bundled into a regular membership fee. Even more important is the sense of community created when a group of bright, energised people get together in one place (see case studies 1.1, 1.2 and 1.3).

CONCLUSION

The nature of work has changed out of all recognition since the 18th century. The Industrial Revolution gave way to a white-collar bureaucracy driven by scientific management, and then today's digitally enabled knowledge economy. Our workplaces have had to adapt to these shifts. As Figure 1.14 shows, office buildings are a product of both their times and the people who commission them, reflecting a complex interweaving of culture, management philosophy, commerce, technology and building design.

But without people, even the glitziest tower block would be an empty shell. People bring offices to life, and without them commerce would grind to a halt. Yet too often their needs are overlooked in the design process. That this situation is changing is a welcome prospect. Architects, designers and corporate leaders should embrace it.

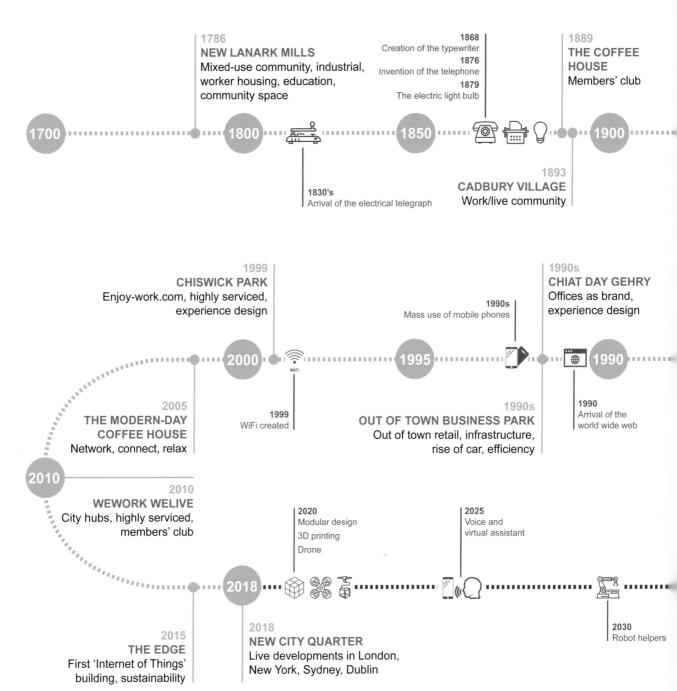

Figure 1.14: From the offices of the past to the office of the future

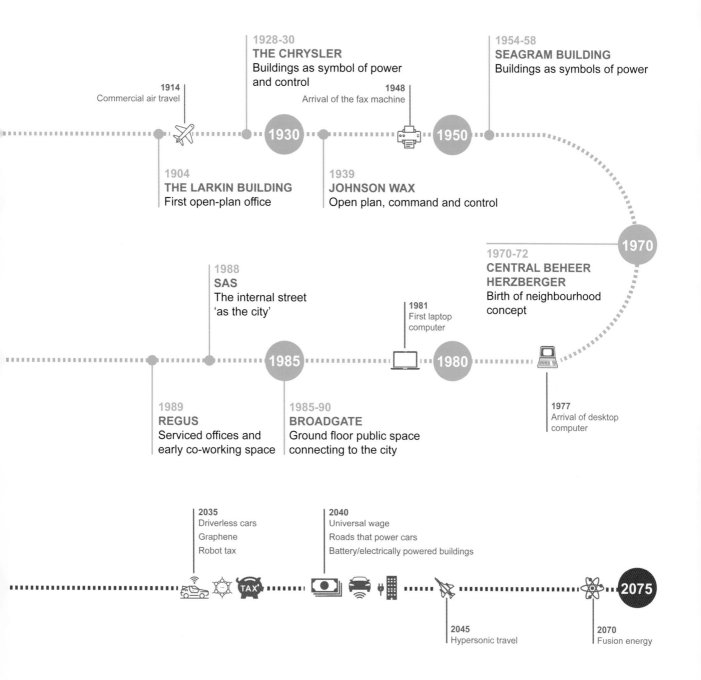

1914
Commercial air travel

1928-30
THE CHRYSLER
Buildings as symbol of power
and control

1948
Arrival of the fax machine

1954-58
SEAGRAM BUILDING
Buildings as symbols of power

1930

1950

1904
THE LARKIN BUILDING
First open-plan office

1939
JOHNSON WAX
Open plan, command and control

1970

1988
SAS
The internal street
'as the city'

1981
First laptop
computer

1970-72
CENTRAL BEHEER
HERZBERGER
Birth of neighbourhood
concept

1985

1980

1989
REGUS
Serviced offices and
early co-working space

1985-90
BROADGATE
Ground floor public space
connecting to the city

1977
Arrival of desktop
computer

2035
Driverless cars
Graphene
Robot tax

2040
Universal wage
Roads that power cars
Battery/electrically powered buildings

2075

2045
Hypersonic travel

2070
Fusion energy

15

LEARNING POINTS

1. Work has always had a social component in terms of the exchange of knowledge or goods between people, and the role of the workplace is therefore to connect people. In early workplace models, work was close to home and community. In later typologies, the two became disconnected. Are we now seeing a return to the earliest models, bringing home and work closer together?

2. The way you manage your people will help determine the type of workspace you want. You need to ask 'What is this building for?' and 'How will people use it?'

3. Architecture is often more concerned with the external envelope than the workplace experience. Questions of engineering and aesthetics take priority over people. Considerations of how people interact with the interior space may add more complexity to a project, but the beneficial impacts on productivity and wellbeing justify the extra effort.

4. The approaches of Erbhard and Wolfgang Schelle and others, focusing on human interaction, signalled the birth of what is now best practice in office design – neighbourhood planning and the attempt to create communities of work. This is about providing teams with a home base that has a variety of spaces, ranging from individual to collaborative, open to enclosed. One size no longer fits all.

5. Consider the role of the office in the city. The idea of what the ground floor is for has shifted. Place is one of the most powerful ways to create experience. Organisations are looking to give something back to their employees and, increasingly, to the local neighbourhood and the environment. There is also a question of what provides the best commercial return for developers on their investment in the ground plane. Organisations are taking advantage of the free, informal meeting spaces that coffee shops provide.

6. Efficiency should not be entirely eliminated from the aims of the design, but neither should it outweigh other considerations. Think about shifting from the 'amount of space' per person to the 'kind of space' per person, with more variety and more collaborative and shared spaces.

7. In the 21st century, are offices finally being shaped by the needs of the people who work there? There's no right answer about which type of office is best – designers must balance technology, people, place, profit and purpose to achieve the optimum result. There has been a shift in how buildings are used and what they are required to do. Staff once had a sharp distinction between their lives in and outside work, with a clear end to the work day. Now there is a blurring between many people's work and private lives, with people working anytime, anywhere. In addition, companies face competition to attract and retain talent. This means a greater focus on wellbeing and flexibility. While people were the central focus of the first offices, they became metaphorically pushed to the perimeter to make way for the means of production. Today, we are seeing a return to people-centred design and community-centred work.

CASE STUDY 1.1

THEBRIDGE, SINGAPORE

LOCATION: SINGAPORE

INTERIOR DESIGNER: SPACE MATRIX

COMPLETION DATE: OCTOBER 2017

Situated in the heart of Singapore Science Park, thebridge at Ascent is a co-working space that breaks the ubiquity of an research and development (R&D) and technology hub with its vision of a modern workspace. It is a beautifully designed place – the contemporary furnishings and high ceilings are typically filled with natural light and flanked by luscious greenery. Amenities within the space include an in-house cafe, 120-person multifunction room, private phone booths and a spacious lounge for networking and meals (as shown in Figure 1.15). Depending on your workspace needs, thebridge offers hot desks, fixed desks and generous private suites which seat up to 40 people.

In a bid to build community within the Science Park, the co-working space also extends programmes and content pertaining to social aspects, learning and wellbeing to the public audience.

thebridge is an extension of Ascendas-Singbridge Group's

Figure 1.15: Ground-floor lobby and amphitheatre at thebridge (Singapore; Space Matrix; 2017)

portfolio of sustainable urban development and business space solutions. Since its inception in October 2017, thebridge has already attracted an eclectic mix of tech entrepreneurs and corporates, as well as hosted industry thought leaders like Vitalik Buterin and Gunnar Lovelace. Building on the momentum of its flagship space, centres like thebridge will be rolled out across Asia in a bid to grow a co-working network, and will be introduced into China and India by early 2019.

17

WEWORK

LOCATION: MULTIPLE

CONCEPT: WEWORK

COMPLETION DATE: ONGOING

It is no coincidence that the rise and rise of WeWork during the past decade coincides with seismic shifts in the workplace. This deep and broad change has included increasing numbers of people working as freelancers and on short-term contracts, the rapid growth of start-ups, corporations seeking to inspire ever more innovation, and the working community wanting flexibility, high-quality tech and, of course, good coffee. Advances in technology, too, have liberated people from their desk and the traditional office.

WeWork is certainly not the first to offer high-quality, flexible, serviced workspace. There have been numerous versions over the years including those operated by companies from Workspace to Regus dating back to the 1980s. However, WeWork's focus on humanising work, creating true business and social communities, its global ambition, approach, conviction of mission and purpose, and its strong brand have ensured it a high profile.

The distinctive features of every WeWork space include high-energy and welcoming communal areas – each inspired by, and responding to, its individual location and community (see Figure 1.16). The social component to this model is key to creating the positive experience that the huge majority of members enjoy. High levels of

service are a hallmark, too – from tech and building management to food and beverage and community activities. Continuous research into changing work patterns and new trends keeps things fresh, as do the networks of sensors around the buildings. Even the furniture is part of the company's iterative approach, as well as the Internet of Things – for example, if a sofa remains unused for a month, it is removed.

The company has also sought innovative ways to streamline the construction process. It has developed a technology platform that supports the full life cycle of property from site selection to design, procurement, build, operation and activation. This is designed to enable the faster and more efficient delivery of buildings, and also to provide the data required to gain new insights from each project. In addition, the technology is used to gather input and feedback from members.

The success of this approach is clearly demonstrated not just by the fact that the workspace racks up an enviable 90 per cent occupancy during main working hours, but also that some 70 per cent of members report that they do business with fellow members. The rapid global expansion is further confirmation of the growing demand.

A view to the future

This model has the potential to be applied to new and very different markets. WeWork believes that wherever people congregate, it can bring its concept of community, technology and design to create a more humane experience. It began with the workplace and has now moved on to wellness and co-living; future potential lies in areas including education and healthcare. There is more growth in the workplace too. For example, for some time now large corporations have located their innovation teams to WeWork spaces, so they can benefit from the creative buzz and ecosystem of start-ups and other creative organisations with which they can partner and innovate – and, conversely, WeWork has created Powered by We. This is where WeWork operates on behalf of big clients to design, build, operate and activate their space.

Commenting on the future, the company's Ronen Journo, SVP, Enterprise Strategy, said: 'At a time where there are so many predictions that artificial intelligence will replace significant numbers of jobs, we see people creating new work opportunities all the time. We are looking past the robots and helping people back into the new workplace, which will be energised and, above all, it has to be where people want to be.'

Figure 1.16: WeWork Euljiro community bar, Seoul, South Korea; 2017

FACTORY BERLIN

LOCATION: BERLIN, GERMANY

ARCHITECT: JULIAN BREINERSDORFER ARCHITECTURE

COMPLETION DATE: 2013

Figure 1.17: Factory Berlin, refurbishment of a brewery building in Berlin-Mitte
(Julian Breinersdorfer Architecture; Berlin, Germany; 2013)

With their rugged aesthetic and functional layouts, former industrial buildings make appealing and inspiring spaces to incubate 21st-century businesses. This is certainly the case with the brick-built former brewery which is now Factory Berlin. In a city centre location, this 10,000m^2 start-up campus is home to firms including Twitter, Soundcloud and 6Wunderkinder, and hosts Google for Entrepreneurs as one of the main partners. The arrival of new industries in a historic industrial complex is reflected in the architectural interventions.

Parts of the main building, the former Oswald Berliner Brewery, date from the 19th century (see Figure 1.17). Its north facade was part of the Berlin Wall (1961–1989), and third-floor windows facing the former West Germany were used for surveillance. After the wall fell, the site was left in disrepair for decades. The building records were destroyed by a bomb strike in the Second World War, which meant that detailed historical and archaeological investigation was required as part of the planning process.

As a result of this research, the weakened structure of the brewery required the construction of a tailored structural system to support the new volumes. It stands on concrete stilts that penetrate the existing building. In turn, these stilts are based on pole foundations that penetrate an old bunker system 15 metres below ground.

Driven by this structural strategy, all interventions have been treated as distinct, in both typology and materiality, and are consequently highly legible against the

Figure 1.18: Factory Berlin, combining the old with the new (Julian Breinersdorfer Architecture; Berlin, Germany; 2013)

existing brewery. The aged, rough materials of the existing industrial building contrast with the simple materiality of the new volumes above (as shown in Figure 1.18).

The campus-like arrangement of the additional top floors adds a new spatial quality to the simple, large open spaces of the existing brewery. These distinct typologies co-existing in one site mirror the programmatic strategy of the Factory in bringing together smaller start-ups with tech giants and public space.

The public programmes in the building and the exterior spaces are connected by a horizontal axis. This axis intersects a vertical exterior circulation axis connecting the different office spaces.

The layout has to be capable of rapidly expanding and contracting as companies grow and collapse. By responding to this dynamic ecology of start-ups housed within the site, an improvisational architecture emerged. The offices of Soundcloud, for example, grew continually

during the planning and construction process and now occupy formerly separate building parts and floor levels that were laced together with open internal staircases, creating a continuous spatial system connecting three floors of office space.

Today, Factory Berlin continues to grow, expanding into adjacent buildings. A building permit has been granted for a new structure on the site by the same architect.

FIT FOR THE FUTURE – SUSTAINABILITY AND ADAPTIVE BUILDINGS

David Cheshire

As the previous chapter shows, the types of buildings we create and the ways in which we design and build them are shaped by the shifting ideas and attitudes, and the needs, of the age in which they were developed. As a consequence, many buildings can struggle to adapt as times change, proving too inflexible and difficult – in terms of cost, design and opportunity – to update and evolve.

The digital revolution, tenants' desire for shorter leases, and an ever-changing market for office space are all driving the frequent refit, refurbishment and, even, demolition and rebuilding of inflexible buildings. Developers are recognising the risk that workplaces conceived now could already be obsolete by the time they are completed. There is also a legacy of buildings proving hard to adapt that are being demolished, despite being less than 30 years old.

A TIME OF CHANGE AND CHALLENGE

This high rate of change is exacerbating some of the systemic problems with the construction industry: the built environment demands more than half of the world's extracted materials and, in the EU, produces around a third of the total waste generated.[1] It is predicted that, by 2030, three billion people globally, who are currently living in poverty, will join the middle-class level of consumption.[2] This will in turn create a corresponding surge in the demand for resources. Global steel demand alone is predicted to rise by 50 per cent by 2025.[3] The raw materials required for our built environment are becoming harder to extract, and their use is putting more strain on the environment as fragile ecosystems are exploited.[4,5] Meanwhile, construction and demolition waste is typically not reclaimed for reuse, but is 'downcycled' into lower-grade products, where most of the value is lost. For example, solid timber is chipped or burnt, structural concrete becomes non-structural aggregate, and even modular, potentially reusable units like bricks are often crushed rather than reclaimed.

Most new buildings are designed with little thought for the future, and are composed of complex components with a bewildering array of different materials and polymers irretrievably melded together. This lack of regard for the future life of buildings risks creating a new legacy of obsolete architecture, with precious resources locked away from subsequent generations.

THE SHIFT FROM A LINEAR TO A CIRCULAR ECONOMY MODEL

The construction industry exemplifies the 'linear economy' model in which materials and resources are mined, manufactured, used and thrown away. A new model is emerging where resources are kept in use and their value is retained: a circular economy.

For buildings, this means creating a regenerative built environment that prioritises retention and refurbishment over demolition and rebuilding. It means designing buildings that can be adapted, reconstructed and deconstructed to extend their life, and that enable components and materials to be salvaged for reuse or recycling.

New business models mean that short-lived elements of the building can be leased instead of purchased, providing occupants with increased flexibility and the ability to procure a service rather than having the burden of ownership. Building collaborative relationships enables manufacturers to invest in product development instead of having to focus on the next sale. Creating a demand for reclaimed or remanufactured components will stimulate the local economy and create new industries, while reducing waste.

Figure 2.1 summarises these circular economy principles specifically for buildings. The inner three circles show that retaining existing buildings is the most resource-efficient option, followed by refits and refurbishments. The outer three circles apply to building elements, where the priority is to design components that can be reclaimed or remanufactured, and only recycled or returned to the biosphere as a last resort. The five segments on the diagram demonstrate the design principles associated with a circular economy.

One of the key design principles is 'designing in layers', as proposed by the writer Stewart Brand and architect Frank Duffy.[6] This approach considers each of the major components of the building to be separate and independent, comprising the Structure, the Skin, the Services, the Space plan and the Stuff. The Structure is the longest lasting, and is independent of the Skin (the facade and roof). The Services is an accessible layer that can be replaced as required. The Space plan and the Stuff describe the short-lived

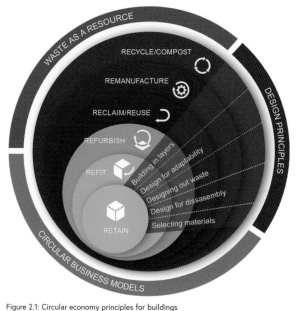

Figure 2.1: Circular economy principles for buildings

elements that can be reconfigured and changed regularly.

Figure 2.2 shows how the different layers can be separated, based on the intended life of each element.

It is easy to imagine how a more circular approach could be taken to these inner layers. Interiors could be designed to accommodate their shorter lifespans by using modular systems that can be reconfigured, or elements could be leased instead of purchased, allowing them to be returned for reuse or remanufacture. But this still leaves the question of how to deal with the longer-life elements – the structure and the fabric of the building.

Can new buildings be designed that have robust, adaptable structures that will endure? A proportion of the building stock has proved to be adaptable more by accident than by design. Georgian townhouses and Victorian warehouses are good examples of buildings that have been adapted for completely different uses in their time.

Refitting or refurbishing an existing building instead of demolishing and building new is often a difficult path to follow, but there is a demonstrable market for buildings with history. Refurbishing existing buildings requires designers to think about the whole life of the building, from the decision to build new or refurbish through to the eventual demolition or deconstruction of an obsolete building.

In the UK, some developers have built their business models around refurbishing existing buildings into attractive places to live and work, for example, Derwent London (see Case Study 2.2).

TO CHANGE AND ADAPT

In *How Buildings Learn: What Happens After They're Built*, Stewart Brand, a writer,

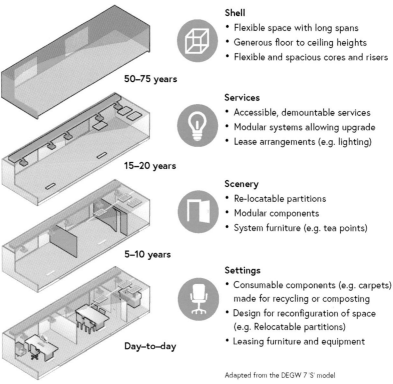

Shell
- Flexible space with long spans
- Generous floor to ceiling heights
- Flexible and spacious cores and risers

50–75 years

Services
- Accessible, demountable services
- Modular systems allowing upgrade
- Lease arrangements (e.g. lighting)

15–20 years

Scenery
- Re-locatable partitions
- Modular components
- System furniture (e.g. tea points)

5–10 years

Settings
- Consumable components (e.g. carpets) made for recycling or composting
- Design for reconfiguration of space (e.g. Relocatable partitions)
- Leasing furniture and equipment

Day–to–day

Adapted from the DEGW 7 'S' model

Figure 2.2: Layers of a building and circular economy principles

proposes some strategies that might allow buildings to be more adaptable to change:[7]

- **Loose-fit structures:** Spend more money and apply more effort to the structure of the building, less on the finishes and more on adjustment and maintenance.

- **Scenario planning:** As Brand bluntly puts it, 'All buildings are predictions. All predictions are wrong.' Using scenario planning to determine the alternative potential futures for the building will help to make the building designers think more about how the building could be used. This should help to lessen the chances that the building is so

tailored to one use that it quickly becomes obsolete.

- **Simple plan form:** The examples in Brand's case study show that, 'The only configuration of space that grows well and subdivides well and is really efficient to use is the rectangle.' Complex building forms often result in buildings that are harder to change, extend and adapt.

- **Shearing layers:** As discussed above, applying the idea that buildings have different, independent layers results in a design imperative that, 'An adaptive building has to allow slippage between the differently-paced systems of Site, Structure, Skin, Services, Space plan and Stuff.'

27

HUCKLETREE, LONDON

LOCATION: LONDON, UK

ARCHITECT/INTERIOR DESIGNER: GRIGORIOU INTERIORS

COMPLETION DATE: 2014

Sustainability in the design and operation of its business has been at the core of the Huckletree co-workspace brand. Based in London and aimed at thriving tech and creative entrepreneurial businesses, the workspaces are designed by sustainable interiors specialist Grigoriou Interiors to inspire and support this dynamic community. Huckletree's first project achieved a SKA silver rating and was designed embracing the Cradle to Cradle® and circular economy principles. Additional workspaces have now been opened elsewhere in London.

The approach is to combine design thinking with product and material selections, choosing sustainable and recyclable materials, always considering their environmental impact and reducing it steadily through design iterations (as shown in Figure 2.3). Most materials were sought with life-cycle assessments, EPDs or other third-party certifications, especially Cradle to Cradle® labelled products and companies.

Building materials such as partition glazing, timber and metal parts were procured through film reclamation company Dresd. The detailing of most built items was aiming for disassembly and recyclability at the end-of-life, which has been achieved to a great extent.

During the design phase, user profiles were created for typical workplace users, both customers and staff, and the design was then harmonised to their needs and those of the brand. Additionally, an environmental psychologist was brought on to the design team to provide an understanding of the workings and needs of occupants, and how to support their cognitive and emotional wellbeing. An occupancy assessment revealed that eight out of ten users felt they were more productive at Huckletree than wherever they had worked before.

Figure 2.3: Huckletree co-working space – interior view (London, UK; Grigoriou Interiors; 2014)

There has been a long history of designing more flexible and demountable buildings in the Netherlands, starting with the Open Buildings Philosophy (proposed by John Habraken in the 1960s) and evolving into the Dutch government's programme that combines standardisation, customisation and adaptability, called 'Industrial, Flexible and Demountable' (IFD) construction. Accordingly, these concepts have been adopted by industry leaders in the Netherlands. For example, Park 20|20 in Amsterdam aims to implement many of the principles of the circular economy. (See case study 2.3).

USING BIOLOGICAL MATERIALS

Another principle of the circular economy is to consider the biological and technical cycles of materials. Biological materials include timber and fabric and should be designed to be returned safely to the biosphere at end-of-life. Technical materials such as metals and plastics should be kept in an industrial loop of recycling or reuse. When selecting building materials and products, the constituents of each component have to be known, and they have to be split into biological and technical materials.

The lifespan of the component can be more closely matched to the materials selected to avoid wasting valuable resources when products are replaced long before their technical lifespan. In buildings, there is an opportunity to substitute technical materials that are difficult to reclaim or recycle at end-of-life with biological materials that can simply be returned to the biosphere. This is particularly relevant to short-life components, such as carpets and furniture. Several carpet manufacturers already have ranges of carpets that meet these criteria, and furniture manufacturers are designing closed-loop products. For example, chair manufacturers are designing their products so that they can be readily recycled, and it is now even possible to obtain cardboard furniture.

CONCLUSION

In the future, buildings could be designed to be more adaptable to enable them to be reconfigured and even changed to new uses without creating huge volumes of waste and a demand for new materials. Applying the principles of 'design for disassembly' and 'building in layers' enables buildings to be reconfigured for different uses: facades can be replaced without affecting the structure; atria and stairwells can be created; and new interiors can be implemented.

The construction industry could embrace the digital revolution, rather than reacting to it. As explored in Case Study 2.4, prototypes of all buildings could be explored and tested in a virtual environment. The idea of designing buildings in a user-friendly 'gaming' environment could be adopted into the mainstream to allow adjustment and reconfiguration by the users, while showing the cost implications of those changes. The design packages can be linked directly to manufacturing facilities that create building components off site, ready for assembly.

Having an intimate understanding of the material ingredients in buildings would help occupants to choose healthier interiors that are not polluted by volatile organic compounds, and would enable building owners to disassemble and repurpose elements of the building with confidence.

And of course, if the building is overwhelmed by the future and is earmarked for demolition, then it can be disassembled and the components reclaimed for reuse, remanufacture or recycling, even providing a positive residual value at its end-of-life. Perhaps the idea should be that buildings endow future generations with the precious resources that they will need to live their lives, and buildings are, therefore, designed to endure, either in whole or in part.

LEARNING POINTS

1. Designing buildings with the future in mind – in terms of the materials used to create them, and their capacity to adapt as our needs evolve – is essential to reduce waste, employ resources more efficiently and ensure greater sustainability.

2. A shift is required in the construction industry from the traditional 'linear economy' model, where materials are generated, used and thrown away, to the 'circular economy' model, which creates a regenerative built environment, promoting retention and refurbishment to extend the life of buildings.

3. Often assembled with modular components that can be switched in and out, adaptive buildings are responsive, cost-effective and sustainable, especially when consistent with the principles of the circular economy.

4. Adaptive buildings have the same user experience as permanent structures, but are designed and built to be changeable, demountable or relocatable as user requirements change.

5. Buildings should be designed for disassembly and the individual components assessed for reuse, remanufacture or recycling.

DERWENT LONDON

LOCATION: LONDON, UK

PROJECTS ARCHITECT: ALLFORD HALL MONAGHAN MORRIS

COMPLETION DATE: TEA BUILDING 2003
WHITE COLLAR FACTORY 2017

Figure 2.4: Tea Building (London, UK; Derwent London; 2003)

The property company Derwent London specialises in breathing new life into old buildings, and has been successful in turning industrial buildings into highly desirable office space. Tea Building in Shoreditch, London is a great example. Built in the 1930s as a bacon factory for Allied Food's Lipton Tea brand, Tea Building was in fact used as a tea-packing warehouse for most of its life. Derwent London converted Tea Building – completed in 2003, and designed by architects Allford Hall Monaghan Morris (AHMM) – into a series of individual office units by keeping the structure and facade, refurbishing the windows and installing new main plant and services (see Figure 2.4 and Figure 2.6).

Derwent London was keen to understand why 100-year-old warehouses converted so well into office space, and asked its design team to study the parameters of these buildings and see if they could be captured in a new building design.

The design team proposed a 'template' model that prescribed the floor-to-ceiling heights, depth of floorplate, structural grid and other attributes, summarised in Figure 2.5.

This base model was then used as a basis for the design along with some other basic concepts, which included using the layers principle to provide an adaptable shell and structure that could be fitted out independently with minimum intervention to the outer layers.

The result is a building that holds true to many of the principles set out in the base model and to its warehouse predecessors, as shown in Figure 2.7 and Figure 2.8.

White Collar Factories: generic design

(A) building height G(5m) + 5 storeys

(B) 45 x 45 m floor plate

(C) 4m floor to floor = tall ceilings

(D) 9m x 9m insitu concrete frame

(E) central core

(F) GIA = 130,000 sqft

(G) NIA = 105,300 sqft

(H) overall NIA:GIA = 81%

(I) typical floor NIA:GIA = 85-87%

(J) Wall to floor ratio = 0.35

(K) No basement, car park or transfer structure

(L) Min. fresh air and radiant slabs

(M) section 20 does not apply

(N) limited sub divisible floors

(O) 1 or 2 tenancies

(P) 8 WCs per floor

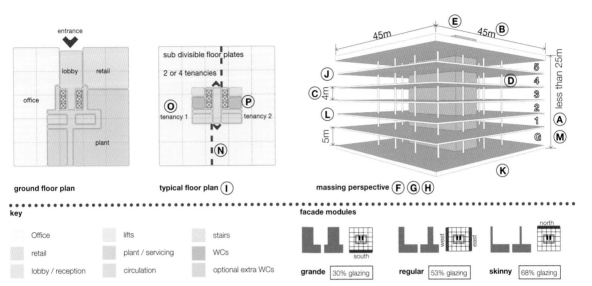

ground floor plan

typical floor plan (I)

massing perspective (F)(G)(H)

key

- Office
- retail
- lobby / reception
- lifts
- plant / servicing
- circulation
- stairs
- WCs
- optional extra WCs

facade modules

grande 30% glazing   **regular** 53% glazing   **skinny** 68% glazing

Figure 2.5: Parameters of the base model for the White Collar Factory (London, UK; Derwent London; 2017)

Figure 2.6: Tea Building, fit-out of Albion Marketing (London, UK; Archer Architects; 2015)

31

Figure 2.7: White Collar Factory – interior view of The Office Group space (London, UK; Derwent London; 2017)

Figure 2.8: White Collar Factory – exterior view of entrance (London, UK; Derwent London; 2017)

PARK 20|20

LOCATION: HOOFDDORP, NETHERLANDS

ARCHITECT: WILLIAM MCDONOUGH + PARTNERS

COMPLETION DATE: 2011

Park 20|20 in Amsterdam is the first business park in the Netherlands to be inspired by Cradle to Cradle® thinking and aims to implement many of the principles of the circular economy. Park 20|20 is the brainchild of Delta Development Group CEO Coert Zachariasse.

Park 20|20 has been consciously designed to be more adaptable to reduce the risk of building obsolescence; the careful selection of materials and components has led to a healthier internal environment as well as according with the circular economy principles, and the buildings should have a residual value by having been designed for disassembly, allowing reclamation of components and materials.

The buildings are designed with abundant daylight and generous interior planting, and the materials selected are all non-toxic (using Cradle to Cradle® certified products and principles). Large central atria provide plenty of space for circulation, breakout areas for meetings and events, and a sense of space and light. Internal green walls and trees provide contact with nature, enhance air quality and bind fine dust (see Figure 2.9).

Occupant satisfaction

The forensic study of all the building materials and their ingredients has provided DDG with a detailed inventory of all the constituents of each component. This is key to a circular economy, as it allows toxic materials to be designed out and facilitates reuse, recycling and composting. The use of Cradle to Cradle® principles also means that the building interiors are healthier for occupants.

DDG is reaping the rewards from focusing on providing a healthy interior environment that promotes occupant wellbeing: it commands higher rents than neighbouring buildings, and Zachariasse has been able to develop some interesting performance-based leasing models. He starts by offering an incentive package to new tenants formed of a rent reduction of 30 per cent, but the amount of incentive is based on the results of the occupant satisfaction survey. The idea is that the tenants are paying a premium for a healthy, productive workspace, and if this positive impact is delivered then they will be happy to pay the full rent.

DDG has set up an arrangement to objectively measure the occupant satisfaction using the Leesman Index, a benchmarking tool that measures workplace effectiveness (see case study 6.2 for further details of Leesman's Global Standard for Workplace Effectiveness). It captures employee feedback on how well the workplace environment supports their activities. DDG uses the benchmarks to create a sliding scale: if the occupant survey achieves a high satisfaction rating, then Zachariasse does not have to pay any incentives; if there is a lower score, then he does have to offer some rent reduction. The aim, according to Zachariasse, is that, 'We let clients/employees judge our work and add an economic model to recognise this.' DDG acknowledges that this arrangement could be manipulated and that tenants could be primed to deliberately respond with a low satisfaction rating, but Zachariasse's focus is to create a great workspace and to cultivate a productive partnership

between the tenant and the landlord that is mutually beneficial.

Adaptable and flexible

The structures of the buildings on the park are designed around an 8m × 8m grid, which works equally well for commercial or residential buildings in the Netherlands. The structural steel frame is modular, and uses standard-sized beams to increase the chances that they may be reused at end-of-life.

As part of the fit-out, DDG has entered into leasing arrangements for some of the elements. There are leasing contracts with LED Lease and BB Lights for the lighting, office furniture is leased from Ahrend, and the carpet tiles are leased from Desso. DDG is also working with HM Ergonomics, which is researching a full interior leasing concept, including partition walls.

Since its construction, the Bosch/Siemens building at Park 20|20 has had a minor renovation and retrofit of the showroom/reception area and part of the office (Park 20|20, Hoofddorp; William McDonough & Partners; November 2011). The circular economy principles were tested during the retrofit, and the interior walls and acoustic panels were successfully reclaimed and used in another building.

The remodelling of this building demonstrates the potential for using a more modular approach to the interiors of a building that would allow spaces to be reconfigured and components repurposed, rather than stripped out and 'downcycled', and then replaced by new materials.

Figure 2.9: Bosch Siemens building – atrium with green wall
(Park 20|20, Hoofddorp; William McDonough & Partners; November 2011)

DOING IT RIGHT THIS TIME (DIRTT)

LOCATION: CALGARY, CANADA

CONCEPT: DIRTT

COMPLETION DATE: ONGOING

Figure 2.10: Virtual reality experience of a space with avatars

Based in Calgary, Canada, manufacturer DIRTT has rethought the whole fit-out process from the bottom up using integrated off-site manufacture. Its proprietary design software makes it possible for users to interact with the space as avatars in virtual reality.

The software, as shown in Figure 2.10, allows clients to design and redesign spaces using a set of components that can be moved, changed and tailored to the users. Jim Pollard, the former

Construction Manager at the University of New Mexico, experienced the design process for himself: 'We were inside a virtual-reality system. You could go in and look at each room and look at each output, look at each fixture, look at the height, look at the colour, look [to see] if the lines match up and change it if it didn't.'

The software automatically generates instant pricing and manufacturing drawings, as well as the 3D fly-throughs

that enable modifications to be made in real time.

The software creates all the information that is required to manufacture the design, and this is delivered directly to the factory floor. Production lead-in times range from two to three weeks, meaning the team can continue designing and sourcing equipment right up to the last minute. 'We were probably making corrections up to the second week before we released the order,' said Pollard. 'Because it's an existing

Figure 2.11: Interior space constructed off-site and assembled on-site (DIRTT)

building, we didn't have all our as-built dimensions, and we had a few things that just needed to change. From a contractor's point of view, and from our architect's point of view, it was so much simpler. And error free.'

Each element of the fit-out, an example of which is featured in Figure 2.11, is manufactured directly from the design software and includes full integration of all the fixtures, fittings and services (including power and data) in the factory. The components all arrive in crates and can

be rapidly assembled by a small number of people.

The modular design of the system means that all of the components can be disassembled and reconfigured in a different arrangement without the dust, noise and waste associated with demolishing plasterboard stud walls, blockwork, plaster and components glued together.

The walls containing the plumbing, technology and equipment are all

accessible by the facilities team, allowing the systems to be maintained, adjusted and upgraded as required.

According to DIRTT, the reduced time on site and the streamlined manufacturing process makes the capital cost comparable to conventional construction. For occupiers with high churn rates, the ability to change the configuration of a space further reduces costs. Building owners can use the concept of an adaptable space to attract tenants.

TECHNOLOGY

PART II

DIGITAL TRANSFORMATION AND THE FUTURE OFFICE

Gavin Davies

As our world becomes ever more digital, gathering and applying data will be essential to ensure the efficient design, construction, maintenance and day-to-day use of the future office. Crucially, as this chapter will discuss, the growing deployment of sensors, big data solutions and digital tools such as building information modelling (BIM) across the workplace can help provide insight and strengthen collaboration between the developer, consultant and contractor throughout the project life cycle – as well as empowering users.

INTRODUCTION

DIGITAL TRANSFORMATION AND BIG DATA

As Professor Flora Samuel, Professor of Architecture in the Built Environment, Reading University, and RIBA Vice-President for Research, argues, 'Much of the humdrum repetitive activity of architectural practice, of which there is a great deal, seems set to be digitised in the very near future by architects or by others if architects don't get there in time. What will remain is the design of user experience, the honing of the processes which enable people to become more involved in the design of their environments, the design of transformations and of change, of both organisations and individuals.'[1]

This means those involved in commissioning, designing, building and managing the operation of offices now need to understand how this extensive volume of data will affect their work, and how to incorporate its impact into their routines and processes. As a flavour of the changes ahead, the UK government is driving the construction industry to adopt building information modelling (BIM) and to work collaboratively on a 3D twin model of a finished project, incorporating data and information that can be used throughout its life.[2]

The result will be that the traditional process of planning and designing a new office will be turned inside out. Rather than focusing on floorplate square metres and the exterior aesthetic, design emphasis will be on the ambitions for the office in use, from energy demand, sustainability and emissions, to the creation of spaces that can be used flexibly and updated easily.

To this end, sensors to gather the necessary data for efficient operation will need to be incorporated into the design early on, for reasons of both neatness and efficiency. This will require a more in-depth understanding by an office's designer and constructor of what owners and tenants want from their new building in use.

Meanwhile, as the growth of machine learning enables computers to take on much of the detailed legwork for engineering design and internal fit-out, this frees engineers and architects to concentrate on the creative aspects that will produce an individual, high-quality office environment. At the same time, data gathered from existing offices in use will increasingly inform the brief for new office buildings. Architects and engineers will need to become adept at understanding data about building performance and use, and demonstrating how such data supports their design ideas.

THE CHANGING DATA LANDSCAPE

Of course, computers have long been used as a design tool – for crunching data and producing information, drawings and models, all of which were once done by hand. But we are now taking the next big digital step. This will involve making intelligent use of the large volume of information-rich data generated during the operation of machinery, products and structures.

For example, considering anything from office printers and phones to air-conditioning systems and building security networks, the capture and interrogation of data will make it possible to diagnose problems, perform self-repair or alert maintenance crews, tailor and personalise environments, continually assess and improve security, and much more besides.

This is just the start. Currently, the construction industry is only scratching the surface of the value that could be created through the use of data. The potential is huge, with the right data gathering and interpretation. Take office occupancy, for instance. Many businesses operate an agile working and desk-sharing system across locations. As AECOM's global database of Time Utilisation Studies (TUS)[SM] shows, often Fridays are the quietest day of the week, and so heating and lighting can be adjusted to the meet the needs of the lower staff numbers, thereby reducing unnecessary costs and emissions (see Case Study 10.2: Time Utilisation Study[SM]).

Similarly, office-space temperatures are often controlled to fixed settings, but the use of live data combined with intelligent use of historical data about the thermal performance of the building under different external temperatures and with differing numbers of occupants could enable the building to be more responsive, providing a more comfortable environment, and resulting in lower bills.

More widely, as data-in-use is gathered and leveraged more extensively, it is not a big leap to assume that the amount of office space required by businesses will reduce and produce real-estate cost savings.

DATA THROUGHOUT THE ASSET LIFE CYCLE – THE 'DIGITAL THREAD'

Digital data is starting to enable more value to be extracted across a project life cycle, but this will only be successful if it is part of a fully integrated approach. Conversely, efficiencies throughout the project life cycle rely on a seamless digital thread which ensures that value is retained and enhanced from design through to construction, then operations and maintenance and beyond.

Building information modelling

Building information modelling (BIM) 'sits at the heart of digital transformation in the built environment' and is 'a core element of the UK government's Digital Built Britain strategy'.[3] The UK government is currently recognised worldwide as a leading proponent of BIM in infrastructure.

According to the BSI's Guide to BIM Level 2, 'BIM involves the use of digital tools to collaboratively manage information and data across the entire lifecycle of built environment assets' including future offices.[4] 'It is a process – enabled by technology – that focuses on outcomes and derives value from open, shareable asset information.'

'At its core, BIM uses 3D models with attached data and information to connect and share information efficiently across the supply chain', reducing the risk of error, maximising the project team's

ability to innovate, and driving efficiency, transparency and productivity.[5]

The UK government mandated the use of BIM Level 2 (see 'The different levels of BIM' below) in government projects from April 2016 in a strategy aimed at accelerating the UK construction industry's general adoption of the software tool. This has been succeeded by a 2020 target to increase the maturity of BIM Level 2 implementation across government to a point that supports development of BIM Level 3, with a view to government adoption at a later date.

'At this maturity level, all disciplines and contributors to a project would be able to access, modify and transact using a single shared project model, held centrally,

which would remove the remaining risks of conflicting information and support the development of whole-life approaches.'

With BIM at this level, the BSI reports: 'We will increasingly see advanced data analytics help to plan, deliver, maintain and operate new and existing infrastructure more effectively, built at lower cost and operated and maintained more efficiently. The use of design and construction automation, robotics, additive technologies and virtual/augmented reality simulation modelling would increasingly become second nature.'[6]

The expectation is that leading organisations involved in infrastructure, including those with their eyes on delivering the office of the future, will be

THE DIFFERENT LEVELS OF BIM

BIM is at the heart of the UK government's industry vision, called Construction 2025. This has set targets, including lower costs – a 33 per cent reduction in the initial cost of construction and the whole-life cost of built assets; faster delivery – a 50 per cent reduction in the overall time, from inception to completion, for newbuild and refurbished assets; and lower emissions – a 50 per cent reduction in greenhouse gas emissions in the built environment.[7]

Level 0 – use of 2D CAD drafting with paper-based or electronic print information and data exchange. BSI says this covers traditional ways of

working that are enhanced only by technology to speed up the production and exchange of drawings. All changes, checks and interfaces across disciplines are manual.[8]

Level 1 – use of a mixture of 2D or 3D CAD backed by a common data environment for electronic sharing of drawings and data with a standardised data structure and format managed to BS1192:2007+A2:2016. This means collaboration is limited between disciplines, with each controlling and issuing its own information, either as 3D models or 2D drawings derived from those models, according to BSI.[9]

Level 2 – collaborative working across disciplines with all parties using 3D BIM models, integrated but not necessarily shared. Clients will have to be able to define and use data, and the industry will need to adopt common ways of working based on standard data file formats. All parties will embrace collaborative working and use 3D, data-loaded models to integrate and exchange information.[10]

**Level 3 – fully collaborative working across all disciplines using a single, shared project model, held centrally and accessible to all to modify and share

data.** BSI explains that this means all disciplines and contributors to a project will be able to access, modify and transact using a single, shared project model, held centrally, which would remove the remaining risks of conflicting information and support the development of whole-life approaches.[11]

Beyond BIM Level 3. The concept of 4D BIM has become a buzzword in recent years. This equates to the use of BIM data to analyse time; beyond this is 5D, which includes cost management, and 6D for facilities management. There is no current timescale for their introduction.

setting their sights on BIM Level 3 and beyond, while the 'trailing edge' of the supply chain, in particular second- and third-tier sub-consultants and contractors, will be pushing to meet BIM Level 2 as soon as possible.

The impact of BIM is likely to be profound; not only will it improve the quality and efficiency of the design process, but it is likely to change the culture and processes of architects and other building specialists, resulting in improved communication, reduced costs and greater certainty for clients.[12]

Designing for data and flexibility

In the past, offices were designed without specific consideration for future data needs. For example, a building management system that controls air temperature may have limited capacity to capture and record data in real time and use it to improve future performance. A more meaningful approach to sensor data capture, storage and accessibility needs to be designed in, both within the BIM model and embedded in the physical office building from the start. This will improve payback, as the installation of sensors is relatively inexpensive if carried out during construction, but they are more expensive and difficult to retrofit. The advice to clients and designers is to consider the data required to operate the office (taking into account, where possible, potential future requirements too), and make sure that the ability to capture, retain, access and use sensors features in plans from the beginning.

The range of sensors for consideration should be broad, and should include not just those in familiar use, such as temperature, air-flow, humidity, carbon dioxide and motion sensors (already commonly used to control lighting), but also more advanced sensors detecting the presence of people, in order to assess occupancy in much greater detail.

In terms of building management services (BMS), data can be used to fine-tune networks and systems, enabling the building to operate more efficiently. The BMS software could potentially learn, continually refining the rules and getting better at delivering an environment attuned to the people working in the office.

And the same BMS, using data from sensors, control gates, cameras, wifi logins and other Internet of Things devices, could be dynamic about improving seating options and supporting team working by grouping people together, displaying in real time which spaces are occupied, and guiding each staff member on where to sit with colleagues, having learned their personal preferences. Mobile devices and apps already capture and act on personal preferences, so this is nothing new. Moreover, reviewing the pattern of space use provided by such sensors over time would help building managers achieve an efficient use of the space while ensuring that individuals are always able to find the type of workspace they need.

Data during construction

The construction industry has made limited use of digital technology to capture data during the erection of office buildings. It has started to use digital engineering to support construction planning for some projects, for example, using virtual construction to demonstrate how a structure can be built in reality. This will soon become the norm, with an increasing level of sophistication. Data gathering on site via scanners or drones will also track progress against plan. And proximity sensors fitted to hard hats are already starting to support health and safety programmes.

For the future successful operation of the office, updates to the digital model during construction are vital, so that owners and operators are handed an as-built twin version in model form. Currently, it is usually the case that those maintaining and operating a building conduct their own audit to put the asset information in a format they can use. In the future, this asset information will be located within the validated as-built BIM digital model.

TOP SEVEN BENEFITS FROM DIGITAL TRANSFORMATION AND BIG DATA

1. A higher quality of environment for individual users.

2. Reduced total cost of ownership.

3. Cost of operation and maintenance will go down with better understanding of data.

4. The ability to learn from how an office performs in a much more systematic way, enabling continuous improvement.

5. Data will facilitate the efficient adaptation of an office building through the understanding it provides of how the building works in use.

6. Digital twin models will be able to run different use scenarios to aid designers' understanding of how to create higher quality environments.

7. The digital twin model will be able to trial options for refit, adaptation and change of use.

SYDNEY OPERA HOUSE – BUILDING INFORMATION MODELLING

CASE STUDY 3.1

LOCATION: SYDNEY, AUSTRALIA

TEAM (BIM): LED BY AECOM, INCLUDES THE UK-BASED BIM ACADEMY, CO-FOUNDED BY NORTHUMRIA UNIVERSITY AND RYDER ARCHITECTURE, AND LIFE-CYCLE SOFTWARE DEVELOPER ECODOMUS

To help guide the design, construction, operation and maintenance of the future office, BIM will play a central role. The potential of this technology as a single source of truth is already being explored for existing and new buildings. An example of its application is in one of the world's most iconic structures – the Sydney Opera House (Sydney, Australia; Jørn Utzon; 1973) (see Figure 3.1).

The new system is web-based, and is being developed as part of the Opera House's ongoing upgrade – called the Decade of Renewal – to celebrate its 50th anniversary in 2023.

As part of creating the new data-driven management system, a vast archive of historic material – from microfiche to original drawings to stacks of manuals and electronic media – has been digitised and drawn together in one central store. Far from being just a historical record, this material is crucial to the future. It has contributed to the ongoing creation of a full and interactive 3D digital model of the building, constructed using BIM, which streamlines maintenance, guides ongoing development and optimises use of the highly complex building. The single interface is a custom and pioneering solution and, together with providing an immediate response to the venue's needs, it also has the capacity to grow and evolve as those needs change.

The information is accessible from handheld devices and is used in a variety of ways. Maintenance workers can use it to receive repair orders for equipment, access technical manuals and other information, make repairs and mark a job as complete. For example, the model makes it possible to call up any element, from an air-conditioning unit to a light fitting, in any part of the building, and there on the screen is its entire history and specification.

The team that helped Sydney Opera House pull together this vast and virtual store of knowledge is led by AECOM and includes the UK-based BIM Academy, co-founded by Northumbria University and Ryder Architecture, and life-cycle software developer EcoDomus. Other team members are based in the United States, Russia and Australia.

Figure 3.1: BIM is playing an integral role in the ongoing upgrade of Sydney Opera House (Sydney, Australia; Jørn Utzon; 1973)

Digitally enabled operations and maintenance

One of the goals when developing a new office should be to maximise staff productivity by enhancing occupant wellbeing, and by making it easier for users to create an environment that works for them. Localised data gathering can, for example, enable temperature control to be changed from a system based on an average for the whole building to a system that allows local adjustments to suit individual needs.

The data-driven building will require a different type of facilities management (FM) that makes much greater use of data science. With data about users and mechanical plant performance gathered by sensors, combined with a digital twin model, the future FM data scientists will be able to detect when building performance is less than optimum, or

when key equipment is about to break down. Using the digital twin and data, the FM data scientist will be able to cut costs, increase staff productivity and add value to an office in a way that will turn building operations and maintenance into one of the leading roles in the office hierarchy.

Capturing data-in-use and using it to inform future projects

Once data-in-use is captured and used by intelligent systems to better adapt the office building to suit its inhabitants, the obvious next step will be to use it to inform the process of office design. The big tech-enabled companies like Google and Amazon which already have an interest in data are likely to be implementing this early, along with developers who have a pipeline of new projects – it's simply good business. If a building is being used more efficiently and

delivering an individualised environment that people like and that adds value, people will want those offices, and it's a win-win situation. Expect office standards to change in response. And designers may need to challenge their own beliefs, because data will show how buildings are actually used, rather than how designers thought they would be used.

CONCLUSION

The data landscape of buildings is changing through the use of building information modelling (BIM), building sensors generating 'big data', and intelligent building management systems (BMS); these technologies will profoundly alter the role of building designers and building managers. The top seven benefits from digital transformation and big data, on page 46 and the box below, show some of the key benefits and important challenges of this digital transformation for building professionals.

FIVE KEY CHALLENGES FROM DIGITAL TRANSFORMATION AND BIG DATA

1. Managing the sensitivity of people around data collection and the use of cameras.

2. At the moment the vision is evolution rather than revolution, but what

are the disruptors – will everyone be working in their kitchens or co-locating?

3. Designers will need to become proficient in using digital engineering

tools such as BIM, which will be the fundamental tool of architecture and design.

4. Engineers will need to develop their understanding of new

kinds of building data.

5. Architects will need to develop their understanding and use of data to support their design decisions.

LEARNING POINTS

1. Data will drive design. Feedback through the capture, analysis and interpretation of data from previous and current projects will impact directly on new projects.

2. Data collection has to be designed in at the start. Retrofitting for data capture and analysis is less efficient and can potentially have less impact than if it is planned from the start.

3. Designers need to be able to interpret data and use it to confirm or guide their design decisions. Tools to analyse and interpret data must produce outputs that are actionable.

4. As the office building becomes more intelligent, users will expect more individualised management of the office environment. Localised control of offices based on personal preferences will be enabled through new technologies.

5. Accurate BIM will be the key to running an office efficiently. An accurate digital twin will enhance office performance both for the users and the operations and maintenance (O&M) teams.

6. Facilities management will rely heavily on data in the future. Data-gathering tools such as the Time Utilisation Study^{SM} will become integrated into BIM systems, enabling a step-change improvement to office FM.

49

THE EDGE – DELOITTE NETHERLANDS HEADQUARTERS

LOCATION: AMSTERDAM, THE NETHERLANDS

ARCHITECT: PLP ARCHITECTURE IN COLLABORATION WITH OVG REAL ESTATE, THE DEVELOPER

COMPLETION DATE: NOVEMBER 2014

Figure 3.2: The Edge (Amsterdam, Netherlands; PLP Architecture; 2014)

An eye on the future

How do you create a workplace to stand the test of time, when the technologies we use and the ways in which we need to live and work are changing so rapidly? This was the challenge Deloitte Netherlands put to PLP Architecture and developer OVG Real Estate when planning its new headquarters in Amsterdam.

The brief was to bring together Deloitte staff working throughout the city into a single central location, and to deliver a space built to the highest environmental standards and fitted with the latest technologies to ensure it would be managed and used in the most productive, efficient, sustainable and healthiest ways possible.

Working in close collaboration not just with the client but also investors, suppliers, regulators and delivery partners, the team designed and delivered The Edge – now recognised as one of the world's greenest and most groundbreaking buildings (see Figure 3.2).

Born in the digital age, The Edge exemplifies the often unseen ways in which technology, environment and human behaviour impact on, and shape, each other. Crucially, The Edge has the capability to adapt as these elements evolve in the days, weeks and years to come.

A smart way to work

If one word sums up The Edge, it is connection. Every digital solution and system that runs through the building –

- ★ A flexible, smart and sustainable building, fitted with 28,000 sensors, and designed to adapt to users' needs
- ★ Built for Deloitte as its main tenant, consolidating offices from across the city, and located in Amsterdam's Zuidas business district
- ★ Secured a BREEAM New Construction rating of Outstanding, and score of 98.36 per cent, raising global standards
- ★ Comprises 40,000 square metres, 25 per cent of which is allocated to meeting spaces
- ★ Provides access to a restaurant and cafe, game rooms, meeting and conference facilities, and parking areas for cars and bicycles

from its lighting and heating to security and drinks machines – is connected to the Internet of Things and controlled by a single network, viewable to the building's managers via central dashboards.

This is made possible by the tens of thousands of smart sensors fitted throughout the building, generating gigabytes of data, which give Deloitte insight into how the building is operating, and its employees' relationship with it.

The Edge's LED lighting system is just one industry-leading innovation. Created specifically for this project, in collaboration with Philips, this IP-based network, which runs via Ethernet, is made up of 6,000 luminaires – 50 per cent of which are fitted with smart sensors – and helps monitor, among other factors, temperature, movement and light within the building.

The information produced is then used to direct everything from the cleaning and maintenance of The Edge to its security and protection. For example, The Edge uses small robots – which can be controlled remotely or run automatically – to roam the floors at night, and identify potential security issues or inform staff of false alarms if the system is accidentally tripped.

A space that works for you

The building's tech empowers occupants on a personal level, too. Via a smartphone app, employees are able to view their work schedules; access the building and its facilities, including the gym; identify and secure parking spaces; track down colleagues; and locate a desk and locker to serve as their base for the day.

With just over 1,000 desks for use by around 2,500 Deloitte staff, the app combined with the range of other areas available for focused, collaborative, in-person or virtual work, ensures that the space is being used as efficiently as possible, and promotes social interaction.

In addition, occupants are able to fine-tune the lighting and heating in their preferred work areas – which will adapt as they arrive.

Setting a new global standard

From top to bottom, the building is working hard to eliminate waste and increase energy efficiency. For example, when sections of The Edge are unoccupied, energy usage in these areas is reduced almost to zero. Meanwhile, the catering facilities rely on real-time data, traffic, weather and other insights to predict lunchtime demand every day – cutting food waste and costs.

The Edge is 'energy positive', which means it produces more energy than it needs, drawing on photovoltaic panels placed on its own roof and south-facing facade, as well as those used by the nearby University of Amsterdam.

The building uses an aquifer thermal storage system to meet its heating and cooling requirements, alongside a heat pump that boosts efficiency, and reuses rainwater collected from its roof and balconies.

The atrium at the core of the building helps to fill the space with light, and every work area is situated within seven metres of a window, while materials such as mesh panels between each floor aid natural ventilation.

ACCENTURE LIQUID STUDIO/ DIGITAL HUB

LOCATION: MADRID, SPAIN
ARCHITECT: AECOM
COMPLETION DATE: 2018

Figure 3.3: Garage doors and a trolley of planter boxes have been used instead of traditional partitions to separate the various working spaces (AECOM; Madrid, Spain; 2018)

Creating the conditions for innovation is a top priority for many businesses today. Professional services company Accenture has invested in a suite of creative spaces where its own team members work and collaborate with clients, digital partners, universities and start-ups. These spaces are in major cities worldwide, from Singapore to Stockholm, and Moscow to Milan. One of the built versions of the company's vision, called the Digital Hub, was completed in Madrid in 2017. The vision is that, 'Digital Hub brings together

key elements of the Accenture Innovation Architecture to invent, develop and deliver disruptive innovations in order to accelerate clients' digital transformation'. The concept is to create a flexible, comfortable, inspiring, digitally enabled and well-connected space that will help accelerate solution finding and delivery. At the Digital Hub in Madrid, Accenture can provide access to more than 500 Spanish start-ups through the Accenture Open Innovation programme, and other players in the ecosystem

including pure digital companies and top university professionals.

The 1,700m² space is devoted to co-creating innovations with clients by bringing together digital technologies with the strongest business ideas. This goal is pursued every day by more than 260 professionals who work there and reflect 'Accenture's diverse universe': the Hub hosts more than 30 different professions, four generations and ten nationalities in more than 20 interconnected teams. Accenture has developed a disruptive methodology and a set of experiences that will help organisations increase the effectiveness of their approach to innovation, accelerate the speed of implementation and improve and measure results.

The space is provided with a kit of parts: modular elements including desks that can be moved and configured into many different shapes for large or small teams, screens, space dividers, shelving, breakout seating, standalone phone booths, and one-to-one meeting modules (as shown in Figure 3.3, Figure 3.4 and Figure 3.5).

In addition to the Digital Hub, Accenture has also developed 21 'Liquid Studios' around the world. One of the first of these is in London, and specialises in artificial intelligence and cognitive processes, as well as offering expertise in augmented and virtual reality, the Internet of Things, the cloud, blockchain and security among other technology solutions.

The Accenture Liquid Studio in Madrid is also part of Accenture's Innovation Architecture, and occupies 900m^2 of an intelligent building. Its design is based on the concept of 'liquid architecture', or flexible reconfiguration, which is more about the experience than the physical place. Liquid Studio teams are grouped in highly interconnected pods or technological areas, working with contemporary development approaches such as agile methodologies powered by DevOps, and disruptive technologies including artificial intelligence, augmented reality, blockchain and the cloud.

Each space is represented in a different way, and the personality of the pods has been created through the use of flexible geometric shapes. In this liquid environment, specialists work fast, turning concepts into products – sometimes in just a matter of days.

Figures 3.4 and 3.5: The Digital Hub meeting room with movable partitions to alternate between open and closed arrangement (Madrid, Spain; AECOM; 2018)

THE CHANGING NATURE OF TECHNOLOGY AND WORK

Dale Sinclair

In our increasingly digitally driven society, the terms of reference for everything around us, including the workplace of the future, are changing. As we constantly adjust to the realities that the digital economy creates, we continue to hanker after people-centric environments – inventing ways of leveraging these new tools, yet moulding them to suit how we wish to work. We look towards new collaborative possibilities; however, it is technology that will shape and shift the way we work.

This chapter discusses some of the emerging technology trends that will affect us as users of office buildings, focusing on developments in three areas: mobility, collaboration and voice. In doing so, it seeks to identify some of the most innovative digital tools on the horizon; it examines how the new ways of designing and managing buildings, discussed in the previous chapter, will influence how we experience our office workspaces; and it explores how these nascent developments might drive and shape the future office, including where and how we work in the years ahead.

INTRODUCTION

MOBILITY

In recent years, the Holy Grail for technology companies has been facilitating mobility. The end goal is our ability to work with anyone, anywhere, at any time. As we commute back and forth from our homes to the city or further afield to meet clients, co-creators or collaborators, we work from trains, coffee houses and airports, rapidly shifting actions from one inbox to another. Mobility, however, facilitates more than working while we move. It creates new possibilities.

An office that feels more like home

Longer and longer commutes, driven by unaffordable inner-city house prices or other factors including schools, communities and access to green spaces, are resulting in an increase in home working. The 'office shed' in the garden is one product that offers some workers the chance to stay close to where they live, while also providing a professional haven away from the day-to-day chaos of their home. This includes the quiet and space to conduct video calls and other virtual meetings, without the fear of uninvited family members suddenly appearing in a live broadcast.[1]

Although convenient for some, the home office exemplifies a tension inherent in agile working between office and home, work and the rest of life. While sometimes, home is the office, at other times, the office almost becomes home. In both cases, there is a difficult balance to strike – especially, potentially, for younger generations in the workforce, who increasingly see work 'as a "thing" not a "place"'.[2]

Home working might provide improvements in work–life balance and productivity, but it also requires a good deal of trust, and pushes the boundaries between the company and the individual. Mobile technology means people are 'always on', replying to emails and calls at all hours. These factors can limit wider support for agile working in many companies.

Out and about

As we shift almost seamlessly from one wifi network to another, we can fail to see the next logical steps of mobility. Home environments are not for everyone. For those seeking liveliness or companionship, the local coffee shop can provide an effective workplace, replicating the buzz and social nature of the office near to home. Yet those who frequently work this way realise that, although the atmospheric background noise of busy baristas and music might facilitate the concentration needed to complete a report, it is no place for making important calls.

There is a need, therefore, for flexible workplaces equipped to bridge this gap between the home office and more traditional workspaces. Such professional 'hubs and clubs' can come in a number of forms and are likely to have a profound effect on the wider market for office space.

In London, for example, mobile technologies are contributing – alongside factors such as the economic uncertainty of Brexit and increased use of co-working spaces – to the flattening of office space rents across London.[3] It is also helping to realise the concept of polycentric cities, with a range of more flexible office locations, such as local community centres, available for use. These operate as workspaces during the day, offering cafe facilities as well as private areas suitable for calls and other immersive experiences closer to home.[4]

Simply, technology creates the opportunity for multiple working spaces – home, office or in-between – and reduces the gap even further between people's professional and personal lives.

Increasingly, this extends to professions traditionally built around, and reliant on, in-person interactions. Medicine is one such example, with doctors and other healthcare professionals increasingly using telecommunication technologies to educate, diagnose and treat patients remotely (telemedicine).[5] This breaking of the in-person bond enables doctors to consult with patients in more far-flung locations. It also makes it possible for doctors to work from anywhere.

For example, a community of doctors in the Lake District could work from home, coming together to share knowledge and experience, and connecting with patients anywhere in the UK.

Looking even further afield, according to parliamentary research, as of September 2017, 139,019 employees within the NHS report a non-British nationality – 12.5 per cent of those staff 'for whom a nationality is known'.[6] Could future consultations, therefore, become global?

Building on this, robotic surgery challenges the connection between surgeon and operating table. Will this lead to the advent of the super-specialist? For example, could all spine operations in the world eventually be handled from a single location, perhaps based at an internationally recognised teaching hospital, with global knowledge pooled in a central location?

While these healthcare examples do not relate directly to the office as we know it, they do point to the future, and underline how technological advances can change not just where we work, but also how we work.

Information at the right time

Mobility and striving for permanent connectivity come with a flip side. As we transition from an analogue to a wholly digital world, we face an increasing deluge of communications. The fax and letter may be almost extinct, but emails, group emails, e-newsletters, social media and blogs bombard us with demands for instantaneous responses, forcing us to live in the world of now, diverting us from longer-term and more strategic tasks. This is a world filled with perpetual demands for instant attention that leads, in turn, to stress and other factors that decrease productivity and job satisfaction. In their book *The Future of the Professions*, Daniel and Richard Susskind succinctly cover this point, noting that in due course some form of AI-driven tool will address this conundrum, feeding us with the right information at the right time.[7] Assuming this to be the case, our focus can be on how we facilitate better collaboration in the places we work.

COLLABORATION

The majority of workplaces are split between the spaces we meet in and the places in which we work as individuals, the latter having shifted away from the personal office to open-plan working on long tables. Companies offering co-working spaces are plugging new business models into the traditional leasing model, providing start-ups and energetic small companies with a diverse range of spaces that allow them to flex up and down to meet project demands. The free beer and prosecco fuel inter-company collaboration, but the environments – save for shabby-chic interior design – are no different from anywhere else. They create a short-term future office rather than stretching the reality of what a long-term future model may bring.

Before considering the office of the future, it needs to be recognised that, as more and more automation consigns the 'easy' tasks to the bin, numerous tasks will be replaced by new software, scripting or coding. As a result, those working in the future workplace will be left with only the difficult and intellectually demanding tasks to do. Those who will provide the

office of the future will need to consider this reality and, importantly, whether these residual and tough tasks will be undertaken by individuals working on their own, or by leveraging teamwork or collaboration. Some firms might provide beanbags in lieu of tables to encourage more creative interactions, but the question that needs to be asked is: how do we use technology to leverage better team work? What is the difference between team working and world-class collaboration? The reality is that a broader spectrum of spaces will be required than are currently provided.

Chapter 3 considers how big data aligned to smart sensors can help building owners manage and adapt their spaces more effectively in response to users' needs, equipping them with up-to-the-minute information on how their buildings are being used, and highlighting different patterns and trends across the working week. Organisations are already using sensors to monitor temperature, movement and light within their spaces, and drawing on the information generated to direct operations and systems from

catering to power and security (see Case Study 3.2: The Edge).

But these technologies have even greater potential to support building users on an individual, and increasingly personalised, level in the future. For example, could the practice of going to a pre-booked meeting room at a set time soon seem archaic? Are traditional meetings really the best way to facilitate invention and innovation anyway? The office of the future will reflect the reality that inspiration can come and go in a second, with smart buildings equipped to monitor the way its spaces are being used in the moment and respond instantaneously to provide the right environment for the activities taking place.

In the years ahead, buildings could use cameras as sensors to recognise the passion and sensitivity of impromptu conversations taking place between colleagues, and dispatch an acoustic bubble to wrap around them, similar to the way in which online retailer Amazon now uses robots to send its shelves of goods to staff to pick from – rather than the more intuitive norm (see Figure 4.1).[8]

Figure 4.1: Acoustic bubbles in use in the workspaces of the future (AECOM)

In the short term, those designing buildings need to consider better ways like this of hacking a building in order to provide the optimum environment. This will be challenging due to the lack of products necessary to facilitate this vision. New innovative tools will be needed that enable faster and even instantaneous adaptations to a building. The use of acoustics and acoustic devices, such as white-noise machines to reduce auditory disruptions and distractions in open-plan spaces, will be a major component of these solutions.[9]

Chapter 3 discusses how buildings will learn about their occupants' behaviour and work styles. A challenge for the learning building will be the tension between providing workplaces for the individual and for the group. This is further complicated by the growing number of global corporate companies that need to communicate and collaborate internationally. Companies are increasingly aware of the financial and environmental cost of flying staff around the world, and are turning to collaborative tools that use wifi instead of air miles to connect. In the context of mobility, individual workspaces could disappear: with valuable city-centre office spaces instead being designed to facilitate team work and collaboration from around the world.

As Chapter 10 details, designers are also using new tools and technologies to create future offices that will make new demands

CASE STUDY 4.1

SOGEPROM, PARIS

LOCATION: PARIS, FRANCE

ARCHITECT: ATELIER 2/3/4 (REFIT)

COMPLETION DATE: 2017

In a world first, the refurbished 15,000m^2 Sogeprom office in La Defense, Paris (as shown in Figure 4.2), has become the pioneer major workplace to use 'Li-Fi' – a high-bandwidth, bi-directional wireless internet connection using lightwaves via LED lighting fixtures – within its meeting rooms.

Sogeprom, the multi-business property development subsidiary of French bank Société Générale, teamed with Lucibel, the French LED lighting specialist, to introduce the system, which has significant advantages over wifi, including security of data and enhanced bandwidth. Development of the technology was by Scottish tech start-up pureLiFi. Employees use a special dongle inserted into

Figure 4.2: Sogeprom office roof terrace, overlooking La Defense skyline (Paris, France; Ateliers 2/3/4; 2017)

on the space in which they themselves work. Architects are moving design reviews with their clients away from the meeting table and drawings pinned to the wall, towards interactive environments where meetings are held inside the building being designed – using immersive, data-rich 3D information where cost and other attributes can be instantly revealed. Those joining the meeting 'inside the design' can do so from anywhere in the world, their avatars and voice indicating their presence inside the building being conceived. These

game-changing possibilities require new types of spaces that allow people to walk safely around inside an environment that is somewhere else.

In sectors with less visually intensive needs, the drivers are the same. The holoportation/telepresence technologies being developed now by a number of companies scan individuals, projecting their hologram into another space, and thus overcome the biggest technological challenge for linking people across

multiple locations: the belief that everyone is 'in the room'.[10] These technologies underline the need to embed the infrastructure for future-facing technologies into a building. This is a challenging task, as the time lag between the design and handover of a building can be many years and technology moves on; adaptive buildings will be a core briefing requirement in the future.

This discussion of the role of technology in collaborative work must also address

their computers and other devices to receive the internet via visible light from the LED lighting.

Across the board, the refreshed office, called Ampère e+, delivers agile and sustainable innovation. Along with Li-Fi (see Figure 4.3), this includes the latest-generation BMS, which connects with users through a mobile application dedicated to comfort, mobility and connectivity.

Another world first is the energy system, which makes it possible to produce (by recovering waste energy), store (by reusing electric vehicle batteries) and control (with an algorithm) energy in the building reflecting the requirements and behaviour patterns of the building's users as closely as possible. A biodiversity ecosystem takes care of air purification, producing optimum indoor air quality for user comfort. In part, it uses natural

micro-bioorganisms taken from forests and spread all over the building – on the walls, the floors, the ceilings, even inside the air-conditioning ducts – to 'eat' and transform all of the pollutant molecules in the air into biomass.

The building's numerous awards and certifications include BREEAM Very Good, NF HQE Excellent and BBC-effinergie®, C2C (circular economy) Inspired Building, WELL Core and Shell/Platinum and Existing Interiors/

Gold, plus the Quartier d'Affaires à Vivre 2017 award in the renovation/reconstruction category at SIMI 2017. It was also the winner of the 2017 international Green Solutions Awards in the Smart Building category.

Figure 4.3: Artist's impression showing LI-FI technology in use

61

one other important aspect: the role of the voice. Just as building technology could learn to recognise the nature of the collaborative activities taking place there and provide the right degree of privacy and enclosure, so it could also provide the ability to record discussions and actions as meetings progress.

VOICE

As research from the US Consumer Technology Association confirms, the sale of voice-activated, artificially intelligent speakers for the home is on the increase.[11] We can command the playing of our favourite song or order a pizza from our couch – yet this technology has not reached the workplace. However, it is inevitable that it will. IBM's Watson speech-to-text software is already capable of automatically transcribing meetings into multiple languages. The skills required to craft a set of minutes will soon be a thing of the past as AI tools pick out actions from meetings, pushing them to attendees' inboxes ready to be picked up when needed, wherever that may be. Verbal comments made will be irrefutable, reducing the need for paper-based contracts and facilitating the use of smarter, voice-based ones. The goal will be for our office buildings to provide environments in which ideas can flow, and to provide tools that can capture these ideas before they are forgotten or the initial passionate vision is diluted.

The same technology can contribute to our wellbeing, too. WELL standards (see wellbeing standards on page 79) point not just to a work–life balance, but also a health–work balance, and it is inevitable that technology will help make us more active in the office of the future. Walking meetings are just one example, and already some companies are turning running tracks into meeting routes to help boost workers' creativity and wellbeing.[12,13] Although dictation is not new, AI-based voice tools will allow a walking meeting to be recorded and action points to be extracted, and immediately and automatically allocated to the appropriate person or team.

Turning to a different example, the offices of product designers: with voice added to immersive environments, the designer will be able to point to aspects of the product, assigning comments to the team, such as 'Could we move this switch to the side panel?' or 'Could we make this disposable part easier for the consumer to fit?' Iterations of the design will be faster and better. Naturally, this will just be a stop-gap on the way to a scenario in which the designer can use voice to change the design in real time, removing the need for another designer to make adjustments. The end game is real-time design interactions with the client, who might be in the same space, or in an office or beach hut on the other side of the globe.

CONCLUSION

Mobility creates new opportunities for places to work. Voice does likewise, but in different ways. Organisations can benefit from these new opportunities, particularly regarding their impact on collaborative working.

Technology will provide robust support for mobile and agile working, allowing people flexibility and choice over where and when they work. Collaboration technologies will enhance virtual meetings and reduce the need for business travel, helping both the environment and people's wellbeing. Voice support for walking meetings will again contribute to people's health.

The workplace of the future will use mobility, voice and collaborative technologies to provide spaces that allow ideas to flow and that capture these ideas in ways that enhance everyone's productivity. The nature of these spaces is likely to vary from individual to individual, project to project and organisation to organisation. Digital technology tools will empower the worker of the future, so that they can be judged on the creativity and strategic nature of their work and the outcomes of their ideas rather than where and when they work. Beginning our section on the theme of people, the next chapter discusses the issues of work and wellbeing.

LEARNING POINTS

1. Mobility technologies allow work to be done anywhere, suggesting a new generation of workspaces in the home, the community and the city.

2. Agile working will change the type of work undertaken in the corporate office, pointing to a greater need for collaborative group spaces and the need for buildings to adapt in response to diverse and rapidly changing requirements.

3. The onset of voice-activated technologies will require a rethink of acoustics, including how individual work settings are configured; it will create new opportunities for working spaces.

4. The need to incorporate sensors and other technologies into a building's infrastructure needs to be considered early in the design process. They must, however, also be designed in a flexible way.

HMRC – GOVERNMENT HUBS PROGRAMME

LOCATION: CROYDON, UK

ARCHITECT: SHED KM (BUILDING)

ARCHITECTURAL/INTERIOR DESIGNER: AECOM

COMPLETION DATE: AUGUST 2016 (FIRST PHASE);
2021 (FULL COMPLETION)

Figure 4.4: Spaces to collaborate (HMRC, Croydon, UK; ShedKM and AECOM)

Government Hubs Programme

The Hubs Programme is fundamental to the Government Estate Strategy to consolidate Civil Service office work into fewer, larger, multi-occupied buildings easily reached by public transport, in strategic locations. By early 2018, the programme – led by the Government Property Agency (GPA), with HMRC delivering phase one of the programme on its behalf – had identified 14 new hub buildings in major cities across the UK and on the periphery of London. The hubs are being designed to provide better working environments that will improve productivity and cost-effectiveness. The programme is expected to save billions of pounds and consolidate the office estate to around 21 strategic hubs across the UK.

Putting the smart in Smart Working

Sharing buildings and regional relocation are nothing new to the Civil Service. The transformational element is digitally-enabled Smart Working, underpinned by the idea that 'work is what you do, not the place you go'.

The hubs will run on Smart Working principles, the first and foremost being that 'work takes place at the most effective location and at the most effective times, responding to the needs of the task, the customer, the individual and the team'.[14] People may not always *need* to go to an office, but will *choose* to because the hub offers the best environments for their work – especially when this work involves collaboration with colleagues.

Hub workspaces are being designed with a variety of zones to suit different types of work and personal preferences. These will largely be treated as shared resources available for people to choose and use flexibly. This flexibility enables people to work at the time and in the place that improves service to the customer and can fit with their own lives. By designing spaces for people and their work, the hubs are responding to physical and psychological needs for health, community, identity, concentration and stimulation. Working in a hub community should lead to a sense of belonging to a larger network within and beyond the hub building itself, and will hopefully inspire a new sense of pride in the Civil Service as a great place to work.

HMRC

HMRC is working closely with the GPA to design and deliver phase one of the Hubs Programme, and will be the major occupier in all of these phase one hubs. Not only is HMRC leading the implementation, but it is making an important statement about the need to 'test and learn' through experience by allowing the British Council for Offices (BCO) to independently evaluate these hubs and publish its findings, so that all may benefit.

Modernisation

In November 2015, HMRC announced the next step in its ten-year modernisation programme to create a tax authority fit for the future, committing to high-quality jobs and the creation of new centres serving every region and nation in the UK. This followed a series of conversations with staff to determine a view of what they would want from new working environments.

Key objectives

- Digital technology will drive customer service, collaboration and efficiency
- 13 new regional centres to improve productivity and wellbeing
- Estate rationalisation to save £300 million by 2025

Creating a modern tax authority

HMRC's transformation programme is the biggest modernisation of the UK tax system in a generation. It involves making fundamental changes to the way the department works and the services it provides. HMRC's ambition is to become one of the most digitally advanced tax authorities in the world – but it can only do this by becoming a smaller, more highly skilled and flexible organisation, making better use of technology and working differently.

A key aim of the programme is to enable HMRC's staff to work more efficiently and deliver better, more streamlined services to the public. Currently, HMRC has an ageing network of offices accommodating between ten people and 5,700. These offices are expensive to maintain and run, and create isolated teams doing narrow ranges of tasks, making it difficult for people to move jobs or build a career.

HMRC plans to replace these old-fashioned buildings with high-quality, modern offices that help employees to collaborate and work flexibly. These sites – 13 regional centres across the UK, along with five specialist centres and seven additional sites to support the transition – will combine adaptable workspaces with a high-speed digital infrastructure and up-to-date learning and development facilities. Together with improving productivity and wellbeing by driving new ways of working,

these environments will have a positive effect on recruitment and retention by offering employees fuller career paths.

Moving to regional centres is estimated to save around £300 million between now and 2025. The programme also aims to deliver annual cash savings of £74 million in 2025/26, rising to around £90 million by 2028.

It started in Croydon

The Croydon Regional Centre is the first new facility. Announced in August 2016, its first-phase opening saw 1,800 staff moving by the end of 2017. Once fully operational, it will have more than 2,700 full-time-equivalent staff in place.

All the new buildings in the programme will follow a design specified through comprehensive employer's requirements, the government's own design guidelines and extensive staff consultation.

In the zone

The Croydon Regional Centre comprises ten floors with a range of different workspaces – or 'zones' – to encourage new ways of working and nurture employee wellbeing (as shown in Figure 4.4):

- **Core space** in which team zones will be based
- **Collaboration areas** prompt better working across teams
- **Concentration areas** for quiet, focused tasks
- **Learning zones** provide modern learning and development facilities, with bookable space where people can come together for classroom learning, small group working or self-study
- **Amenity spaces** are for refreshment, reflection, relaxing and engaging with colleagues

Figure 4.5: IT to enable agile working (HMRC, Croydon, UK; ShedKM and AECOM)

- **Access space** to allow safe and secure entry to and exit from the buildings; these areas are wifi-enabled and allow people to meet in an informal setting outside of the operational areas

Sliding or folding screens allow adjacent open-plan spaces to be used individually, as a group setting or as a town hall, as required. To avoid long rows of desks, smaller neighbourhoods have been created by locating collaboration spaces between every three or four banks of desks, providing each neighbourhood with a level of privacy. The ratio of space allocated to group or shared settings, compared to individual workspace (desks) is around 45/55 per cent.

IT is great (and reliable)

These inclusive, sustainable and adaptable designs are underpinned by good-quality IT, ensuring that the latest technology and tools are used in conjunction with an infrastructure that enables 'smart' or 'agile' working. Cloud-based technology (including a new, easy-to-use room booking system) means staff can work in the zones best suited to their needs (see Figure 4.5). Touchscreen laptops connect to applications via building-wide, high-speed wifi.

A major upgrade to the network infrastructure delivers a secure and resilient system of fibre-structured cabling, providing the building's IT backbone and linking to duplicate communication rooms (N+1, providing network redundancy if one fails) and two secondary communication rooms per floor.

Hearts and minds

Engaging HMRC employees and giving them a clear understanding of the benefits of the locations programme was critical to success. The Croydon Regional Centre's design was the result of HMRC's long-term interest in, and evolution of, new ways of working. Employee feedback was positive; they felt happy, professional, proud and optimistic about the new workspaces.

HMRC also rolled out several 'Test and Learn' sites in Newcastle, London, Salford and Nottingham, giving staff the opportunity to experience this new working environment and provide feedback on layout and set-up. Responses were positive, both to the overall design and to the new ways of working.

By the end of 2018, 'Test and Learn' sites will be open in every region. Some 1,400 digital ambassadors will also be embedded in teams around the UK, supporting colleagues as they transition to new ways of working and ensuring they make the most of these digital technologies. A range of mobile devices, including Surface Pros and smartphones, have also been issued to staff, which – alongside access to dual screens, wifi, and Windows 10 and Office 365 capability – are enabling staff to work smarter and more collaboratively across the organisation.

Design highlights

- Office layouts support zones for collaboration, concentration or relaxation

- Moveable furniture and partitions make spaces adaptable for different uses

- Desk sharing ratio of 64 per cent

- Robust, resilient IT infrastructure supports smart working

- Cloud-based applications and fast wifi aid collaboration

- BREEAM Excellent rating achieved through efficient water, energy and lighting systems

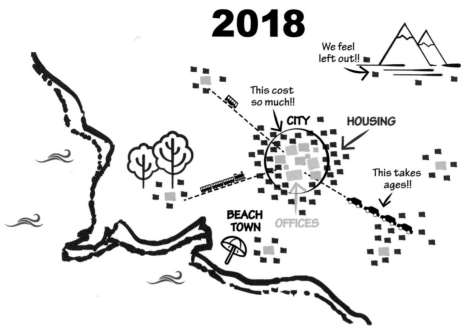

Figure 4.6: The world of work as it is now, in 2018, as drawn by the winning AECOM Hackathon team

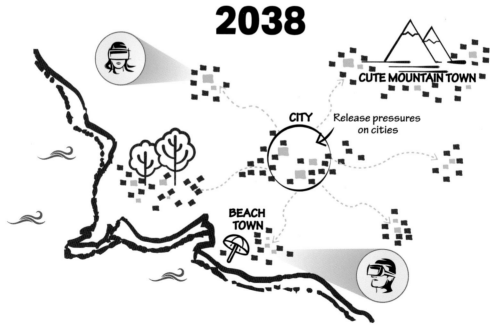

Figure 4.7: The future of work in year 2038, as envisioned by the winning AECOM Hackathon team

FUTURE OFFICE CHALLENGE – AECOM

LOCATION: ANY
CONCEPT: AECOM
SUBJECT: HACKATHON WINNER

As part of ongoing research and investigations into the future office, a number of multidisciplinary UK AECOM teams participated in an intense four-hour, head-to-head hackathon challenge to propose a vision for the future of work and the workplace in 2038. Here is the winning narrative.

'Live in your community and plug into work'

It is the year 2038. New ways of living and working have emerged, driven by economic, societal, technological and market changes. In response to overcrowded cities, increased commuting times and rising costs, a lack of adequate and affordable living and working space, and the influx of artificial intelligence (AI) and smart technology into everyday life as detailed in Figures 4.6 and 4.7, the reality of the office has changed. Offices no longer have their familiar building form, patterns of use or workplace culture.

Physical space, virtual identity

Work has left the city and organisations no longer provide a built workplace. Small communities furnish the physical space in which local people work, while a virtual reality environment carries the organisational identity (see Figure 4.8).

A new generation of workers has emerged, who work where they choose to live, sharing co-working space with people with shared interests from other organisations, and logging in to their company daily.

Co-working hubs grow in seaside locations, the countryside and in cultural city hubs. New technologies are an integral part of this new office. Virtual reality headsets issued by each company are pre-loaded with relevant work environments, as shown in Figure 4.8. Artificial intelligence systems assist in everyday tasks, and smart sensors monitor and shape the environment.

A better balance

A focus on wellbeing, sustainability and technology has driven this change. The office now leverages virtual and augmented reality, exploits the advantages of co-working hubs, and triggers the benefits of work and living co-location. The future worker has a better balance between working and living. Their role is to focus on strategic and creative thinking, while smart technology and AI execute routine tasks.

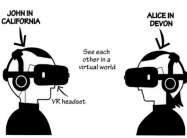

Figure 4.8: A vision of the virtual world – VR headsets, preloaded with each company's branded virtual environment, connecting employees from different parts of the world

PEOPLE

III

PART

WELLBEING

**Nicola Gillen, Hilary Jeffery and
Charlotte Hermans**

More than just the absence of illness, wellness and wellbeing are complex and increasingly important factors in the workplace. In recent years, concerns about health and wellbeing have marched up the agenda as topics of equal and urgent interest to designers, employers and employees. For the purposes of this book, our focus is on wellbeing as a desirable level of comfort for people to work well.

The impetus for this focus comes from a number of sources, but at its core is the fact that a happy worker is generally an engaged and productive worker – and that worker is less likely to take sick leave or look for other jobs.[1] So an effective wellness agenda that helps businesses to be profitable and successful means that investment in great design is essential in the modern workplace. It's a simplistic summary, but it rings true in every workplace, in every industry worldwide.

Beyond this simple outline, however, the debate about the impact of wellness in the workplace is becoming ever broader. An organisation's focus on the wellbeing of its employees can have a positive impact on brand perceptions and can be woven into corporate responsibility, enhancing the organisation's appeal not just to existing and future employees, but also to clients. It can also be a differentiator in attracting investors, and have positive impacts on employees' families, friends and entire communities.

INTRODUCTION

HEALTHIER AND HAPPIER

The increasing concern about wellness has come about as the result of several factors: first, because we are learning ever more about the impact of buildings on our health and wellbeing; second, because we are more aware of mental health issues and all want to lead healthier, longer lives; and last, because the younger workforce of millennials has a big interest in this area – wanting more flexibility and control over how, when and where they work – and will vote with their feet if the work environment does not meet their expectations.

Design and wellbeing

There has been an extensive and long-running debate about how our environment affects people mentally, physically and spiritually. As part of this discussion, there is a particular interest in the impact of the workplace environment. However, understanding and measuring the impact of workplace environmental factors on issues such as motivation, productivity and mental health is complex. For example, individuals can respond in many different ways when undertaking exactly the same tasks in the same environment.

That said, there are three key 'hygiene' factors, now well-recognised, that can have an impact on wellbeing and productivity.[2]

- **Noise** – particularly unwelcome and stressful are sounds that are loud, sharp, unpredictable and uncontrollable. Paradoxically, too little noise can impact concentration – perception is a key differentiator of people's reactions to noise.

- **Light** – prolonged periods of exposure to artificial light and lack of control over glare or access to daylight can also cause issues.

- **Indoor climate** – an environment that is too hot, too cold or too humid, with a lack of controls available for moderating it, decreases people's sense of comfort in the workplace.

More is known about these 'hygiene' factors than other more complex or intangible factors and, as such, it has become accepted practice to incorporate them into office design. But an environment purposely designed around wellbeing must address a wider range of factors, reaching beyond physical and environmental aspects, and including social and psychological dimensions as well.

TAKING A HOLISTIC APPROACH

The global discussion on work–life balance and the importance of good-quality offices has shifted. With the environmental aspects of wellbeing now well developed and accepted, it has become clear that wellness embraces many factors that extend way beyond these. Wellbeing is increasingly thought of as a state of having 'the psychological, social and physical resources' needed to face particular challenges in life, according to the *International Journal of Wellbeing*.[3] Taking an even more holistic perspective, some theories posit that workplace health and wellbeing are, in addition, affected by intellectual, spiritual and material factors, and that all of these factors need to be considered to truly inspire and support employees, and create a healthy and resilient organisation.

While design alone cannot provide all the answers to promoting wellbeing, good design can create a supportive environment that actively facilitates best working practices, improved workflows, innovation and creativity, and reduced stress.

In response to the latest research and thinking, this holistic approach provides an up-to-date model for workplace wellbeing. This broad approach, set out in Figure 5.1, focuses on six facets of wellbeing through which wellbeing at work can be

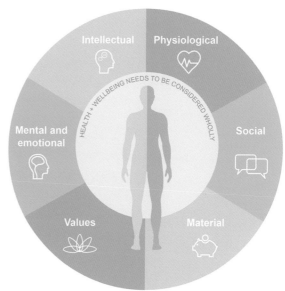

Figure 5.1: Wellbeing at work is more than just physical health; a holistic wellbeing assessment at work embraces six dimensions – health that is physiological, psychological, social, intellectual, spiritual and material

understood, supported and improved, truly holistically:

1. **Physiological health** allows us to feel fit and get through our daily activities without undue fatigue or physical stress.

2. **Psychological health** incorporates mental health and emotional wellbeing, which includes job-related happiness, satisfaction and a positive–negative emotional balance.

3. Being **socially well** means one is well connected with others at work, feels part of a community or communities, and has access to support networks.

4. People who are **intellectually well** at work have the ability to use their knowledge and skills to perform well and are given the right input and stimulation to develop their skills further. Intellectual wellbeing refers to the level of satisfaction with the intellectual challenge that their work provides.

5. Feeling **spiritually well** refers to the match between an individual's personal values and ethics and those inherent in their work activities and the organisation.

6. **Material wellbeing** relates to financial rewards, such as income or other remunerations. People who feel materially well are satisfied with the quality or quantity of rewards they receive for their work and experience a sense of fairness around the distribution of rewards.

RESEARCH ON PREDICTORS OF WELLBEING IN THE WORKPLACE

Academic investigations into predictors of wellbeing and performance in the workplace to date have typically taken a uni-dimensional approach, focusing on influences of design, perception or culture in isolation. However, as multifaceted as the concept of wellbeing is in itself, so are the factors that influence people's productivity and feelings of wellness in the workplace. What has so far been missing in the literature is a holistic research account that considers the impact of multiple influences in a single model, so that their respective impacts can be measured simultaneously, allowing key predictors to emerge.

To fill this gap, a recent body of research set out to test a new comprehensive model, as detailed in Figure 5.2, to investigate key predictors of workplace wellbeing and performance in office worker populations.[4] An international workplace consultancy partnered with Kingston Business School and Zurich University of Applied Sciences' Institute of Facility Management, to interrogate a series of factors such as design, management style and culture, with the aim of providing design guidance through understanding the impact of such factors on wellbeing at work.[5]

This comprehensive model was used to investigate a multitude of relationships between work, workplace and wellbeing. Specifically, the model tested how environmental facets of the workplace (e.g. quality and variety of work settings, noise, light, air quality), assessed both objectively (i.e. quality standards) and subjectively (i.e. perception based), as well as work-related factors (e.g. job design, management, culture), predict physical, mental, social, intellectual, spiritual and material dimensions of wellbeing, performance and satisfaction.[6]

Two waves of data collection (samples of 407 and 221 data points, respectively) across the utilities/ engineering and engineering/design sectors were used to gather, validate and generalise findings. Data was gathered via online surveys, and contrasted with objective expert assessments of the physical office environment in a selection of samples.[7]

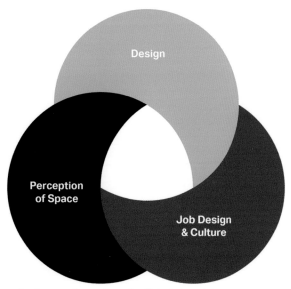

Figure 5.2: A comprehensive approach to predictors of wellbeing in the workplace

Initial findings and learning points

1. *Manager capability is a key indicator for satisfaction and wellbeing*
Managerial support appears to be a key ingredient in promoting wellbeing in the workplace. The results of the study indicate that people who feel supported by their managers experience higher levels of mental, social, intellectual and spiritual wellbeing, and report better job satisfaction. The link with intellectual wellbeing may be due to a monitoring function of line managers in overseeing career development and stimulating positive professional growth: managers who are capable of detecting skills and abilities in people are more likely to offer opportunities to nourish and develop these, with a likely positive effect on the individual's experienced intellectual wellbeing.[8]

2. *Protocols as vehicles to objective conversation – agreeing on ways of sharing workspace*
Preliminary study results indicate that adherence to protocols is positively associated with mental, social and spiritual facets of wellbeing, as well as workplace satisfaction. The link with social wellbeing is particularly interesting: it seems that people feel a greater sense of social wellbeing when protocols about the use of space are agreed and adhered to. This may be due to protocols being used as objective norms of office behaviour, helping to facilitate difficult conversations and reduce social tension. For example, if disturbing behaviour is noticed in the office (a classic example being noisy phone calls at the desk), a conversation about breaching protocol terms is likely to be held more easily than one with a more personal implication about that person's general behaviour in the office.[9]

3. *People want to be proud of their workplace*
Space goes beyond an attractive look and feel: employees report being more satisfied with their workplace when the office creates a strong, positive experience for visitors through an

Figure 5.3: 'Thank You For Letting Me Be Myself Again', an artwork created by Doug Shaw during a presentation about wellbeing.[10]

WELLBEING STANDARDS

The realisation that buildings have an impact on our health and wellbeing has given rise to the creation of performance indicators and rating system tools, to measure health and wellbeing within the built environment. Clients, designers and occupants are discovering the benefits that these interventions can deliver across the design, construction and operation of buildings. The codification of measures proven to enhance occupant wellbeing can now be found in the WELL Building Standard™, Fitwel®, RESET™ and more.

Each of these certification approaches has its own specific focus, relating to phases of development and requiring differing levels of detail and verification. WELL addresses intervention within seven categories, spread across nearly 100 measures, and is suited to projects with large capital spend, such as an office move or a major refurbishment. Fitwel® is a benchmarking tool that was designed for the existing building market and works by identifying opportunities for improvement, especially through large real-estate portfolios. RESET™ is an air-quality performance standard premised on the continuous collection of real-time data in buildings, using sensors and long-term maintenance of targets.

Whichever tool is selected, health and wellbeing standards broadly seek to examine quality of the interior environment through the following parameters:

★ Air quality, including the amount of fresh air within the space and controlling for contaminants that enter the space, during construction and into operation

★ Quality of water supply

★ Having access to views, promoting natural light, decreasing glare, and ensuring that the installed lighting is appropriate for the type of activity being undertaken in the space

★ Examining how an individual is supported by their company and how the building supports staff in operation

★ Encouraging good/healthy behaviour, fitness and nutrition

★ Promoting thermal and acoustic comfort, and accessibility of spaces

Securing full certification can be a win-win for developers and occupants: spaces designed to promote health and wellbeing appeal to new tenants and attract potential employees to organisations that see wellbeing as a priority, which boosts the productivity and happiness of staff. Where completion of a certification scheme presents a cost barrier – either in terms of capital cost upgrades or certification costs – an organisation can still deliver meaningful health and wellbeing measures without pursuing formal certification, which can have a long-term strategic impact on the health of building occupants.

The criteria used in certification schemes have shifted the definition of best practice for occupants, and the increasing availability and affordability of monitoring equipment and wearable technology is enabling them to track their health and wellbeing and challenge organisations on the quality of internal spaces.[11] Certification schemes such as WELL help to bridge the gap between design teams and operation, and the rapidly developing sensor industry will prompt a re-evaluation of how we measure and communicate indoor and environmental quality. As more sensors and new technologies are integrated into the built environment, it will be important to ensure that monitoring devices are properly installed, calibrated and maintained, to ensure data validity.

What all of these approaches share is a commitment to deliver improvements with positive and demonstrable environmental benefits to workplaces for the people who use them. Providing the wider industry with proof that introducing health and wellbeing measures is yielding positive benefits makes a strong case for certification – and one that will surely grow.

FIVE POINTERS FOR THE FUTURE OF WELLBEING AT WORK

It is possible to argue that the work environment can enable a healthy work culture. This may be achieved through the following approaches:

1. A research-led design approach. Starting with a clearly defined design brief will help clients to articulate what they want and architects to design the right kind of spaces.

2. A workplace that offers a variety of social spaces vertically and horizontally throughout the building can stimulate people to take a break from the desk, talk to colleagues and, in this way, establish better connections. Best practice today tells us that 50 per cent of an office should be collaborative space. Strong interpersonal bonds are known to function as support networks and create a sense of safety for people by allowing them to 'bring themselves to work'.

3. Providing the right mix of spaces. People do a variety of activities at work, and so the office should provide a variety of spaces – open and enclosed, formal and informal. An effective office is not just about collaborative spaces, but also about spaces to work quietly and seek privacy. People often come into the office to engage with others, while needing to intersperse this activity with time alone to think and reflect.

4. Encouraging mobility and including standing work settings are key to wellbeing. The human body is not designed to sit in one position for eight hours a day. The best offices deliberately provide a variety of spaces to encourage people to move around during the day, based on what they are doing. Sit/stand desks allow people to adjust the height of a desk to a standing position for periods of time. Standing meetings are building a reputation for being faster and more efficient than the traditional seated variety.

5. Open and shared team areas that remove physical boundaries can foster a culture of equality, break down hierarchy and help employees develop trust in the organisation through transparency (i.e. decisions not being taken behind closed doors, and leadership figures not only more visible on the work floor, but also more reachable). A work culture of equals helps people to feel respected – which, in turn, motivates them to contribute to and identify themselves more with their teams. In this way, tangible, visual symbols of equality can help people develop a culture of equality.

appealing look and ambience. With work representing a significant part of people's lives, it seems intuitive that people want to be proud of what they do and able to show it to the world – a great workplace helps create this sense of pride. For organisations, this signals that the workplace is the biggest canvas for their brand, and an important contributor to staff satisfaction levels.[12]

4. *Choice and control as drivers of wellbeing*
A crucial indicator of wellbeing at work is the degree to which people feel autonomous, and that they have freedom over how and where they do their work (as represented by Figure 5.3). Space, therefore, needs to

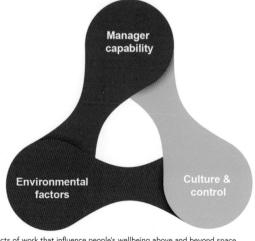

Figure 5.4: The aspects of work that influence people's wellbeing above and beyond space

facilitate the whole spectrum of types of work – the buzz of a stimulating environment, as well as effective spaces to do more concentrated work – so that people are free to choose according to their individual needs or preferences. However, choice goes beyond picking the right place in the office to work from for a specific task – the results of the study indicate that people report higher physiological wellbeing, i.e. perceiving themselves as fitter and healthier, when they have control over their job. It seems that having the freedom to choose how to do one's job, when to take breaks and how to design the work day, supports individuals in making healthy choices and taking better care of their wellbeing.[13]

CONCLUSION

Architects, designers, developers and clients need to acknowledge the aspects of work that influence people's wellbeing above and beyond space. While an objectively perfect space could be designed that offers optimum support for wellbeing, the positive impact of such a space would be significantly lower when aspects of work design and culture are not satisfactory (see Figure 5.4). For example, an office that fulfils all requirements of a fully biophilic workspace would not have the same positive effects on people's wellbeing if managerial support were lacking or job demands too high to cope with.

LEARNING POINTS

1. Wellbeing is no longer just a fad or temporary trend – it is here to stay as a new standard and differentiator that workplaces of the future will adopt. Organisations will respond by including wellbeing on their strategic agendas.

2. There are well-researched 'hygiene' factors that should always be considered in design, including light, noise and indoor climate. Satisfying these provides a necessary baseline for organisations to be able to support wellbeing holistically.

3. As the office is a highly complex place, leading-edge design will need to embrace more than just environmental factors. An understanding of organisational culture, work tasks and patterns, and employee expectations should all feed into the design.

4. A 'well-designed' office environment must address the more complex aspects of wellbeing such as satisfaction and social connectivity. Job design needs to work in concert with space design to create environments for optimum wellbeing.

5. As perception is key, choice and control lie at the heart of creating workplaces for wellbeing – to promote wellbeing effectively, people need to be engaged and involved, and feel empowered to co-design a work environment that speaks to their personal wellbeing needs. Change management can act as a catalyst for this engagement, and gives people a voice to express what they need in order to feel well at work.

BARANGAROO – LENDLEASE GLOBAL HEADQUARTERS

LOCATION: SYDNEY, AUSTRALIA

ARCHITECT: ROGERS STIRK HARBOUR + PARTNERS

INTERIOR DESIGNER: HASSELL

DEVELOPER AND BUILDER: LENDLEASE

COMPLETION DATE: JULY 2016

Figure 5.5: Lendlease's Barangaroo development has regenerated an area that was once docklands (Sydney, Australia; Rogers Stirk Harbour + Partners; 2016)

On the southern end of Sydney Harbour Bridge, a new city district called Barangaroo is rising from a 22-hectare site that was once docklands (see Figure 5.5). With sustainability and wellbeing at the core of this regeneration development, the project's developer Lendlease has shown its commitment to the place by establishing its head office there. For its new base in International Towers Sydney, Barangaroo South, Lendlease wanted to create a dynamic, high-performance workplace that exudes energy – a place where people want to be, where they

feel inspired and where collaboration comes naturally each day (as shown in Figure 5.6). The move was made to one of three commercial buildings on the site, with design practice HASSELL engaged to create an agile workplace for the international property and infrastructure group.

Top facts

- 92 per cent are proud to bring visitors to the workplace – compared to a benchmark of just over 50 per cent

- 88 per cent believe the culture is supporting them to work in a more flexible way – against a benchmark of around 57 per cent

- 73 per cent said the workplace makes them more productive[14]

Making health a priority

The interior design responds to the company's aim to 'encourage greater connectivity between our leaders and people' and to make health a priority in all

Figure 5.6: The site includes spaces for people to meet, socialise and shop (Sydney, Australia; Rogers Stirk Harbour + Partners; 2016)

aspects of the workplace, which brings together around 2,000 employees from five different locations.

Internal stairs are a key feature of the workplace design, which occupies levels eight to 19. Dual stairs between floors promote the important values of connectivity and health by visually linking each floor, and encouraging constant movement and spontaneous interaction.

Places to cooperate, places to concentrate

Within the workplace, employees are not tied to individual desks. Instead, they belong to a 'team studio' or 'neighbourhood' of 15 to 20 people. Each of these zones has access to a wide range of functional spaces for everything from group brainstorms to tasks requiring quiet

concentration. The design also blurs the distinction between inside and outside, with natural light and greenery visible and accessible from all parts of the workplace (as shown in Figure 5.7). The space has more than 10,000 indoor plants, which includes a breathing wall featuring 5,000 plants at the reception. These plants not only look great, but also purify the air, balance humidity and absorb high-frequency sounds (see Figure 5.8).

A square in the sky

The efficiencies that were developed and tested through the design and planning process allowed for one floorplate to be freed up for use as a hub for staff and their guests. This hub includes event and bid spaces, a health hub, an IT service helpdesk and an externally operated cafe at the heart of it all.

Keep moving

The workplace promotes movement throughout the day, starting with shared end-of-trip facilities (1,100 cycle racks, showers, lockers and towel service) that encourage employees to actively commute to work or exercise at lunch. Work settings vary in height and include fixed-height standing, adjustable, and fixed-height seating. All of the meeting rooms have a 'lean rail' that encourages people to change positions during long meetings, and the floors are interconnected with stairs, allowing people to move vertically throughout the workspace and connect socially. This focus on health also includes a dedicated wellness hub on level 13, with consulting rooms for visiting medical professionals – enabling wellness checks to take place in the workplace.

Figure 5.7: Natural light and greenery is a key feature of the Barangaroo development, both inside and out, linking it to its surroundings (Sydney, Australia; Collins and Turner; 2016)

Figure 5.8: The breathing wall at Lendlease's Global Headquarters (Sydney, Australia; 2016)

Design highlights

- Dual internal stairs through all 11 floors promote constant movement and interaction

- Vertical villages or social zones near the stairs are visible from above and below – drawing people through the workplace encouraging social connection (see Figure 5.9 and Figure 5.10)

- Garden zones at the perimeter of every floor form a working 'retreat' full of greenery and natural light for focused, concentrated work

- Australia's first breathing wall with 5,000 plants is the heart – and literally lungs – of the office

- Diverse spaces include 'working walls' for visual communications and 'pods' for quiet working

- Six Star Green Star Office Design rating from the Green Building Council of Australia

- International Towers Sydney, Towers 1, 2 and 3 at Barangaroo South, became the first projects globally to achieve a WELL building certification at the Platinum level for Core and Shell. This represents more than 250,000m^2 of office space, making Barangaroo South one of the world's healthiest workplace destinations.

- Additionally, Lendlease's global headquarters at Barangaroo is undertaking performance verification for its tenancy at the Platinum level, representing the world's best practice for wellbeing in the workplace.

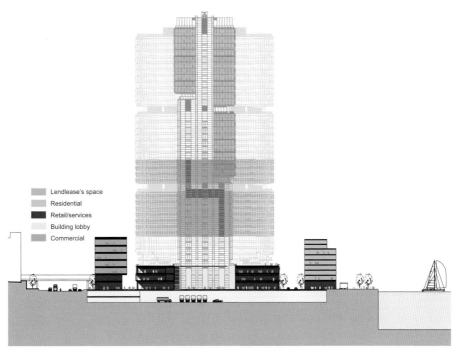

Lendlease's space
Residential
Retail/services
Building lobby
Commercial

Figure 5.9: An illustrative section of Barangaroo (Sydney, Australia; Rogers Stirk Harbour + Partners; 2016)

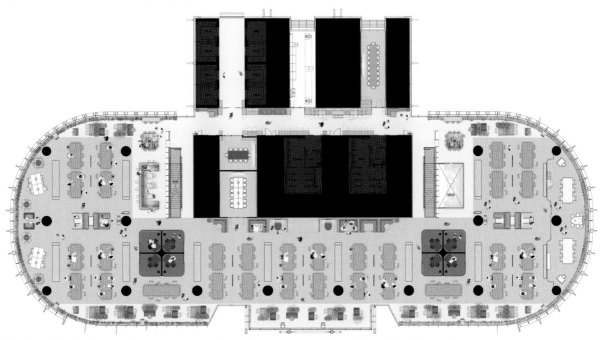

Figure 5.10: Typical floor plan illustrating collaborative areas and connecting spaces around central core (Sydney, Australia; HASSELL; 2016)

ROLLS-ROYCE TRENT XWB PROJECT HALL

LOCATION: DERBY, UK

INTERIOR DESIGNER: AECOM

COMPLETION DATE: 2013

Live well, work well

To deliver a global high standard of wellbeing at work and take better care of its people, Rolls-Royce introduced a LiveWell accreditation scheme. It requires all sites with more than 50 people to meet rigorous health and wellbeing standards, in line with bronze, silver and gold levels of accreditation. The aim is for all eligible sites to be gold accredited by 2020.

Small changes, big difference

Led by Rolls-Royce's Chief Medical Officer, Dr David Roomes, LiveWell is designed to maximise physical, mental and social wellbeing. It helps facilitate the change of unhealthy behaviours, demonstrates that Rolls-Royce takes wellbeing seriously, creates an environment where employees are motivated to make healthy choices, and is a step towards creating a high-performance culture within the business.

Sites can achieve bronze accreditation through simple initiatives such as implementing flexible working and no-smoking policies, and by offering resilience training, for example by preparing people for dealing with stressful situations.

To achieve silver or gold accreditation, more advanced requirements include providing showers, cycling racks and subsidised gym facilities.

Eating well is an important focus, too. A nutrition policy at Rolls-Royce requires all catering suppliers to comply with nutrition standards, and food is divided into three types: 'eat more of', 'eat less of' and 'avoid'.

According to Dr Roomes, the LiveWell accreditation provides a framework for sites to make specific and targeted investments in the workplace that are supportive of wellbeing. He notes that research published in the *Harvard Review*'s 'What's the hard return on employee Wellness Programs?' shows that wellbeing schemes typically bring a return on investment of three to one.[15]

Helping people be their best

So, what's the single biggest or most effective thing an organisation can do to ensure workplace stressors are addressed, and that health and wellbeing becomes a priority in workplaces? Dr Roomes believes that successful schemes must have someone who owns the agenda and

champions it. Getting the policy framework right is also important, inexpensive and likely to lead to sustained improvement.

AECOM devised and rolled out workplace strategies and design and change management initiatives across Rolls-Royce sites globally.

Wellbeing was one of the core elements in this project for Rolls-Royce at its facility in Derby, UK (see Figure 5.11). To improve global communication, efficiency and productivity across Rolls-Royce, and help it bring products to market more quickly, a strategic brief and design was developed for its project hall in Derby, which houses around 400 staff working on the Trent XWB project, creating the world's most efficient jet engine.

By placing all workspaces near windows, natural light helps regulate the staff members' natural body clocks. In addition, varied workspaces, including dedicated quiet spaces, mean people can escape noisier areas and work undisrupted, while vibrant group and social spaces create a stronger sense of community, enhancing people's social wellbeing. Crucially, a change management programme helped those moving into the new workspace to embrace agile and more collaborative ways of working.

Figure 5.11: Rolls Royce Trent XWB project hall (Derby, UK; AECOM; 2013)

GLAXOSMITHKLINE – ASIA HOUSE

LOCATION: SINGAPORE

ARCHITECT: HASSELL

COMPLETION DATE: 2017

A place to thrive
With its fitness facilities, a cafe offering healthy menus, luscious greenery and impressive levels of natural light, the global healthcare company GSK wanted its new base in Asia to boost staff wellbeing as well as facilitate its cutting-edge work.

Designed by HASSELL, in close collaboration with GSK employees, Asia House is a purpose-built facility located in Singapore's growing biomedical, technology, and research and development community at one-north.

Open to people and ideas
Covering 14,330m^2, this is an accessible and inclusive place. The ground-floor reception area is open to the public, hardwiring GSK's connection to the local community (see Figure 5.12).

It is also GSK's first certified Disability Confident building and features a visually approachable exterior, convenient parking for people with disabilities and meeting spaces designed around everyone's needs.

The design also focused on an immersive experience of wellness, with nursing rooms for working parents, a health clinic on site, a fitness centre, and a retreat and tranquillity space.

This is a clear demonstration and reinforcement of GSK's commitment to employing and empowering a diverse workforce.

Smart design, smart working
Asia House's horseshoe-shaped floors are built around a central atrium and spiral staircase, and designed with activity-based working in mind.

With no designated offices, employees have a range of fully wifi-enabled work areas and meeting spaces to choose from. These can be adapted to meet their particular work needs, whether it is for focused work, creative collaborations or more informal discussions, with features such as adjustable workstations to promote movement and mobility.

World-class facilities
Asia House is designed to foster creativity, communication and collaboration among staff, with access to a wealth of outdoor recreational spaces, and excellent transport links close by.

It also provides world-class facilities to drive healthcare learning and research and strengthen connections between GSK and its partners and stakeholders.

This includes a Global Learning and Development Centre, to train the future generation of leaders, help nurture local talent and promote best practice; the Shopper Science Lab, which uses VR technology to digitally recreate different retail experiences and generate unique consumer insights; and a Digital Broadcast Centre with full broadcast and production capabilities to boost communication and engagement with GSK's stakeholders.

Green design
Sustainability is another integral element of Asia House's design. The building's sculpted roof, recycling facilities, natural ventilation and other green features help to keep the building light, save energy, reduce waste and improve air flow – ensuring GSK employees stay fit, happy and well.

Figure 5.12: GSK Asia House (Singapore; HASSELL; 2017)

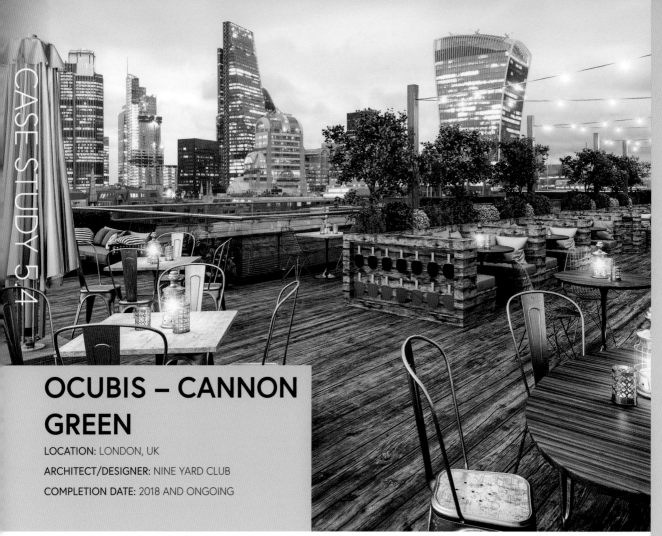

OCUBIS – CANNON GREEN

LOCATION: LONDON, UK

ARCHITECT/DESIGNER: NINE YARD CLUB

COMPLETION DATE: 2018 AND ONGOING

Figure 5.13: Pavilion roof terrace with a view of the City of London
(London, UK; Nine Yard Club)

A relatively recent player to join the co-working sector, Ocubis is a property developer/owner/manager specialising in refurbishment and expansion of existing commercial buildings that mix high-spec offices with a business club. Combining raw industrial materials and exposed services with bespoke furniture and luxurious finishes, these are offices designed to impress.

In the heart of the City of London, the recent 7,600m² Cannon Green building

project comprises eight floors of sleek, refurbished offices, plus a four-storey City Pavilion business members' club tailored to consultants and entrepreneurs. Lead designer was Laura Keith of Nine Yard Club. In addition to the complete refurbishment of the 1960s shell, the most dramatic intervention is the addition of a large glazed podium extension complete with poured-concrete staircase. The podium reception design is based on an old telephone exchange, and features

an aged oak reception desk which was constructed in situ using 5m-long reclaimed beams. The club offers facilities including a members' lounge; a selection of board rooms and meeting rooms; and print, recycling and coffee areas. In addition to the hot-desking, the club also includes a Drake & Morgan bar and restaurant and Gymbox gym all under the same roof.

Only Pavilion members can access the Pavilion spaces, including the hot-desking

Figure 5.14: Interior office space with industrial aesthetic (London, UK; Nine Yard Club)

lounge, meeting rooms and roof terrace with dramatic City views (see Figure 5.13). Other building tenants have the option to pay to use the meeting room and terrace facilities. While the style borrows much from the start-up industrial aesthetic, including plenty of exposed concrete, the attention to detail, quality of finishes, contemporary sculpture and artwork, and high-spec furniture are certainly pitched at the city-slicker, top-tier consultant (as shown in Figure 5.14).

RESEARCH-LED DESIGN

**Nicola Gillen, Dimitra Dantsiou
and Carolyn Whitehead**

The previous chapter describes how employee wellbeing is becoming increasingly important to organisations. However, it is only very recently that wellbeing in offices has started to be actively considered during the design process, as shown by the recent proliferation of wellbeing standards for buildings.[1]

Until now, office design has more typically focused on structure, safety, sustainability and costs. Engineering and aesthetics govern the exterior, while efficiency and the goal of making best use of the floorplate guide what happens inside. As a result, most office buildings constructed today adopt the familiar open-plan style created more than a century ago, rather than providing the variety of spaces required now.

INTRODUCTION

New building techniques and materials have developed over the years, and the design process has evolved to accommodate them. More significantly, the world of work has changed, too. Better IT enables people to collaborate and share information more easily than ever before. Companies value clever, joined-up thinking instead of a strict adherence to set tasks. Policies and practices that emphasise employee wellbeing support these new ways of working, with research showing that paying attention to staff satisfaction and productivity can create value for an organisation.[2,3]

Yet, despite this significant change, office design – stuck in that open-plan mode – has been slow to catch up. Often clients, developers and architects struggle to figure out how best to match workspaces to user needs. In an attempt to prepare for an unknown future, clients can find themselves building too much or the wrong kind of space.

A data-led briefing process could help to avoid such cases. This would involve design teams taking time to understand what their client wants upfront, and then incorporating this into designs through an ongoing feedback loop in order to inform the next project. A strong, data-led design brief is based on engagement with occupiers and evidence that draws on both objective and subjective data. This will usually be achieved by a team effort. Clients may not always be able to articulate their future requirements in detail at the very start, so architects and design teams will need to be proactive and supportive. This will bear fruit later, as clear design objectives and metrics are defined, and it will avoid the design process unravelling if value engineering is required. Figure 6.1 shows how a typical briefing process could be aligned to RIBA's Stages of Work.[4]

TOOLS TO GATHER DATA ON USER REQUIREMENTS

It is also important to consider what tools and techniques will be needed to gather this data. For subjective information, interviews and focus groups will be useful – focused around the occupants' daily

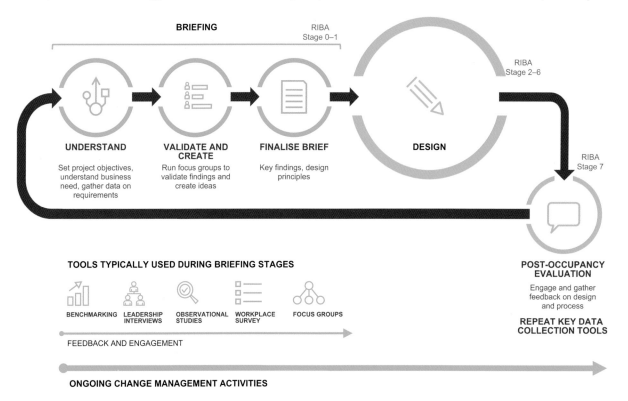

Figure 6.1: The data-led briefing process, matched to RIBA's Stages of Work

activities and the challenges they face in their work environment. If there is a large population of workers to interview, online opinion surveys are an efficient way to engage them in the design process.

Objective data could be gathered through observational studies of how workspaces are used over time. Good examples are the Time Utilisation Study (TUS)[SM] (see Case Study 10.1: Time Utilisation Study), which is a tool that AECOM (legacy DEGW) created almost 30 years ago, or, for benchmarking, the office density and utilisation reports designed by the British Council for Offices (BCO) in 2009, 2013 and 2018. The TUS challenged the common misconception that workers were at their desks 'all of the time', showing that people were, in fact, at their desks just over 40 per cent of the time (see Figure 6.2). This evidence prompted many clients to implement agile working strategies, in which employees share desks within allocated team areas, to address this under-use of workspace.

The adoption of agile working, where people do not have allocated desks, brought to light some complexities in the gathering and use of occupation data. BCO's (2018) report *Office Occupancy: Density and Utilisation* found that agile working practices had spread widely

across its sample of 133 office buildings, and there was an overall increase in the utilisation of open-plan desks by around 10 per cent in agile work environments compared with traditional environments.[5] It also found that open-plan desks were left temporarily unoccupied more of the time in agile working environments, as workers took advantage of the different work settings (informal breakout areas, quiet booths, cafes and huddle spaces, etc.) available in these offices.

Reflecting this, the report concluded that, as agile working becomes more widely adopted, the number of people in a building is likely to fluctuate significantly. In addition, desk occupancy is becoming a poor indicator of how many people are in a building at any point in time. The BCO's findings show that as our ways of working in offices evolve, the tools we use to gather data must keep pace.[6]

THE 'PERFORMANCE GAP' AND POST-OCCUPANCY EVALUATION

One of the most important aspects of data-led design is post-occupancy

evaluation (POE). POE has been used, in one form or another, since the mid-1960s, with successive refinements culminating in Wolfgang Preiser's 1989 framework for assessing how buildings perform when built.[7]

Although building users were included from the start, as methodologies developed, the emphasis shifted to the design of the building and how its systems worked.[8] Much attention was paid to the building's energy 'performance gap', i.e. the difference between design aspirations and the reality of energy use in the finished building.

Evaluations were aimed at facilities managers and building owners to enable them to make the most efficient use of their asset. Users were still consulted, but mainly to identify how successfully the various heating, air-conditioning and ventilation systems worked. In this sense, POE could provide facilities managers with a benchmark for the systems installed, and incentivise them to achieve optimal workplace efficiency.

As POE studies have matured, there has been more widespread adoption by building owners and developers. In the UK, projects such as the Chartered Institution of Building Services Engineers' (CIBSE) Post Occupancy Review of Building Engineering (PROBE), the Carbon Trust's 'Sharing Our Experience' series and Innovate UK's (formerly the Technology Strategy Board) Building Performance Evaluation programme have helped to introduce rigour and consistency into the evaluation methodology.[9,10,11] POE is also now often mandatory for public-sector construction projects. Furthermore, RIBA's Plan of Work includes POE as part of its Stage 7, 'In Use'.

Professor Flora Samuel, Professor of Architecture in the Built Environment, Reading University, and RIBA Vice-President for Research, is clear on why this is important: 'To be professional is to lay claim to a distinct body of knowledge.

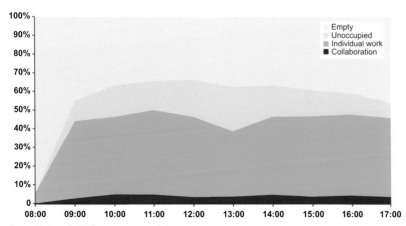

Figure 6.2: Example TUS[SM] output – average daily activity pattern

In the case of architecture, this should be knowledge of methods for ensuring the best possible fit between people and their environments. This knowledge can only be honed through the constant loops of review and feedback – in other words, post-occupancy evaluation – not just to do with energy, but also to do with more intangible things such as community, identity and wellbeing. It seems however that only about three per cent of architecture practices undertake regular POE, largely because of cost and belief that clients won't want to pay for it, but clients have so much to gain from knowing about the behaviour of their building and its impact on running costs, the environment, staff retention, absence, productivity and indeed brand.[12]

A POE is most effective when clear project objectives have been established upfront and metrics have been gathered on the existing ('before') environment during the briefing process. For the POE to be meaningful, the project team needs to understand what it is measuring and why those elements are important. The key data collection tools used in the initial data-gathering and briefing phase should also be repeated three to six months post-occupancy to enable benchmarking of the 'before' and 'after' results.

However, while providing essential benchmarks, POE in this form tells only part of the story. POEs will be most valuable to the organisation when they focus on the areas where the quality of the environment has its biggest impact – namely, the people working in the building.

Although metrics, parameters and definitions vary by industry and by study, and debate about a precise figure continues, making firm conclusions difficult, the literature tells us that the cost of people can equate to well over half of the total running costs of organisations.[13] Understanding how a building affects its workers' productivity and wellbeing is key to minimising

those costs. Hence, a POE that focuses on these effects will provide the most benefit to the organisation. Yet sometimes POE studies are inadequate in terms of assessing these areas, partly because they are often much more difficult to measure than, for example, air change rates or electricity consumption. Existing sustainability and performance benchmarks need to be supplemented by indicators of wellbeing and productivity.

Lately, new types of POE are emerging that put people at the centre of the evaluation process. Evidence points to increases in productivity and wellbeing in offices following investigations of this type, and relevant input in workplace design and culture. A reimagined POE could be a key tool to help architects understand better who they are designing for, and to guide developers towards creating healthy and productive work environments.

A NEW TRAJECTORY

What would a POE that includes productivity and wellbeing look like? These areas are not always well served by quantitative metrics. Productivity is difficult to measure in today's knowledge-based economy. Many factors – organisational culture, an individual's skills, management style, and personal motivation – affect employee productivity in addition to the physical surroundings.

The choice of a productivity measure is dictated by who is asking the question (or holding the budget). While the finance director may want hard financial measures, the human resources team may be interested in examining employee engagement and wellbeing as well as more obvious measures of performance.

Teasing out the relationship between productivity and the workplace is challenging, but it is important. There needs to be a balance between people

and technology measures. People metrics, rather than technology metrics, will have more value for corporate occupiers. Fortunately, there are precedents for this way of thinking. Since the 1980s, the state of California has examined how classroom design affects student performance, looking at how students' cognitive ability is affected by factors such as natural light.[14]

Gradually, the focus and content of POE is acknowledging the effect of building design on employees and their performance. Furthermore, research-led design has been found to produce better workplaces and improve the culture in organisations.[15] The relationship is complex and so evaluations often blend several research methods and tailor the tools and methodologies to individual organisations and buildings.[16]

POE studies such as these enable organisations to benchmark their workplace transformation projects, supporting wider roll-outs across their estate. What is lacking, however, is a consistent loop back to architects and developers. Lack of time, limited budget and the fear of failure that might be revealed with a project's assessment often overshadow the feedback process.[17] But without these lessons learned, the design community could become out of step with what clients want.

BUILDING A CULTURE OF KNOWLEDGE EXCHANGE

Currently, there is an imbalance in the relationship between the architects, contractors and developers responsible for creating a building and the organisations and individuals who occupy them. For the former, the belief prevails that a project is finished as soon as the keys are handed over to the client. On the other hand, corporate clients running programmes of work are more interested in measurement and driving improvement through to their next projects; there is little focus on feeding this knowledge back into the construction sector.

The challenge

This is partly about cost. POE is often not included in the client's capital budget. Even though awareness of its benefits is growing, implementation is sporadic and confined to the more sophisticated corporate organisations. Most client organisations ask to see POE results, but not enough are investing in data

gathering. If POE is not included in the budget, it won't happen.

It is also about education. Architecture as a discipline has been challenged for the quality of its teaching, its focus on individualism and its failure to address global issues.[18] We can add to this list a lack of awareness around the daily practices of building users. A student may graduate with the ability to create stunning 3D visualisations of an office complex, yet will have no conceptual basis for thinking about the people or processes going on inside. Occasionally, postgraduate courses cover POE, but these are

isolated courses for those who want to specialise, and are often focused on physical environment factors.

Office buildings may be designed by architects, but they are containers for people. Architects need to draw on knowledge about a building's use to avoid perpetuating design mistakes. In-depth POE studies – in combination with new standards like the WELL Building Certification[TM], which emphasises the importance of health and wellbeing in the design and construction process – may help to build these essential linkages between architects, corporate clients and building users. For example, Soft Landings,

---

CASE STUDY 6.1

UNIVERSITY OF EAST LONDON'S STRATFORD LIBRARY

PROJECT: UNIVERSITY OF EAST LONDON – STRATFORD LIBRARY

LOCATION: LONDON, UK

ARCHITECT: HOPKINS ARCHITECTS

COMPLETION DATE: APRIL 2013

A performance-based strategy was the approach taken for the University of East London's Stratford Library (Hopkins Architects; 2013), to help ensure the building met strict energy and environmental targets when in use. The client had helped set the green criteria early on, and a Soft Landings engineer was deployed at the commissioning stage to brief client maintenance teams on how to optimise performance. Work continued after handover, with a special monitoring programme to help fine-tune systems, and regular meetings between project engineers and client teams during the first year of operation.[19]

Figure 6.3: University of East London, Stratford Library

LEESMAN'S GLOBAL STANDARD FOR WORKPLACE EFFECTIVENESS

CONCEPT: LEESMAN

While methodologies such as POE and Soft Landings provide vital frameworks for organisations to gather data on the effectiveness of their buildings, it is perhaps natural that they're often less than keen to share this information. Architects and designers may be unwilling to give their peers sight of ideas that haven't worked. And, on the client side, few organisations would want to give up the competitive advantage delivered through improved productivity with their rivals.

Activity complexity

Data as at Q4 2017

10.3

Our research consistently points to work activity complexity providing the strongest marker of an employee's workplace infrastructure needs. The average number of activities across all employees is 10.3. Demographically those aged 45-54 have the highest average activity complexity at 10.9 but those aged 35-44 have the lowest Leesman Lmi workplace effectiveness score.

Figure 6.4: Work activity complexity – the strongest marker of an employee's workplace infrastructure needs

Leesman is a leader in measuring workplace effectiveness, with its survey and benchmarking tool providing insight into how well work environments support employees. Leesman examines, in detail, how workplaces support employee experience and the key drivers of employee experience, productivity and engagement within organisations (see Figure 6.4).

In 2010, Leesman developed an online survey which evaluates how effectively the workplace is able to support employees to carry out the role they have been employed to do. The tool examines five key areas, including the ability of a workplace to support those activities that individual employees class as important to their role.

Although the tool was targeted at architects and designers, it was the facility management (FM) world that became the trailblazer, recognising the value in being a better-informed client to the designers whose services they were buying. Now more than 85 per cent of Leesman's client base comprises end-user occupiers – facilities management and real-estate teams – trying to better understand how their workplaces support their organisations.

This focused approach has allowed Leesman to collect data on how more than 2,250 workplaces in 67 countries support more than 300,000 employees in work. The data provides a detailed examination of employee needs and exposes how well those requirements are being met by the hard and soft infrastructure (examples are shown in Figure 6.5). The output allows occupier clients, their suppliers and their advisers to develop a roadmap of short- and long-term goals, with specific interventions to help meet overall corporate objectives.

Today a typical large project would extend to a client's global workplace portfolio. One such organisation* measures all its key assets every two years. The data collected informs their employee workplace experience framework. The Global Workplace Experience Lead at this organisation is responsible for the biannual survey, and cascading the findings out to regional property and facilities services leads. He says, 'It's a substantial task, but the data we obtain allows us to test and verify that our workplace experience programme is delivering

benefit for both our employees and for the business.'

For a large number of clients, however, the data reveals that organisations are repeatedly not getting what they should from their corporate workplaces, with opportunities being consistently missed and the impact on employees of the physical and virtual infrastructure of workplace grossly underestimated.

An elite group of employers bucks this trend, delivering individual workplaces that brilliantly support employee experience across most activities employees are undertaking. Some of these spaces – those that comply with strict qualification criteria – are given the Leesman+ 'high-performing workplace' certification.

This independent mark of outstanding employee workplace experience has increased in influence over the past years. Leesman is focused on understanding what makes these locations distinctive, and how their physical and technical infrastructure differs from those with lower Leesman workplace effectiveness scores, as per Figure 6.6.

*Anonymous for business confidentiality purposes.

Differences based on productivity agreement

Data as at Q4 2017

Most would agree that any examination of productivity must focus on outcomes not inputs. So, understanding what an employee is doing across the breadth of a working day is central to creating an infrastructure to support those activities. But our research also points to specific activities having greater impact on an employee's perceived sense of productivity. The chart below shows the agreement / satisfaction differences in opinions of those who agreed, those who were neutral and those who disagreed that their workplace enabled them to work productively.

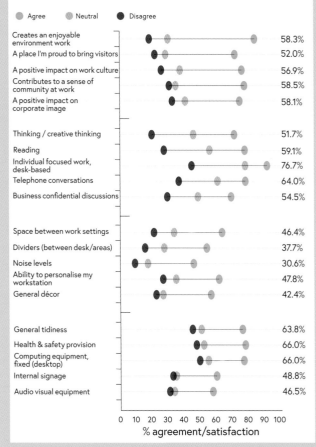

● Agree   ● Neutral   ● Disagree

Creates an enjoyable environment work	58.3%
A place I'm proud to bring visitors	52.0%
A positive impact on work culture	56.9%
Contributes to a sense of community at work	58.5%
A positive impact on corporate image	58.1%
Thinking / creative thinking	51.7%
Reading	59.1%
Individual focused work, desk-based	76.7%
Telephone conversations	64.0%
Business confidential discussions	54.5%
Space between work settings	46.4%
Dividers (between desk/areas)	37.7%
Noise levels	30.6%
Ability to personalise my workstation	47.8%
General décor	42.4%
General tidiness	63.8%
Health & safety provision	66.0%
Computing equipment, fixed (desktop)	66.0%
Internal signage	48.8%
Audio visual equipment	46.5%

0 10 20 30 40 50 60 70 80 90 100
% agreement/satisfaction

Figure 6.5: Differences based on productivity agreement

How Leesman+ spaces out-perform the rest

Data as at Q4 2017

Difference
+3.7%

The design of my workplace is important to me:

Leesman average	85.1%
Leesman+ agreement	88.8%

Difference
+15.0%

My workplace contributes to a sense of community at work

Leesman average	58.5%
Leesman+ agreement	73.5%

Difference
+20.4%

My workplace is an enjoyable environment to work in

Leesman average	58.3%
Leesman+ agreement	78.7%

Difference
+15.7%

My workplace enables me to work productively

Leesman average	58.8%
Leesman+ agreement	74.5%

Difference
+29.2%

My workplace is a place I'm proud to bring visitors to

Leesman average	52.0%
Leesman+ agreement	81.2%

Figure 6.6: How Leesman+ spaces outperform the rest

101

a process that encourages architects and contractors to consider how a building performs in use, could help to formalise this way of thinking.

These debates around how to make POE more people-focused are part of the wider discussion about how to bridge the gap between the designer (and constructor) of a building and its maintainer (and occupier). Architects, contractors and developers need to take the long view, across the building's whole life, incorporating a sense of how people work and socialise into the design process from their very first sketches – and, critically, developing an awareness of how this usage changes over time.

A wider view – Soft Landings

Soft Landings is a UK initiative that aims to address some of these issues. It was launched following the PROBE programme in the late 1990s, which found that many buildings weren't performing to the level set out in their design specifications, leaving occupiers unimpressed with the finished product.[20] The programme showed that, more often than not, this was down to inadequate consideration of what users expected and needed from their building.

Launched in 2009, by a cross-industry group – the Building Services Research and Information Association and the Usable Buildings Trust (both non-profit) – the Soft Landings framework champions better links between the different organisations involved in planning, designing, constructing and operating buildings. Although often viewed as a method to make building handover smoother, the Soft Landings process covers the whole property life cycle, from emphasising user needs and expectations at initial briefings through to ensuring that POE takes place. Aligned to RIBA's Plan of

Work, it can be used for private- or public-sector projects.

According to the 2018 Soft Landings Framework guide, 'Soft Landings starts by raising awareness of performance in use in the early stages of briefing and feasibility, helping to set realistic success criteria and assign responsibilities. It then assists the management of expectations through design, construction and commissioning, and into initial operation, with particular attention to detail in the weeks immediately before and after handover. Extended aftercare, which can take up to three years after occupancy, includes performance monitoring and evaluations. This can help the client and the project team better understand how successful their project has been and how the building's performance can improve. The lessons learned can be used in future projects. Extended aftercare can also help the end users make better use of their buildings. Soft Landings can run alongside any procurement process, potentially in any country. It also provides a natural route for post-occupancy evaluation (POE) and feedback.' [21]

Seen this way, POE is just one element of an iterative, user-focused design, build and operate strategy, in which a constellation of stakeholders collaborate to deliver a project. This may seem daunting to those accustomed to the clean break represented by completion and handover. Architects can no longer walk away at the end of a project. Indeed, the idea of an 'end' may itself need redefining, replaced by the idea of an ongoing relationship with a building's occupier and maintainer. The latter will become involved in a project earlier, too, and will need to prepare themselves for making potentially far-reaching design decisions upfront.

While POE has been around for decades, it has been sporadically implemented. Soft Landings is also still in its infancy. And both tend to focus on the more tangible elements of building services, rather

than on the complexities of employee productivity and wellbeing.

Building on this, the aspiration is for the focus of Soft Landings to widen, into a more sophisticated understanding around those harder-to-measure elements of people and behaviour. There are already signs of this in the UK government's Soft Landings Framework for public-sector building projects, which includes criteria around 'functionality and effectiveness' and internal conditions such as comfort that are linked, albeit implicitly, to wellbeing.

Adopting the standards and processes discussed in this chapter could trigger deeper thinking about productivity and wellbeing before a construction project even gets on site. Design and construction decisions will be informed by a longer-term view, engendered by Soft Landings and based on lessons learned from POE studies. This, in turn, could prompt architects to embrace a more user-focused curriculum and skill set. A virtuous circle of learning, with user-centred design at its heart, suddenly becomes achievable.

CONCLUSION

Although there is some history of more enlightened corporate clients running POE, first to make their office buildings more efficient and, more recently, to support the productivity and wellbeing of their workforce, this people-centred thinking has struggled to establish a foothold in architectural design practice and education. With a growing body of evidence suggesting greater productivity and wellbeing in well-designed offices, the need to exploit and build on evidence is clear. The time is right for clients and the design community to take notice.

This is not just a box-ticking exercise. Architects could benefit from re-orienting their thinking away from technology-centred solutions, towards a more human-centred approach. Architects study as individuals, but at work they are part of a team – managing a web of complex relationships, with clients, partners, users and the wider world. Initiatives such as Soft Landings and the sustainability standards help them make the most of these relationships, prompting them to ask the right questions early on and to bring building occupiers into the process at the right time. They also provide a context in which to make the most of the rich data harvested by POE studies.

Those evaluations will not follow a common pattern or template. They will need to be adjusted to the specific needs of the project. There will still be a requirement for those tried-and-tested POE tools – the user satisfaction survey, energy-use assessment and details of the existing physical and managerial circumstances – but a new POE should

incorporate sophisticated metrics that align with new ways of working. It is important that productivity and wellbeing are assessed along with sustainability and building performance.

What may result is a whole new way of looking at workplace construction programmes. Contractual relationships may need to be redrawn to include early involvement on the part of the occupier, and post-occupancy responsibility for the delivery team. Corporate clients will also need to review their real-estate strategies. Although a number of global facilities managers are taking an increasingly employee-centric approach, supported in some organisations by a Head of Employee Experience, the norm more widely is still towards a programmatic, FM-heavy method for rolling out new sites – based on a corporate 'bible' of fit-out guidelines that may not deliver offices that stimulate innovation, clever thinking and agile working.

Even greater effort is required, therefore, to ensure that clients' real-estate functions evolve beyond just FM concerns to encompass and help address human-resource and productivity issues as well. In this new, connected world, workplaces that can bring together sustainability, efficiency and wellbeing will become real drivers of value for an organisation.

This chapter has focused on using research to help create better workplaces, but the ultimate objective is for organisations to do better work, to create stronger and more creative teams, to produce better products and services – and simply providing better workplaces will not necessarily achieve this. The next chapter looks at how the workplace can be a catalyst for a change in organisational culture and behaviour.

LEARNING POINTS

1. A data-led briefing process – with architects and design teams working together to enable clients to identify their requirements upfront, and then incorporate them into designs as early as possible – can help ensure a workspace matched to users' needs.

2. As our ways of working in offices develop, the tools we deploy to measure users' needs must evolve alongside them.

3. When designing a new office, investment in supporting people (comfort, wellbeing, engagement, etc.) is likely to yield much greater rewards than

   focusing only on real-estate costs.[22] Existing sustainability and performance benchmarks need to reflect this, and should include indicators for wellbeing and productivity.

4. A shift in attitude and approach is required to ensure

   a consistent focus on POE, covering wellbeing and productivity, and to share and embed the knowledge this generates.

5. It may be time to redefine project 'end', replacing it with an ongoing relationship between the building occupier and maintainer.

NATIONAL GRID

LOCATION: WARWICK, UK

ARCHITECT: AECOM

COMPLETION DATE: 2014

Figure 6.7: In National Grid's Warwick site, employees are able to adapt the work space to their needs (Warwick, UK; AECOM; 2014)

For more than eight years, National Grid and AECOM have worked to update National Grid's office portfolio – with adaptable and stimulating spaces, including its Warwick site.[23]

This work is an example of how sophisticated data-led design and POE research can help validate and benchmark productivity benefits from a workplace transformation project.

The team redesigned the office environment in line with changes in ways of working. This included introducing shared work areas, moveable walls, project rooms, a variety of support spaces and places for employees to socialise, as shown in Figure 6.7. The first project was undertaken as a pilot, designed to experiment with the future of the workplace for National Grid. This piloting approach is a great way to test design ideas live and measure their impact. Following the success of the first pilot, each floor at their Warwick site was transformed into a new way of working.[24]

It was a major project, and assessing how the new surroundings had made a difference to employees was crucial. Traditional POE didn't have the breadth or nuance to capture the information the client and designer needed, so they teamed up with a leading UK university to create a bespoke study. The research drew comparisons between the perceived (subjective) and actual (objective) productivity levels of employees in redesigned floors, and those of employees in floors that had not yet been redesigned in the same building.

Research methods

The research team knew that a single indicator of productivity would not provide a complete picture of improvements at National Grid. They developed an integrated approach using several research methods, including:

- **Work performance survey:** This measured a range of attributes proven to be key indicators of productivity. Data was collected from more than 500 employees.

- **User focus groups and interviews:** These tested and validated data from the survey, and helped the team to understand more about why certain things were happening.

- **Observational studies:** These gathered live data on space use and work activities at National Grid over time.

Over time, it became clear that these metrics were useful for steering the workplace programme, but the team needed to dig deeper to try to measure productivity benefits. To this end, the research team ran a series of cognitive performance tests to complement the subjective data provided by these surveys and studies, and to provide an objective measure of performance.

Before and after findings

Data was collected in the existing open-plan environment and was compared to data collected in the new smart working environment, which included shared desks, project areas, quiet rooms and informal meeting areas in areas assigned to specific teams. Results revealed that comfort and satisfaction with the work environment at the redesigned offices was eight per cent higher than those in open-plan offices that had not been redesigned. This was also positively associated with perceptions of team performance. The higher teams rated their comfort and satisfaction with their work environment, the higher they rated their performance.

As part of an industry-first study, the team also looked at the 'before' and 'after' effect on productivity through cognitive testing. Those in the new environment performed eight per cent better than those in the old one. Employees also said that their ability to concentrate was better. A higher percentage of people in the new space agreed that the environment helped them and their team to be more productive. The study showed that five per cent more productive time was gained through easier access to meeting spaces.[25]

Additionally, a five per cent increase in collaborative activity per person was found in the new office environment, along with better connectedness between teams, effective team working and an increase in knowledge sharing.

Further analyses around variables that could have influenced the relationship between the work environment and productivity revealed that the less positively employees perceived their workplace culture, the less positively they rated their individual performance.

An in-depth picture of productivity

While there is no magic formula with which to calculate exact revenue increases due to changes to an employee's work environment, this series of studies gave National Grid a rounded, in-depth picture of productivity. It demonstrated that improvements to the design of the workplace helped to improve productivity, but also that change management was crucial to the success of the project. Improving and measuring productivity must be done in the round, with as much investment going into how the people and space are managed as the physical design of the office itself.

WORKPLACE AS A CATALYST FOR BEHAVIOUR CHANGE

Hilary Jeffery, Charlotte Hermans and Kelly Bacon

7

Change is a constant in all industries, sectors and parts of the world. It is also getting harder to predict and happening at an exponential rate – with products, design approaches and services that were revolutionary two years ago becoming obsolete if they are not adapted fast enough.

The previous chapter looked at how research can help us create outstanding workplaces. This chapter focuses on how the development of such workplaces can act as a powerful lever for organisational change. It also examines the role that change management has in ensuring that the users of a workspace understand the vision for ways of working and can use the environment for maximum benefit. The topics and case studies provided here are intended to be relevant to both the occupier and the designer.

INTRODUCTION

CHANGE AS A CONSTANT

Change readiness has been a hallmark of successful start-up companies that are small enough to be nimble and adaptable, while FTSE 100 organisations have struggled to change course quickly enough for today's markets. But competitive advantage, no matter the size of the organisation, can perhaps now be defined as the ability to see what is coming down the line, and being willing and able to respond. That said, there is a delicate balance between responding to passing trends and staying focused on what is proven to work and get results. This is the line that the world's most successful companies tread.

However, the reality is that identifying the need to change, and then implementing it, is so often fraught with challenges that few change efforts are entirely successful. Most change takes longer to achieve than anticipated, can negatively impact morale, and often costs a great deal in terms of money, time and emotional upheaval.

Organisations must seek support for change from every corner of the business. Change readiness and responsiveness means having the right people in the right roles: building capability, prioritising innovation, speeding up decision making, reducing waste, and creating a culture of trust and openness. The challenge is in providing the right conditions to make that happen.

Buildings and places have a role to play in catalysing and optimising change for organisations. Traditionally, property has simply been a drain on the balance sheet, but organisations are increasingly tapping into the power of the physical environment as a lever for transformation. With this comes an increasing need for the built-environment industry to take organisational development and change management seriously, and build it into the DNA of its processes and projects.

There is a need for a greater link between workplace designers, change managers and those who ultimately operate and manage facilities once a project is complete. The risk in not connecting these traditionally siloed disciplines is that the building or workplace created will not be used optimally, resulting in superficial change to the organisation.

THE PHYSICAL WORKPLACE AS A CHANGE ENABLER

One of the most visible and powerful levers for change in an organisation is its physical workplace. The most mature organisations unite people, culture, technology and place to create a climate for change. Instead of the working environment adapting and reacting to change, forward-thinking organisations now recognise that it can be a powerful enabler in itself.

Seeing the workplace as a tool for transformation means organisations such as Estée Lauder, when they have identified an opportunity for change, seek to align their behaviours, technology and workplace strategies in support of it. They look for ways in which they can achieve improvements, such as better supporting leadership qualities and capabilities, responding to a changing regulatory environment, or changing how teams operate and make decisions, increasing the speed to market. When managed well, the workplace can be an important contributor to making these changes happen.

CHANGE NEEDS TO BE MANAGED

Change strategies have the potential to fail when a structured approach is not adopted by the client organisation, so successful and sustainable implementation requires proactive management. Change management improves project adoption

and long-term success. An estimated 70 per cent of failures are not due to poor strategy, but rather poor execution.[1] Change management reduces this risk and closes the gap, because it focuses on the solution, not the benefits of the solution. Without an intelligent change management programme, timelines often extend, resistance increases and apathy spreads.

A 2013 study by Booz & Company surveyed more than 2,200 workers from various industries and found that 67 per cent said change management processes had a positive impact on their experiences of change at work.[2] An earlier 2002 study by McKinsey also validated the need for strong change management programmes in organisational transition. Based on research with 40 operations, from financial institutions to hospitals, it revealed that only 42 per cent of companies were successful in large-scale reorganisation, while 58 per cent of companies did not achieve their objectives; 20 per cent secured a third or less of their expected return on investment. Companies with poor change management practices had the lowest returns.[3]

One of the key issues can be misaligned business strategies that commonly result in contradictory directions for an organisation. For example, a strategy may focus on the long term, but a company's rewards systems are set up for short-term wins. These kinds of misalignments are rarely visible to any one person in the organisation. Change management works to connect an organisation's separate components via a holistic and integrated perspective that enables the organisation to work collaboratively across divisions towards a unified vision and goal.

BUILDING A CHANGE CULTURE

When it comes to driving workplace change, one of the biggest challenges is the relationship that cultural change inevitably has with a build project that has a fixed start and end date, and follows the principles of project management. This creates an emphasis on timelines, milestones, risk mitigation, build quality, the supply chain and, importantly, budget. Managing the organisation through a cultural change, within this context, requires buy-in at the very top of the organisation to ensure the right balance between project and change management. One has a definite end date, while the other continues far beyond practical completion.

Organisations undertaking workplace change have the opportunity to build a change culture, rather than manage a one-off change event. However, too often, workplace change initiatives miss this opportunity. Returning to the points made at the beginning of this chapter, to create an organisation that thrives in an environment of constant change, organisations need to see change initiatives as an opportunity to build capability within the organisation. It should be seen as a place where people embrace change, can maximise it for the good of the business and can leverage it to address broader organisational challenges. Taking this approach means the organisation will become more change-ready, giving it the skills to tackle the next change that will inevitably come, later on.

To attain these goals, workplace design must be grounded in an understanding of the organisation, its culture, its employees and the work they undertake. A thoughtfully designed workplace, coupled with a strong change management approach, can improve organisational performance and deliver returns on investment far greater than the initial costs. Improved productivity, improved wellbeing and more innovation or creativity are just as valuable returns on investment as using every square metre well. In essence, the success of a design project should be measured in terms of how well it works for the organisation and how happy the occupiers are.

CONSIDERATIONS FOR MANAGING CHANGE IN WORKPLACE TRANSFORMATION

Start early and position it right

Change management works to remove barriers that impede a project's success by shifting attitudes and organisational resources, and providing opportunities for the workforce to get involved early. Therefore, for change management to be successful, it needs to be part of the project from the beginning and continue beyond completion and the moving-in date. By aligning resources upfront, organisations can ensure that engaged staff can provide valuable feedback to avoid major blind spots. This will help the organisation to address negative perceptions and rumours early on, so that resistance to change is managed and productivity loss during the transition phases is minimised.

Balance structure and process while staying agile and open

The nature of change means that those managing it successfully need to stay agile. Managing change means being in a place of exploration and continuous learning. For example, as the journey of change progresses, good change managers will uncover opportunities to link workplace change to other parallel change programmes, as well as seeking to learn from them. This means that change managers need to plan well and create appropriate plans and structure, but also remain flexible to changing circumstances, demands and priorities.

Because change is an organic process, it cannot be planned from beginning to end. The role of the change manager is to stay alert and react to circumstances as they arise, while maintaining continuity and minimising feelings of instability by keeping the project on track and working towards milestones.

Leverage parallel change programmes

Linked to the points above, a major enabler of successful change is forging a link with other change programmes in the organisation. The skill is to leverage them so that they reinforce each other. Workplace change will be just one aspect of the overall change ambition within an organisation. So, workplace changes have to be woven into the overall vision, with any clashes in resource, ability and enthusiasm identified and worked through. For example, change programmes seeking to implement flexible working will have a direct impact on workplace planning and need to be connected to it, while an overload of change creates the risk of talent leaving the business. Change management contributes to getting the balance right.

See change management as facilitation, not project management

Change managers need to balance driving change and being the face of it. The role of change managers is to help others grasp and leverage change. In many ways, the change manager is a facilitator, a trainer and coach. This approach will contribute to building change capability, as previously mentioned. A welcome compliment for a change manager is when leaders, managers and employees take credit for the success of the change – this signifies a job well done.

Transfer ownership for change and building capability

Building on the above point, a major part of a successful change management programme is transferring ownership of the change to leaders within the business. With skill, it can be used as a leadership development opportunity, with people given the task of delivering the change as part of their development. Rather than being considered a challenge, the change journey should be seen by business managers as an opportunity for self-development – and, by the organisation, as a chance to identify leaders and managers with the skills to lead change. This learning process helps the organisation to build capability around change.

Research by the Center for Creative Leadership identified three leadership competencies – communication, collaboration and commitment – as being central to successful change programmes, because they bring together the 'process' and 'people' parts of change that 'make or break' these programmes.[4]

Communication is about 'knowing what to say and how to say it to build and sustain commitment to the change'. Crucially, the research points to the importance of clearly articulating the 'why' of change as well as the 'what'. The design process is a powerful change and communication tool. The challenge for the architect is to utilise this to engage occupiers in the process.[5]

Collaboration covers 'bringing people together to plan and execute the change'. Those leading successful change programmes drove high levels of collaboration by building strong teams, finding ways to work across traditional boundaries and empowering people within the organisation to take ownership and tackle challenges.[6]

The final competency, commitment, relates to leaders 'changing themselves in service of the change goal'. In other words, adapting their own beliefs, methods and behaviours in line with the change they are leading – for example, displaying enthusiasm and a positive attitude towards the changes they're implementing, thus acting as a powerful role model to the wider organisation. This is about the client stepping forward, engaging in the change directly and setting an example of change leadership.

Know that success lies in bottom-up engagement as well as top-down leadership

While engagement with leadership teams is crucial to successful change, change managers need to continually play a top-down *and* a bottom-up game. These two efforts need to run in parallel while staying connected. People across the organisation need to be authentically involved in the change to accept, adapt and ultimately influence it. Only when they feel they have played a real part in its shape and development and got an understanding of 'what's in it for them' will they be willing to own the change and adapt their behaviours and attitudes. Therefore, to be sustainable, change cannot only be managed top-down; it needs to be driven from the bottom up and carried by all layers of the organisation. An intelligent change management programme will build in lots of opportunities for dialogue at every level of the organisation, through interviews, workshops and other engagement activities.

Invest in people and build relationships

Change management will not work if it is impersonal and indirect. Workplace change can be difficult, and has a significant impact on the people in an organisation. Change management is not a tool for avoiding the difficult conversations that need to happen. It is important that communication is honest and transparent about the goals and driving forces of the changes. Leaders have to work with employees to help them embrace change at their own pace, and they need to work hard to listen to those affected by the change. Change mangers need to design change programmes that allow space for investing in people and hearing their concerns, while positively challenging convention.

Recognise that change needs its own strategy

Successful change programmes also invest time in developing a clear and deliberate change approach, and strategy based on knowledge about the organisation and its culture. This will involve articulating what the key change messages are, who the key stakeholders are, and what mechanisms will be used to trigger dialogue across the organisation about the change. In contrast, a communications plan is typically one-directional, with the aim of distributing information in a structured way; a change strategy is a two-way process that is informed by staff engagement.

TOP TEN TIPS FOR WORKPLACE CHANGE MANAGEMENT

1. **Relationships, not process:** The most important change moments often happen outside set meeting schedules. The most valuable use of your time will be to get alongside those you are working with and build relationships in an informal way. Putting these relationships in place in the early stages will make the project easier in the longer term.

2. **Sponsorship needs to be visible:** If the senior leadership team is not committed to the change or do not show that they sponsor the ongoing process, the project is more likely to fail. It is also true that employees tend to trust their leaders and follow them more easily if they see that the new behaviour is expected, recognised and valued.

3. **Success comes when you transfer ownership:** A sense of ownership of the solution will create a sense of pride among those affected by a changing environment, and will create a culture where problems and issues are managed by the organisation rather than being passed back to the project team.

4. **One size doesn't fit all:** Just as each building is different, so are the business units you will encounter. Different groups have different expectations and start from different positions. Furthermore, they tend to like to receive information and get involved in different ways. For example, a construction team will like to be involved in developing the programme for the project, while an engineering team wants to have significant involvement in the design phases. Change management needs to be tailored to suit the different audiences.

5. **Know your audience and speak their language:** Get to know the business units you are leading through the change, and communicate in a way that they are used to and understand. It is not about what you tell; it is about what they hear.

6. **Don't hear what you want to hear; be prepared to learn:** It is easy to forget to listen to the people you are taking through the change process. It is important to always listen out for legitimate concerns that need to be considered as the solution is developed. Often some of the best ideas come from those going through the changes – make sure you don't miss them.

7. **Build confidence by taking the little things seriously:** Lots of conversations in a change management programme will be about small details in relation to workspace. It is crucial to understand and respond to these queries in the same way as you would for the 'bigger ticket' items. The success of projects often comes down to the details, so spending time getting them right will pay off in the long run.

8. **Always answer the question 'what's in it for me?'** While there are often obvious benefits to the organisation from change, the change management programme needs to focus on the benefits that individuals and teams can expect from embracing the change. It is a good idea to write a response to the 'what's in it for me?' question as part of the project brief and vision stage. This will help distil the project objectives and provide a considered response when people do ask the question.

9. **A strong change agent network is crucial:** This will help cascade information and change management activities to the wider community. Choosing the right person for the role is crucial. Key characteristics are:

   ★ They are well known and respected in their team

   ★ They have an in-depth understanding of the culture and dynamics of the business

   ★ They have a positive outlook

   ★ They have good interpersonal and communication skills

   ★ They have the ability to challenge their peers

10. **Change isn't easy for anybody; change is hard, even when you choose it:** Some of the resistance you may face during the change process will simply be a reaction to change, or it could be that people don't have all the facts. Make sure your change programme gives people the information they need.

113

WHAT SCALE OF CHANGE MANAGEMENT EFFORT DO YOU NEED?

Answering the following questions will help determine the scope and effort required when planning a change programme.

1. **Consequence:** What is the worst-case scenario if the change doesn't happen? The answer determines the level of urgency and resources needed to move the project on.

2. **Scale:** How large is the project? What is the size of the organisation? Does it involve one site or several? The larger the project, the more pieces will need to be managed, the more people will need to collaborate and engage, and the stronger the communication will have to be.

3. **Financial feasibility:** How do consequence and scale get balanced against the available budget?

4. **Resources:** What kind of resources will the organisation need? Do the change management budgets align with the scale of change? Is an internal team able to handle all of the changes? Does the organisation need the help of external experts?

5. **Time:** How much time does the organisation have to adapt and implement the strategy? Longer timelines allow more flexibility and decrease urgency.

6. **Culture:** Are the changes welcome? How much training is involved? Is the change about shifting the way people work, or about teaching them new skills?

7. **Opportunities:** What other benefits come from the process?

IMPORTANT ROLES IN CHANGE MANAGEMENT

A significant element in establishing the right change management approach is identifying key roles across the organisation. The roles outlined below play perhaps the most significant part in making change successful.

- **Sponsors** need to be the top level of authority in an organisation, and are the ultimate owners of the change. They have the ability to direct the resources needed to deliver the vision. There may also be sponsors in local departments who have an important role in driving change within their part of the organisation.[7,8]

- **The design team** has a crucial role to play in bringing change alive for the organisation. Design teams who grasp the connection between design and change act as powerful ambassadors and drivers for the change. They have a unique ability to involve occupiers in co-creating solutions by bringing design ideas to life through images, 3D visuals, animated walk-throughs and stories – rather than traditional 2D plans that don't fully convey the change story and are difficult for occupiers to understand.

- **Implementers** are the people who ultimately make the change happen. Sponsors delegate the delivery of the change to this group of people – they are often the first to flag any barriers to the change strategy, and will recommend options for how to move forward.

- **Change agents** help to facilitate the change. They often come from different levels within the organisation but have certain characteristics in common – they are supportive, positive, well-networked, understand the organisation, and are available for people to talk to. They can often act as a bridge between the wider population and the sponsors, as well as supporting the implementation team by acting as sounding boards and advisers as the change progresses.

- **Early adopters** are those people who are 'ready to embrace the change' and understand the vision. Again, these people can come from different parts of the organisation but tend not to be in positions of power, so need genuine support from the sponsors. Early adopters tend to be solution-oriented and can naturally motivate and energise others around them.[9]

CONCLUSION

This chapter has explored how the physical workplace can be a catalyst for a change in an organisation's culture and people's work behaviour, and completes the section of the book that is focused on people. Turning to delivery, the next chapter relates back to the concerns about sustainability discussed in Chapter 2: examining the materials and energy used in developing and running our office buildings, and how careful specification can help us create more sustainable workplaces.

LEARNING POINTS

1. In the world of work, change is constant and occurring at an exponential rate.

2. The physical workplace is a powerful catalyst for organisational change.

3. Organisations have an opportunity to use workplace change to build change capability in their leaders and employees, readying them for the next change coming down the line, ultimately creating a culture of change.

4. Change is a positive. It is an opportunity to address longstanding issues, link with ongoing initiatives and introduce innovative ways of working.

5. Change can only be successful when managed well.

6. Design teams need to find a sensitive balance between driving projects by the principles of project management and the principles of change management.

7. Change management doesn't stop at the point of practical completion, but needs ongoing commitment from occupiers.

8. Gaining management/ leadership buy-in to the process is essential, as is the involvement of all key stakeholders, from architects and designers, and buildings and facilities managers, to IT, HR and staff.

9. Designers have a key role in bringing change to life for occupiers and engaging them in the process – the design process is a powerful change tool.

10. When change management is successful, investment in the physical environment brings rewards in terms of improved productivity, satisfaction and wellbeing.

AIRBNB

LOCATION: SAN FRANCISCO, US

ARCHITECT: WRNS

CREATIVE: AIRBNB ENVIRONMENTS TEAM

COMPLETION DATE: 2017

A Russian forest cabin, an English country house, a castle, a boat and a bootcamp: all part of the rich inspiration which has been incorporated into a new Airbnb office building in San Francisco (see Figure 7.1). Home to 1,000 staff from teams including customer service and the legal departments, the eclectic design style was conceived to reflect the company's global brand and its 'belong anywhere' ethos.

Working with local studio WRNS as the architecture firm of record, Airbnb's own Environments Team began implementation of the project by stripping an existing building back to its essential structure. In its previous guise, the building was divided into cellular offices and let in little natural light. The new design and fit-out is steeped in a sense of adventure and travel, and is flooded with natural light. At its heart, the building's atrium features The Castle – made of pinewood strips, this is conceived to dramatise the vertical space and visually link the four floors. Above this sits The Boat, a highly functional structure with spaces for quiet and privacy.

Each of the four floors is given a distinctive city theme – Buenos Aires, Kyoto, Jaipur and Amsterdam. The public spaces are finished in colours, patterns and materials that reflect the respective city culture. Additionally, the interior design of each meeting room is inspired by existing Airbnb listings around the world to enable employees to 'travel' throughout their day.

The main workspaces are divided into 18 neighbourhoods with identical components, for up to 55 people each. Every neighbourhood comprises desk space with large custom-made communal tables and standing desks, three phone rooms, and personal storage. Another feature is the 'garage' – a meeting room for up to 30 people which can be adapted for different uses by opening and closing a room divider with a garage-door mechanism.

As part of Airbnb's ongoing global office design strategy, the Environments Team engaged with local employees in an Employee Design Experience (EDX) programme to help with the finishing touches to the design of the meeting rooms. For example, the Russian forest cabin features pine-clad walls with tapestries, pillows, books and games. Staff added items sourced from Little Russia in San Francisco and New York to bring in fun prints for the pillows and smaller accessories, as well as a decorative iron stove that stands in one corner.

The variety of workspaces encourages healthy ergonomic movement, and increased socialising and engagement. Employees' suggestions also resulted in the incorporation of a bootcamp space, yoga room/wellness centre with a Japanese Zen theme, and an 'apothecary' of wellness-related items.

Figure 7.1: The design style of Airbnb's San Francisco office reflects the company's global brand and its 'belong anywhere' ethos (San Francisco, USA; WRNS; 2017)

THE ESTÉE LAUDER COMPANIES

LOCATION: LONDON, UK

INTERIOR DESIGNER: MCM ARCHITECTURE

WORKPLACE STRATEGY AND CHANGE MANAGEMENT: AECOM

COMPLETION DATE: 2016

Figure 7.2: Clinique brand space at The Estée Lauder Companies' headquarters (London, UK; MCM Architecture; 2016)

Using design as a change tool

Strategic workplace design and supportive change management can encourage creativity, foster wellbeing and increase job satisfaction. The goal is to create spaces and cultures that people want to spend time in and be a part of, and that also enable them to innovate, collaborate and feel – and do – well.

This strategic approach is exemplified in the new UK and Ireland headquarters of The Estée Lauder Companies (ELC) in London. The success was evident seven months after ELC moved into its new office, when staff workplace survey results showed almost 90 per cent workplace satisfaction, up from 30 per cent before the move.

The opportunity was to establish a new UK and Ireland HQ in London, and bring 400 employees and around 20 brands together under one roof for the first time.

Before the design team was brought on board, ELC commissioned a strategic brief. The purpose of this was to work with the business to develop a vision for its workplace, and to understand its requirements and how it would work in the future. This was a creative process of engagement with staff and leaders that resulted in a high-level design concept of the business.

Crucial to the evolution of this new environment were interviews, surveys and focus groups to understand the company's people, workplace culture and current ways of working, and its future wants, needs and the overall vision for its workplace. The results were clear. The vision was to create a new home, designed with employees at its heart, that would support collaboration, creativity and innovation, and strengthen the company's commitment to work–life harmonisation. The space also needed to be flexible enough to grow with the company as its people, technology and ways of working evolved.

The immediate design impact was to move from anchored desktops to agile working, and from segregated workspaces to open plan. This would require new protocols for behaviour and a change management process to guide employees as they transitioned from old to new.

To ensure the new physical workspace matched the company's vision, wants and needs, the strategic brief was developed and signed off before interior designer MCM Architecture started the design implementation. Once the design team was up and running, a parallel change management team was established, led by human resources and communications teams, to prepare people for their new environment. This initiative ran alongside the detailed design process, move-in and post-occupancy evaluation. The client team understood that move-in day was when the project really started for staff, and they invested in making sure they were prepared and excited about their future workplace.

Project highlights

Managing change

Working with the human resources and communications teams made it easy to connect with the company's inherent focus on employee wellbeing, and to provide the ongoing change management and support. A blog was established early in the project and became one of the key communication methods for staff. Closer to move-in, a welcome pack was created for employees that outlined the location, concept and purpose of their new workplace spaces. Employee change champions within teams gave staff a friendly face to speak to and ask questions of throughout the transition. FAQs were regularly updated and became a resource for staff and leaders alike.

Strategies to feel and live well

Wellness, health and happiness have always been important at The Estée Lauder Companies. In the new HQ, employees can book services from manicures to haircuts at the in-house salon, and there's a contemplation room for quiet reflection or meditation. Other benefits include subsidised gym membership, bike storage, showers and a flexible event space designed for yoga classes. The intelligent lighting system and temperature-controlled air improve employee comfort, and there is an in-house cafe with healthy food options and two outdoor terraces.

From anchored to agile

Agile working was introduced, with most employees using a laptop, giving them the freedom to work across teams and locations, whether in the office, at home or elsewhere. Spaces for collaboration, concentration and one-on-one meetings coupled with seamless IT enable employees to stay connected while on the move. A clear-desk policy means that employees pack up at the end of every day and store their belongings in a locker. This was a particular focus for the change management process: listening to staff concerns and questions, and working with the change champions to co-create solutions that would make the new environment work.

Technology as an enabler

New IT, including digital meeting-room booking systems and tablets, helps staff to be more productive. A physical 'IT Salon' helpdesk helps fix IT problems quickly and easily, while also encouraging more face-to-face interaction across departments.

A sense of community and belonging

An important part of the project was creating spaces that balanced The Estée Lauder Companies' overall corporate identity with individual brands, while encouraging employee interaction and collaboration. This fundamental shift from 'me and mine' to 'us and ours' encourages people to share knowledge across brands to spark innovation and build a sense of community (see Figure 7.2). People are at the heart of the concept for this office. A short and powerful video was created of move-in day, which featured leaders telling the story of the project and showing staff reactions upon arrival.

Space to communicate

The move to open-plan working has facilitated much easier connections between individuals and teams. Along with informal breakout areas, and more than 50 large and small meeting rooms, there are flexible collaboration spaces.

DELIVERY

IV

PART

ENERGY, MATERIALITY AND SPECIFICATION

Ant Wilson, Mike Burton and Simon Lerwill

This chapter shifts the focus from a concern with how people use their office buildings, covered in Chapter 7, to the issue of the physical performance of the buildings themselves, and how the specification process can help improve this.

Alongside look and feel, energy efficiency is fast becoming a prime feature on the new-office wish lists of many funders, developers and occupiers, driven by a desire to reduce energy costs and the need to comply with global climate change targets. As a result, developing low-energy buildings that also ensure the health, safety and wellbeing of workers will be a core challenge for architects and engineers, and central to design and specification, in the coming decades. Within the UK, for example, there is much debate about how the situation post Brexit may lead the UK government to review and simplify the legislation around energy efficiency and climate change.

INTRODUCTION

WHAT IS DRIVING CHANGE?

The 1997 Kyoto Protocol requires developed countries to reduce greenhouse gas emissions, in order to restrict global temperature rise to 2°C – coming into force from 2008 and running until 2020. The Paris Climate Change Agreement, which followed in 2016, commits both developed and developing countries to the same aim from 2020 onwards. Individual countries also have their own targets for emissions reduction to contribute to the overall ambition, such as the UK Climate Change Act, which seeks to ensure the country achieves an 80 per cent reduction in greenhouse gas emissions by 2050 from a 1990 base.[1]

Easy wins in the developed world have been achieved by focusing on the carbon load of more powerful gases than carbon dioxide, for instance, by capping methane-producing landfills, as well as switching energy supply away from high CO_2-producing 'dirty' fuels like coal and, controversially, outsourcing heavy industry to other countries. This approach has allowed the use of energy sources such as biofuels and biomass, because they have lower CO_2 emissions.

Now, however, the focus is shifting to tackling carbon dioxide production more substantially. In the UK, CO_2 production accounts for around 82 per cent of greenhouse gas emissions, and is driving policy to decarbonise the power grid altogether,

with cleaner renewables such as solar, wind, tidal and nuclear being used to generate greener electricity.[2]

In addition, carbon emissions from non-domestic buildings, including offices, have fallen only slightly since Kyoto. According to research, non-domestic buildings account for 17 per cent of UK carbon emissions.[3] It's a similar picture across the rest of Europe, with 'buildings responsible for approximately 40 per cent of energy consumption and 36 per cent of CO_2 emissions'.[4]

'Currently, about 35 per cent of the EU's buildings are over 50 years old'. By improving the energy efficiency of buildings, it is estimated that total EU energy consumption 'could be reduced by

KEY EU LAWS

The 2010 Energy Performance of Buildings Directive and the 2012 Energy Efficiency Directive are the main pieces of EU legislation covering the reduction of the energy consumption of buildings.[5]

In 2016, the European Commission (EC) 'proposed an update to the 2010 Directive to promote smart technology in buildings and to streamline the existing rules. The Commission also published a new buildings database – the EU Building Stock Observatory – to track the energy performance of buildings across Europe.'[6]

In 2017, agreement was reached to add a series of measures to the

current directive, aimed at accelerating the cost-effective renovation of existing buildings. There will also be updates to provisions on smart technologies and technical building systems, including automation, and e-mobility will be introduced into the scope of the directive. 'The legal texts of this political agreement will now be finalised and formally adopted by both the European Council and the European Parliament in the coming months.'[7]

Under the existing Energy Performance of Buildings Directive:

★ 'Energy Performance Certificates are to be included in all

advertisements for the sale or rental of buildings

★ EU countries must establish inspection schemes for heating and air conditioning systems or put in place measures with equivalent effect

★ All new buildings must be nearly zero-energy buildings by 31 December 2020 (public buildings by 31 December 2018)

★ EU countries must set minimum energy performance requirements for new buildings, for the major renovation of buildings, and for the replacement or retrofit of building elements (heating and

cooling systems, roofs, walls and so on)

★ EU countries must draw up lists of national financial measures to improve the energy efficiency of buildings'[8]

Under the Energy Efficiency Directive, EU countries must:

★ 'Make energy efficient renovations to at least three per cent of buildings owned and occupied by central government

★ Only purchase buildings that are highly energy efficient

★ Draw up long-term national building renovation strategies that can be included in their National Energy Efficiency Action Plans'[9]

5–6 per cent and CO_2 emissions could be lowered by about 5 per cent'.[10]

This reality has led the EU to seek a step-change in the energy efficiency of buildings, exemplified in its commitment that all new buildings must be nearly zero-energy buildings by 31 December 2020, and supported by Energy Performance Certificates (EPC).[11]

So what are the big trends emerging in sustainable office space as a result? And what tools, materials and approaches can architects and designers employ to help realise these ambitions for a greener future for both clients and governments alike?

EMBODIED ENERGY

In the drive to achieve emission targets, embodied energy in office building materials will become more important than energy in use. Materials that require less energy to produce will be preferred. Equally, the reuse of materials will become essential, with the expectation that buildings will be able to be reconfigured easily or even adapted for a completely different use in the future, such as residential or hotels.

As the idea of the circular economy takes hold in current thinking about sustainability, the aim is to keep materials in high-value use for as long as possible, and it is likely that future developers will not only want floor spaces that can be reconfigured for new uses but the opportunity to reuse elements of the structure. This would require, for instance, steel frames that can be unbolted, dismantled and reused on other buildings (please see Chapter 2 for more details on the circular economy).

THE FUTURE IS ELECTRIC

In terms of energy use, in the future, more buildings will need to be fuelled by electricity and generate their own power from solar panels or implement low carbon and energy efficient solutions such as heat pumps and heat recovery. As a result, gas- and oil-fired boiler rooms will no longer be required, and will be replaced with spaces for battery storage, as buildings that are energy self-sufficient become the norm. Computer rooms in the office will become a thing of the past, with data held in the cloud or in separate data centres. And, after years spent making ducts and pipes smaller, big is making a comeback. It requires much less energy to blow air or move water through bigger ducts and pipes.

Some progress is already being made, resulting in a more holistic approach to the design and specification of office environments. Architects are designing for good daylight with tall ceilings, a range of interesting views out and lots of fresh air. Similarly, as workers demand ever more adaptable spaces, mixed-mode options will become more common, with heating and cooling options fit for all weather – from the hottest summers to the coldest winters.

Taking into account the announced intention of the US government to withdraw from the Paris Climate Change Agreement in 2017, and the uncertainty over Brexit in the UK, the future picture becomes less clear, but there will continue to be a demand for low-energy buildings across the world.[12]

SEVEN WAYS TO ACHIEVE A NEAR ZERO-ENERGY OFFICE

As well as being low energy, to attract the best talent, office buildings will also need to be inspiring, enjoyable places in which to work – with staff being attracted to employers who focus on promoting wellbeing and the environment, and occupiers and employers recognising the link between spaces that support wellbeing and boost productivity, creativity and staff retention.

To help achieve this:

1 Orient and design for daylighting – maximise north light, and shade south and west to minimise solar gain, but design for natural daylighting in the building.

2 Insulate – minimise heat loss with a well-insulated fabric that keeps in heat during the winter, but keeps out the heat of summer. To reduce cooling demand, provide glass only where needed for views and daylight. The built fabric will include photovoltaics and solar thermal collectors, with the energy generated used to power the building.

3 Use good glazing, low-emissivity coatings and inert gases to stop energy loss and heat gain. And, while much of the spectrum can be eliminated, remember to allow for visibility. Below 40 per cent visibility and more lights will be needed – and, consequently, increased energy will be required. Higher-quality glass will contribute to the building's energy performance and the comfort of its occupants, but it will be at a higher price.

4 Provide low-energy systems – lighting, heating, cooling and ventilation systems with heat recovery and occupier demand controls.

5 Don't forget storage – thermal mass for absorbing heat and controlling temperature swings, and batteries to store energy generated during the day or when temperatures are high, for use in the dark or cold.

6 Make the building airtight, paying attention to the junctions/interfaces – controlling unwanted airflow to stop unwanted heat loss and/or gain.

7 Use smart controls to provide energy only where people are/when needed, and use energy-efficient equipment.

WATCH OUT FOR GRAPHENE

Graphene is being hailed as the new wonder material whose potential is only just being explored. This single layer of carbon atoms arranged in a hexagonal lattice is 200 times stronger than steel and the thinnest material on earth – one million times thinner than human hair. It is a superconductor. Graphene could take the place of cables and dramatically increase the lifespan and storage of lithium batteries or help create spray-on solar panels.[13]

Graphene coatings could be applied to steel so it never rusts, or to brick or stone to weatherproof buildings. In addition, graphene can be added to paint, potentially enabling walls to radiate heat and light. Graphene could also be used in clothing, giving individuals wearable heating and cooling solutions to meet their personal requirements and making radiators and air-conditioning obsolete in the future. Its uses are only just being explored, but the built environment will inevitably change because of it.

SPECIFICATION

The specification defines the requirements for the materials and systems used in the construction of a building. It is a key document that communicates the design intent to others, and specification has emerged as an expert discipline in its own right.

As the design evolves from concept to realisation (the completed building), the specification should also evolve and develop to provide a robust data set. This data will reflect the design intent and include a level of information commensurate with the architect's appointment, the procurement route and the work stage. The specification must also be coordinated with the deliverables from the wider design team to prevent duplication or omissions in the information. Ultimately, the quality of the information contained in the specification is fundamental to realising the design.

Prescriptive and descriptive specifications

Broadly, there are two specification types:

- **Prescriptive:** This type of specification is a detailed materials and workmanship specification reflecting the architect's design solution. The contractor may be required to submit some drawings and technical information, but design responsibility remains with the architect.

- **Descriptive:** A specification which, when read with the design drawings, indicates the requirements with which the contractor must comply when undertaking the detailed design. The contractor retains full responsibility for completing the design and execution of the works and for achieving the specified requirements.

It is important to note that the descriptive approach, while passing responsibility for completing the design to the contractor, still requires significant input from the architect if the design intent is to be realised.

For example, the architect may design a glass panel, and specify this using the descriptive approach with particular performance requirements. The architect must be confident that a panel that achieves such requirements can be procured in the market. If not, the contractor will be at liberty to provide alternatives that may not achieve the architect's intended visual requirements, or may have cost and programme implications. As a further aid to clarity, the specification may include indicative products that the architect considers – based on their knowledge and experience – would meet the visual and performance requirements. This gives the contractor a general direction, and they may choose to use the indicative product or another comparable product that is acceptable to the architect.

The development of either the prescriptive or descriptive approach will be defined by the design responsibility split (architect/contractor), which should be agreed early in the design process, with a design responsibility matrix preferably being included in the architect's appointment. Thereafter, the architect should develop the design information to reflect the agreed design responsibility split, being careful not to take on more design responsibility than they are contracted to. This is particularly important when developing the design intent information for contractor design elements. While rightly checking that the design intent is robust, the architect may be tempted to include more information than is necessary, particularly in the building information modelling (BIM) environment. This could potentially attract design liability to the architect, which should sit with the contractor.

Specification development

The specification typically starts out as a descriptive data set and is developed through the design and construction phases, Work Stages 2 to 5, to be fully prescriptive to reflect the completed building.

At **Work Stage 2 (Concept Design)**, the architect endeavours to communicate initial ideas to the client, fellow design team members and other key stakeholders. At this stage, the specification, in its simplest form, may comprise a drawing annotated with initial thoughts on form, function, adjacencies, material options and key performance requirements.

As the design develops through **Work Stage 3 (Developed Design)**, a more detailed outline specification will be prepared. The procurement route and programme will dictate the level of information required and how, in turn, that is presented. Where the project is being tendered at Work Stage 3, typically using a design and build procurement route, the outline specification will be predominantly descriptive in format. There will be few prescriptive work sections, and only where systems or materials are known. The document will include performance requirements, submittals and testing requirements, materials and execution clauses.

The architect and the wider design team may be engaged by the client to continue to develop the design beyond Work Stage 3 – i.e., the project is not being tendered at this stage. In this case, the outline specification may take the form of a schedule of systems and components with key performance requirements and manufacturers' information. A specification in this format is easy to manage and will be used to prepare the cost plan and seek client approval.

At **Work Stage 4 (Technical Design)**, fully developed specification work sections will be prepared for tender purposes, in accordance with the agreed design responsibility designations.

Through **Work Stage 5 (Construction)** the specification will be further developed, with descriptive work sections being developed by the contractor, or their subcontractors on their behalf, to reflect the contractor's design solution. These documents will be subject to acceptance by the architect via the submittals process. There may be little change to prescriptive work sections other than to pick up alternative products put forward by the contractor. However, it should be noted that the architect does not have to accept such alternative products. Accepting such changes may involve the architect in significant research, yet create savings for the contractor, and it is therefore reasonable that a fee is agreed for reviewing such proposed changes. More importantly, the architect needs to remember that once they have accepted changes they may be liable for the products used. Therefore, if they have any doubts regarding such alternatives, they should say so.

Procurement routes

Different procurement routes have typical industry-accepted design responsibility splits that drive the preparation of either prescriptive or descriptive specifications.

Design build – employer's requirements

The architect is employed to prepare employer's requirements documentation for tender purposes. The documentation will include a specification that is typically descriptive in form, but may include a limited amount of prescriptive elements where the client's requirements are clearly defined, e.g. a defined corporate requirement for a particular material or finish.

Design build – post tender

The contractor is required to take the employer's requirements and develop the design for construction purposes. This design work will typically be completed by the contractor's specialist subcontractors, the architect who completed the employer's requirements documentation novated to the contractor, or another architect selected by the contractor. Where the architect is novated to the contractor or an architect is appointed by the contractor, the design responsibility split with the contractor must be agreed. In this situation, it is important to understand the design capabilities of the subcontractor(s), noting that passing

FIVE TRENDS SET TO IMPACT MATERIALS AND SPECIFICATION

1. Augmented reality and virtual reality will be widely used to make choices about buildings, design, layout and systems.

2. All-electric buildings will be powered by renewables, with no reliance on fossil fuels, no chimneys and no big boiler rooms.

3. Total connectivity: all devices will work quickly wherever you are, via cloud-based systems, with no need for computer rooms in the building.

4. Control systems for lighting/security/building management systems/IT, etc. will be fully integrated, and used to improve the efficiency and comfort, safety, health and wellbeing of users. As such, they will enable the personalisation of workspace regarding heat, light and cooling.

5. Artificial intelligence (AI) and data analytics will be used to design and improve the workplace; buildings will be more intelligent and robots will be the norm in design, construction and operation.

design responsibility down the line to the subcontractors using the descriptive approach can only be done if the proposed trade contractor has design capability and carries professional indemnity insurance.

Traditional procurement routes

The architect is typically employed on a full service agreement with a standard form of contract or construction management appointment. With most projects, there will be elements of the design that will be subject to contractor design. Again, the design responsibility split (architect/contractor) will need to be agreed, preferably as part of the appointment negotiations. The decision on the split between prescriptive and descriptive specifications will based on

the complexity of items being designed, the capabilities of the contractor/subcontractors and the size of project.

The future for specification data

We are now at the point where designers are building libraries of specification data sets that are linked to BIM object data to make the process of developing the BIM model and specification more efficient. Moving forward, the link between the object data and specification data will become increasingly dynamic, with changes to the BIM model automatically updating the specification data set and vice versa.

Potentially, design changes discussed and agreed by means of a virtual reality (VR) design review will be automatically reflected in the data sets contained within or linked to the BIM model, with cost and carbon data being updated and available in real time to aid the design process.

The future trend will be for the document to be kept live and passed to the facility manager to assist with the building management. The specification will be a valuable addition to the traditional project file.

Having looked at energy, materials and specification during the design and construction of our office buildings, the next chapter looks at the process of procuring office space.

LEARNING POINTS

1. Increasingly, office buildings will need to be designed for near-zero or net-zero energy use.

2. The future of office power is electricity, and offices will be required to generate and store their own electricity.

3. Design tips include:
   ★ Consider orientation; design for daylighting;

improve insulation and glazing.
   ★ Provide highly efficient heating, cooling, and ventilation systems and lighting with intelligent integrated controls.
   ★ Look at solar PV and solar hot water heating.
   ★ Consider atriums, skylights and light

shafts to improve ventilation, control heat gains and diffuse natural light.
   ★ Consider solar shading or dynamic glazing to control solar gain.

4. The specification is a key contract document. It should address design responsibility issues and should be developed to an appropriate

level of information commensurate with the work stage.

5. Refer to appropriate specialists for issues, such as for fire and acoustic reports.

6. Use the correct terminology appropriate to the contract form.

Figure 8.1: Informal areas within the Sky Central building (London, UK; AL_A, PLP Architecture and HASSELL; 2016)

SKY CENTRAL

LOCATION: LONDON, UK

ARCHITECT: AL_A, PLP ARCHITECTURE AND HASSELL

CAMPUS MASTERPLAN AND CONCEPT DESIGN: AL_A

EXECUTIVE ARCHITECT: PLP

WORKPLACE DESIGN: HASSELL

COMPLETION DATE: 2016

Figure 8.2: A vast 100m-long street runs east to west through the Sky Central building, connecting the main entrances and creating informal community spaces (London, UK; AL_A, PLP Architecture and HASSELL; 2016)

A space to collaborate and create

Collaboration, creativity, community and a place for staff to do the best work of their career – all are part of the design ambitions of Sky Central in West London, the new home of the broadcast giant, bringing together 3,500 people (see Figure 8.2).

As one of the UK's biggest agile workplaces, the numbers are impressive.

This new building is a large and open-plan workplace of 45,000m² over three floors. It includes two atriums, some 18 team 'neighbourhoods' for around 200 people each, 15 different work settings, 5,000 places to sit and almost 25,000 plants, including a small olive grove.

The neighbourhoods are supported by 'home zones' – arrival spaces that include small kitchens, meeting tables and casual sitting areas. These more 'residential' settings blur the boundaries between work and home, and bring

an intimate, human scale to Sky's expansive workplace.

The palette

One of the keys to making this an enjoyable and productive place to work is the materials palette. The concept was driven by a hospitality/residential approach where all finishes were chosen to create an authentic, warm, comfortable environment reflecting Sky's brand. There was a desire to have a workplace that reflected a friendly residential feel with classic longevity.

The vast size of the floorplate and internal ceiling heights needed effective space planning to ensure that human scale, authenticity and comfort were achieved. Key principles were put in place that drove many subsequent design decisions, and continued to underpin the project through stages of change, right through to completion.

One key planning principle was the Bürolandschaft-inspired '20 metre rule', which dictated that at every 20 metres of the floorplate there would be a 'landmark' that served as a wayfinding device, but also to break down the scale of the floorplate. Looking down the floorplate, the eye travels to these landmarks and isn't lost in the vast scale of the building.

The flexible workplace principles were also another key driver for the planning direction of the neighbourhoods; however, the workplace setting types were tailored to Sky's needs (see Figure 8.3). Through detailed briefing and mock-ups in the Live Lab pilot space, the type and proportion of setting types were refined to suit each neighbourhood population. Being modular, with repeated elements, it was essential for the materiality to maintain a cohesive whole.

Taking cues from the base building's cross-laminated timber, steel and concrete palette, there is a deliberate sophistication to the pared-back textural materiality, and this gives a consistent and timeless quality throughout all areas. There is generous use of natural timber, canvas screens, fingerprint-proof black laminate, and soft upholstery in a mixture of neutral and rich block colours, but also in certain areas featuring monochrome patterns.

Landmark elements such as the coloured rope meeting areas, central mezzanine destinations and the olive grove in the north atrium are structures that achieve distinction through colour and texture, acting as key wayfinding points on the large floorplates. These have also formed

the cues for the signage approach, which references the materiality, linking a character to each neighbourhood.

The signage, by Acrylicize, was developed to be clear and simple, and easily distinguishable from a distance. Large numbers follow the system used for identifying neighbourhoods and ensure that the large floorplates are easy to navigate.

Build quality, durability and maintenance

As a single-tenant-occupied building, the Sky Central workplace demands a high level of durability for longevity of use. Taking materiality cues from the base building, architectural language also ensures that high quality and high levels of durability are consistent throughout. Where possible, materials with solid cores are utilised in high-traffic areas – for example, Corian worktops in wet areas, and solid timber at the edges of key circulation junctions. Longevity is also built into the

way of flexible working, where density can fluctuate according to business needs without requiring the standard level of physical churn.

A 'Kit of Sky Parts' was created for the agile workplace settings to create modularity throughout the large floorplates. This was a measure to optimise budgets through repetition and ease of off-site construction. The level of standardisation from neighbourhood to neighbourhood also ensured that finishes and construction types were consistent, to maintain an equal offer across the workplace.

All settings – including home zones and resource points, meeting rooms and collaborative settings – were made from modular components. Where possible these components where made from off-the-shelf systems customised to suit Sky's needs. The use of shop-fitting systems that could be modified as needs changed is an example of the extensive thinking that went into ensuring the longevity of every item designed or specified for the workspace.

Figure 8.3: The open spaces promote wellbeing by encouraging movement and facilitating ad-hoc meetings between colleagues, whilst also providing informal filming spaces (London, UK; AL_A, PLP Architecture and HASSELL; 2016)

133

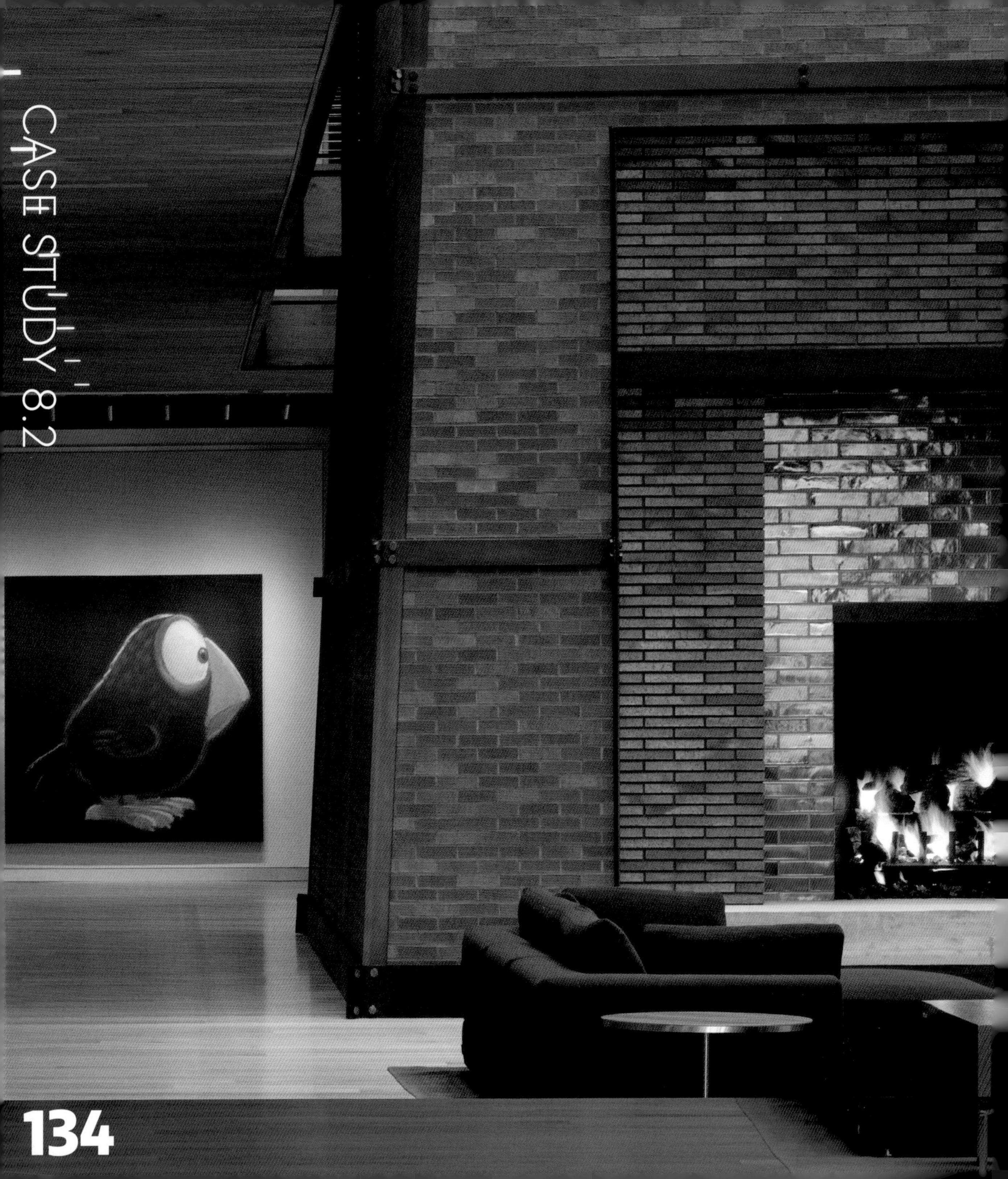

PIXAR

LOCATION: EMERYVILLE, USA

ARCHITECT: ALLIED WORKS ARCHITECTURE

COMPLETION DATE: 2011

It's entirely fitting that there is a powerful storyline woven into the animation studio building created for film-maker Pixar at its California campus. The designs by Allied Works Architecture were created in collaboration with Pixar's former Chief Creative Officer, John Lasseter, and his team of writers, directors and animators, to embody the process and culture of the company. Known around the company as 'Brooklyn', the building responds to the industrial history and character of the Emeryville neighbourhood with the warehouse-style building constructed using the classic trio of concrete, brick and steel.

The interior engages with the city's urban grid, with streets and alleys breaking up the building massing, and supports Pixar's work and culture with a range of spaces tailored to the feature animation process. Against the rugged industrial backdrop, the interior palette and detailing are a delight (see Figure 8.4). Highlights include the welcoming red-brick hearth at the core of the building, and the extensive use of timber to 'wrap' parts of the steel structure and which also plays a starring role in the exquisite spiral stair. Other details directly reference Pixar's history: a custom conference table/display case

for a treasured collection of Matchbox cars, stainless-steel silhouettes of iconic characters inlaid within the terrazzo floors, and a bronze screen punched with a geometric pattern derived from 'Luxo Jr.' – the animated lamp that has become Pixar's de facto mascot.

In complete contrast to the great hallways and public spaces, intimate lounges which serve as informal meeting spaces are rich and lustrous, featuring dark bricks, high-gloss tiles, backlit golden onyx and club-style furniture upholstered in leather and plush fabrics.

Figure 8.5: Pixar campus – one of the restaurants (Emeryville, USA; Allied Works Architecture; 2011)

Figure 8.4: Pixar campus – a lobby area (Emeryville, USA; Allied Works Architecture; 2011)

Figure 8.6: Pixar campus – interior palette and detailing (Emeryville, USA; Allied Works Architecture; 2011)

136

Figure 8.7: Pixar campus – terrazzo floor detail (Emeryville, USA; Allied Works Architecture; 2011)

Figure 8.8: Pixar campus – meeting room (Emeryville, USA; Allied Works Architecture; 2011)

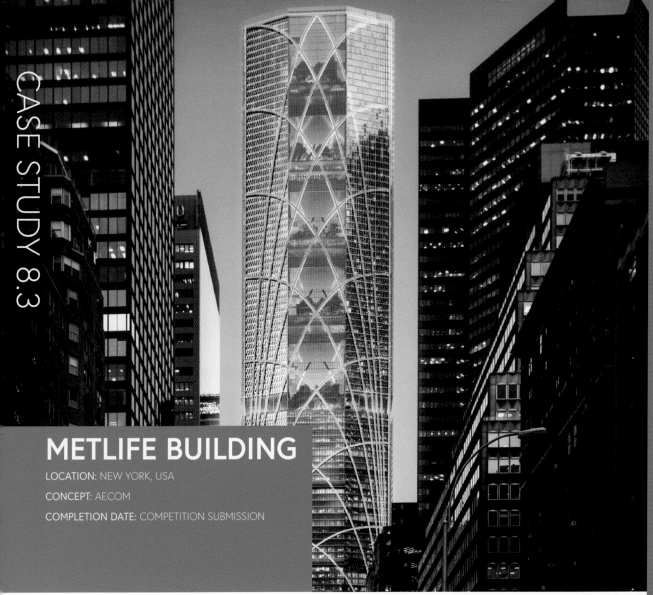

METLIFE BUILDING

LOCATION: NEW YORK, USA

CONCEPT: AECOM

COMPLETION DATE: COMPETITION SUBMISSION

Figure 8.9: MetLife Building – reimagining a New York City icon (New York, US)

Breathing wall

Imagine taking one of the world's 100 tallest buildings and making it twice as high. At the same time, you'll slash annual utility costs, load upper floors with gardens, improve the health and wellbeing of occupants, and boost workplace productivity.

This vision is for the future of the New York City's MetLife Building (formerly the Pan Am Building), and won AECOM the 2016 'Reimagine a New York City Icon' competition, sponsored by *Metals in Construction* magazine and the Ornamental Metal Institute of New York. The proposal to enhance the building's performance included elements from

a deep energy retrofit with different mechanical systems for every season, to using the roots of plants to filter and freshen the air as it comes into the building (as shown in Figure 8.10).

Inspired by the goal of radically reducing energy consumption in the built environment, the competition mandate

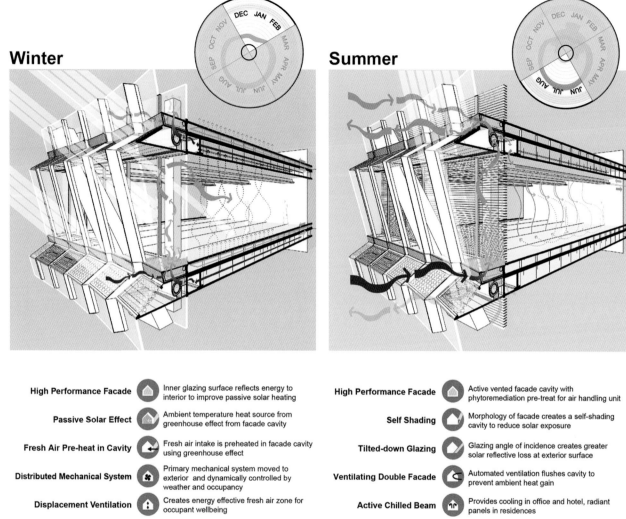

Winter

High Performance Facade — Inner glazing surface reflects energy to interior to improve passive solar heating

Passive Solar Effect — Ambient temperature heat source from greenhouse effect from facade cavity

Fresh Air Pre-heat in Cavity — Fresh air intake is preheated in facade cavity using greenhouse effect

Distributed Mechanical System — Primary mechanical system moved to exterior and dynamically controlled by weather and occupancy

Displacement Ventilation — Creates energy effective fresh air zone for occupant wellbeing

Summer

High Performance Facade — Active vented facade cavity with phytoremediation pre-treat for air handling unit

Self Shading — Morphology of facade creates a self-shading cavity to reduce solar exposure

Tilted-down Glazing — Glazing angle of incidence creates greater solar reflective loss at exterior surface

Ventilating Double Facade — Automated ventilation flushes cavity to prevent ambient heat gain

Active Chilled Beam — Provides cooling in office and hotel, radiant panels in residences

Figure 8.10: A deep energy retrofit with different mechanical systems for every season (New York, USA)

was to reimagine 200 Park Avenue with a resource-conserving, eco-friendly enclosure – one that creates a highly efficient envelope with the lightness and transparency sought by today's office workforce – while preserving and enhancing the tower's historic profile (see Figure 8.10).

The design applies available air rights from the new Midtown East rezoning to envision a 'vertical city'. It doubles the height of the building by wrapping the existing and new tower sections in a unified exoskeleton, using a diagrid structure inspired by the Michell truss. In support of NYC sustainability goals, the

design increases density over a major transit terminal to reduce travel demand and, by removing the base building, creates a new garden, offering natural light and public space to the streets around Grand Central Station.

139

WWF LIVING PLANET CENTRE

LOCATION: WOKING, UK

ARCHITECT: HOPKINS ARCHITECTS

ENVIRONMENTAL DESIGN CONSULTANT: ATELIER TEN

STRUCTURAL AND CIVIL ENGINEERS: EXPEDITION ENGINEERING

MAIN BUILDING CONTRACTOR: WILLMOTT DIXON

COMPLETION DATE: 2013

Figures 8.11 & 8.12: Timber is one of the core materials used at the WWF Living Centre (Woking, UK; Hopkins Architects, Expedition and Atelier Ten; 2013)

An environmentally sensitive build

When the nature conservation group WWF-UK made the decision to move from tired, rented offices and commission a new UK headquarters, it set out the bold ambition to create an environmentally sensitive building using responsibly sourced materials. The group had the good fortune of receiving a substantial £5 million donation towards the building, and then raised further monies specifically for the project, so that no funds were diverted from vital conservation projects.

The guiding principle from the start was passive design – incorporating elements such as natural ventilation, effective insulation and low energy consumption, so the building itself would contribute to its own energy-efficiency and low-emissions operation. The completed Living Planet Centre in Woking, Surrey has achieved an A-rated energy performance certificate and is a showcase for low energy and low emissions.

Energy to spare

An eye-catching design, the two-storey structure is constructed over an existing, and operational, council-run car park. It is built of timber, concrete and steel, and has a distinctive 80m by 37.5m arched zinc-surfaced roof that works for its living. The 4m-high wind cowls suck air out of the building and are integral to the building's passive ventilation system. Accompanying them is 500m^2 of solar PV panels to generate power for the building. And to

increase thermal mass, Energain® tiles sit behind birch-ply panels inside the diamond shapes of the internal roof grid to absorb and release heat.

Behind a thin layer of aluminium, these tiles contain 'phase change material' – in this case, a kind of wax that melts when it warms up, and is mixed with a polymer so it won't leak out of the panels. When the wax melts at around 22°C, it absorbs heat from below and stores it. When the temperature drops to 18°C, the wax solidifies and the stored heat is released back into the room.

This is a mixed-mode ventilation building. The windows open, but a mini traffic-light system – of green and red LED lights – beside them signal when they should be opened or closed to regulate heating and cooling.

Along with the wind cowls, there are ground-source heat pumps and earth ducts that work to regulate internal temperatures. The earth ducts, or earth tubes, are six large-diameter pipes – almost big enough to walk through – with a combined length of 400m, and are buried about a metre under the building. Air is drawn into these pipes at the surface and circulated underground, where the temperature is a fairly constant 12°C. Colder air entering the ducts is warmed up to 12°C, whereas warmer air will be cooled to that level. The air is then fed into the building's air-handling units, assisted by the ground-source heat pumps, for further heating or cooling as needed.

The ground-source heat pump system is made up of 20 water- and antifreeze-filled polyethylene pipes in boreholes going 100m underground. The fluid acts as a heat transfer unit; when the fluid is cold, heat energy from the ground is transferred into it through the pipes. The fluid then passes through a heat exchanger, which compresses it and raises the temperature further, and the resulting heat is then removed for heating use by the building's air-handling units.

The centre's power supply comes in part from the solar PV panels and, when there is power to spare, it is fed back into the local electricity grid to earn extra income and offset some of the cost. Additional load is drawn from the local CHP plant.

Materials palette

Assiduous attention to detail in specification means that 98.5 per cent of the building's materials were certified as responsibly sourced (and the few that weren't were mainly small ancillary components that couldn't be certified).

Timber formed a large proportion of the material (see Figures 8.11 and 8.12). All timber in the construction was Forest Stewardship Council (FSC) certified or from recycled sources. This included spruce (European whitewood) in the more than 800 'glulam' roof beams, and no-waste, economical, construction-strength laminated veneer lumber (LVL) for external soffits. Birch features as plywood panelling in the ceiling and walls, cabinets and other joinery. Internal timber doors were also finished in FSC birch to match the wall panelling. Larch was used for external louvres/brise-soleils, and bike and bin stores.

Concrete was an important element too, with about 2,500 tonnes used in all. Offsetting the energy-intensive production process, the material was specified with a high proportion of recycled aggregate and was reinforced with 98 per cent recycled steel rods.

Glass and aluminium feature predominantly in the roof, windows and doors. The curved roof is a 2,000m² Ziplok standing seam system made from aluminium panels with an anti-corrosion MicroZinc coating that replicates the look of a traditional zinc roof. Glazing in the roof and the walls is mainly glass curtain walling held in thin frames containing 80 per cent recycled aluminium. Glass is finished to cut solar radiation by more than 75 per cent.

In terms of flooring, furniture and fittings, considerations included the environmental credentials in manufacture and sustainability of the materials, as well as emissions that may be released during use. Selections included hard-wearing composite ceramic tiles that contain 75 per cent recycled natural stone chips (marble and quartz), and carpets made from 100 per cent recycled yarn including old fishing nets. Where possible, furniture items were FSC certified with FSC Chain of Custody.

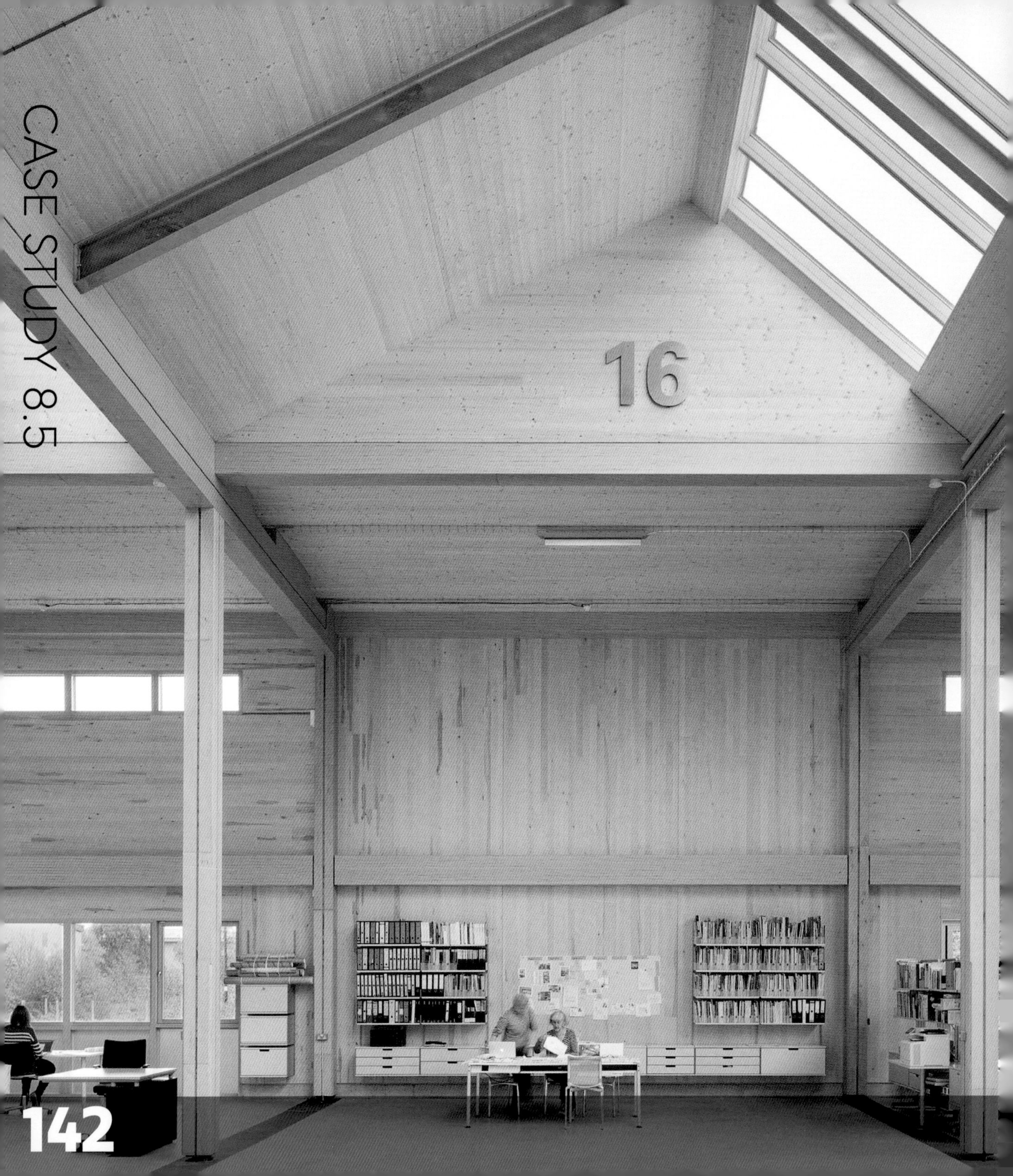
16

VITSŒ — NEW HEADQUARTERS AND PRODUCTION BUILDING

LOCATION: ROYAL LEAMINGTON SPA, UK

DELIVERY TEAM INCLUDED: VITSŒ TEAM WORKING WITH YACHT DESIGNER MARTIN FRANCIS

ARCHITECT (DELIVERY): WAUGH THISTLETON ARCHITECTS

ARCHITECT (LANDSCAPE): KIM WILKIE AND WILDER ASSOCIATES

STRUCTURAL ENGINEER: ECKERSLEY O'CALLAGHAN

BUILDING ENVIRONMENT AND SERVICES ENGINEERS: SKELLY & COUCH

COMPLETION DATE: 2017

A commitment to responsible design

The new headquarters for British furniture manufacturer Vitsœ has been created as an extension and reflection of its brand and values based on a commitment to responsible design. Conceived with a focus on low energy use and the wellbeing of its occupants, it is a place that lifts the spirits, is elegant and respects the planet. It even has a collaborative partnership with Motionhouse, an innovative dance-circus company that has taken up residence in the building. The collaboration brings the arts and manufacturing together to create a vibrant working community.

A beautiful shed

Based in Warwickshire, Vitsœ's new home (see Figure 8.13) has been described as a 'beautiful shed'. A rectangular and predominantly timber structure, some 135m in length, it is simple yet exquisitely detailed. The design of the roof determined the building's character and the quality of light. Rooflights were stretched to maximise the light, and a simple steel I-beam was used to support the roof. The 18 bays of the grid and the resulting pattern of beams create a satisfying visual rhythm.

The space is naturally ventilated and naturally lit during daylight hours via its north-facing, sawtooth rooflights. Lux levels are at 1,000 most of the time. Prevailing breezes provides cross-ventilation, while the high ceiling allows heat to rise for comfort in summer. Windows bring in views of the outside, connecting employees to the surrounding landscape, while passers-by may glimpse activities within. The kitchen and dining area face north, offering a panoramic view of silver birch trees in the adjacent urban community wood.

Since 1959, the company's ethos has been to create furniture that enables its customers to live better with less, and that lasts longer. Like the company's definitive 606 Universal Shelving System, the new building is an extension of Vitsœ's long-term system thinking. Key elements include the use of newly developed beech LVL – essentially timber beams, and an aluminium timber-connection system. Built as a kit of parts, it can be refined and adapted in response to the changing needs of all it serves – company, people and environment – for many decades to come. The building may be easily modified in the future, as the structure, walls and roof are made of wood – a naturally adaptable material.

The new HQ has been realised by an in-house Vitsœ team working with yacht designer Martin Francis, and others including structural engineer Eckersley O'Callaghan, delivery architect Waugh Thistleton Architects, landscape architect Kim Wilkie and Wilder Associates, building environment and services engineers Skelly & Couch, and industrial-sustainability academics EPSRC Centre for Industrial Sustainability, University of Cambridge.

Figure 8.13: Vitsœ's headquarters with a structure and features designed to maximise character and light (Royal Leamington Spa, UK; Waugh Thistleton Architects; 2017)

DESIGN LEADERSHIP
IN PROCUREMENT

**Sandra M. Parét and
Martin Kellett**

Too often in the past, design and procurement teams have operated separately, only coming together on workplace projects in perceived opposition to the other's ambitions for either an attractive design or cost-effective solution. But, as this chapter will cover, it doesn't have to be this way. With designers taking a lead role and bringing procurement teams into the process early, they can ensure designs that deliver long-term value, while also boosting productivity and employee wellbeing.

Globalisation has changed corporate life irrevocably. As organisations have expanded into different regions, both in search of new markets and to reduce their cost base, procurement functions have used extended supply chains and strategic sourcing to maintain efficiency and quality. This has been good for corporate real-estate teams, as global procurement policies bring cost certainty and brand consistency to international office roll-outs. But an awareness of long-term value is often missing, replaced by a focus on the lowest-cost delivery.

It is hard to argue with this financial common sense. But the importance of the longer-term view is growing, spurred in part by developments such as agile or activity-based working, where an office provides a range of environments tailored to different kinds of work. An office or a floor or a building may need to be reconfigured several times over its life to match changes in organisational structure. Adaptability needs to be built in from the start to avoid costly refurbishments every few years.

INTRODUCTION

While architects could help address this problem – using smart thinking to build in adaptability and efficiency over the lifetime of a building – opportunities for design leadership in global real-estate programmes are rare. This is due, in part, to how real-estate delivery teams are structured. The days of architects running project teams and administering contracts have passed. Increasing scale, complexity and specialisation mean that project managers take the leadership role traditionally occupied by architects. The office sector is mostly driven by programmes of work across geographies, rather than individual standalone projects in corporate real-estate portfolios. These project managers usually report into a programme management office (PMO) that provides an organising structure to bring appropriate resources into projects as they are needed.

The procurement function usually oversees these programmes. But central procurement departments often lack the technical skill to deliver best design value, and their decision-making criteria also tend to prioritise cost and time over design quality. Architects are at the mercy of the cost plan and schedule, working with frameworks or guidelines established at a corporate level. It must be the architect's job to change this mindset, providing design leadership instead of merely delivering against plan.

Engaging with facilities managers is also critical. While the traditional facilities management (FM) emphasis on building maintenance shares procurement's preoccupation with standardisation and the bottom line, more enlightened organisations are starting to see employee experience as another important element, as discussed in Chapter 6. These FM teams take a holistic view that considers occupier needs and the organisation's wider business objectives alongside the usual criteria of cost and quality. Architects can add value here, too, by explicitly aligning their designs to the requirements of these FM teams.

BRINGING VALUE BACK

The current situation gives us an indication of how the future will look. Organisations will continue to have to do more with less, and cost-effective procurement will be a key mechanism to enable this. Real-estate teams and their FM counterparts will be looking for ways to reduce costs and still maintain quality. Architects and their designers must balance this by developing an understanding of long-term value in terms of capital expenditure, everyday operating costs and productivity.

What would this design leadership involve? It could, for example, help organisations manage the changing requirements of the workplace with ease. As discussed throughout this book, concepts such as agile working (see page 149) require office spaces to be flexible enough to suit different ways of working, and adaptable enough to be reconfigured to suit a variety of needs without additional capital outlay. Architects can help to build this flexibility into the design at the specification or tender stage. Changes can then be implemented in a straightforward way – in effect, 'plug and play' – instead of requiring a comprehensive refit every few years.

TAKING THE LONG VIEW

Early involvement and long-term thinking are key to design leadership. During procurement and associated capital spend, project leaders can reduce operating costs by thinking about the longer-term picture. But this all needs to happen upfront, before the tender documents are written. During the bidding process the procurement team will be focused on achieving the lowest cost, so the tender evaluation criteria

and scoring will be focused on this. It is no good arguing about how you create value five or ten years later if corporate procurement policy weights bids purely on how quickly and cheaply a contractor can finish the construction phase and hand over the job.

Architects must be empowered to influence the criteria and scoring schemes, bringing in core client business leaders if necessary. Those early discussions are the time to talk about keeping operating expenditure down by, for example, including key performance indicators on contracts that demonstrate savings during operation through strategic design decisions.

This shouldn't be a difficult conversation. The approach is ideal for a global roll-out programme that privileges long-term benefit over short-term gains. In effect, architects should act as catalysts, bringing procurement and FM teams together, and linking design and construction to the entire life cycle of a building portfolio.

INVOLVE, DON'T IMPOSE

The most obvious place for architects to make their presence felt is through the corporate design guidelines. For many organisations, this is a done deal – there's no debate about allowing experts to specify essential criteria around the office build and fit-out. However, it's still worth remembering as a way to demonstrate thought leadership from the start, embedding long-term value, productivity, sustainability and adaptability into the programmme.

Architects can also address the issue of design freedom within guidelines, accommodating regional differences in work styles or architectural thinking. Ways to allow creative thinking from local design teams while maintaining compliance can also be considered, removing potential design risks early.

It is important to track how design guidelines evolve over time. As part of the programme leadership team, architects can ensure that changes in corporate brand, regulation, workplace style and so on are integrated into the guidelines in a structured way.

FOCUS ON VALUE

In addition, architects can bring expertise to bear on the procurement process itself. They can help specify construction materials as well as fine-tune global contracts for furniture, fixtures and equipment. Depending on the corporate structure of the buying group, procurement teams will write the tender documents at either the global or regional level, and score their bids accordingly. But, because they may not know much about the practical application of the product within the wider programme, there's a risk that the scoring criteria will emphasise the wrong things.

Design input at the pre-tender stage can help, providing qualitative advice to complement procurement teams' commercial expertise. Architects can advise on quality benchmarks, which can be cascaded from the corporate to the regional level as required. They can even evaluate or interrogate manufacturers' responses, if required. True, this may require more input and sign-off at the start of the process, and more meetings once the supplier bids are submitted, but the end result is that the technical burden of procurement is lightened.

PEOPLE, NOT JUST PROCESS

As well as materials and products, procurement teams will also have to tender

for professional services. Procurement routes may vary according to corporate strategy, programme requirements or regional practice (see Figure 9.1 for how commercial arrangements vary around the world) but, in reality, good design is about people. That includes the people who will be delivering the design, and so the procurement function needs to understand the professional relationships between the different disciplines for which they are tendering.

Again, architects can support this. They can provide insight into what's important about the skill sets for each discipline. They advise on how the professional team will meet the objectives of the programme and individual projects. Should they procure an integrated team, for example, or enlist separate consultants? What are the advantages of each approach? Some organisations will have in-house design teams who can provide this expertise. If not, they may wish to consider a mini-procurement exercise to recruit this advice, balancing the cost and time of this against strategic objectives and cost constraints.

AGILE WORKING

Agile working provides an ideal opportunity for architects to add value to the work of procurement, corporate real-estate and FM teams. Their expertise will help embed ideas of long-term adaptability into the tender, construction and operations phases of a real-estate programme, ensuring that the benefits of activity-based working are realised.[1]

In an 'activity-based' or 'agile' working culture, the office provides a range of environments tailored to different kinds of work. Formal and informal meeting rooms are interspersed with quieter areas. Desk areas are often shared, and amenities such as cafes encourage a diverse workforce to meet and socialise.

This approach to office space is on the increase, driven by occupiers who want to optimise the use of their space, and by workers demanding flexible offices that support collaboration and enable them to share information wherever they are in the building. Often, it is the starting point from which workplace strategies and office layouts are generated.

Reflecting the changes in approach, workplace terminology is constantly evolving too. In the 1990s, what was commonly called 'new ways of working' became referred to as 'activity-based working'. More recently, the term 'agile working' has been adopted to describe people working across a range of locations such as office, cafe, home and a variety of work settings within the office including at a desk, in project areas or in quiet rooms.

Best practice today is to allocate 'neighbourhoods' of space, or team bases, to specific departments. Again, a variety of spaces are provided within these neighbourhoods including desks, informal meeting areas and quiet areas, and these spaces are shared by those allocated to that neighbourhood or team area. It is intended that the same team would use this area every day; this is where their storage is and where they will find their colleagues. Larger amenities such as restaurants and conference rooms would be shared between several neighbourhoods. This neighbourhood-based approach is a distinct move away from hot-desking – used to describe a system where people can sit anywhere in a building.

DESIGN FOR TECH

There are several ways in which architects can support organisations looking to implement agile working environments. For example, without an IT infrastructure that enables people to share information and communicate wherever they are in the building, new ways of

AFRICA

Fit-out procurement is predominantly traditional and it is rare for a client to use design and build (D&B). However if D&B is selected, an independent (employer's agent) is commissioned to validate work, including cost management oversight and validation.

New office builds are also procured traditionally, however in South Africa some clients are increasingly looking at a turnkey procurement via the contractor, with the contractor then appointing the professional design team as part of a joint venture.

AUSTRALIA

Commercial office developments can be procured through either the design and construct or traditional route with some of the larger developers managing the design and the construction themselves. Typically a developer will engage an architect and consultant team (the procurement of architects can vary from state to state) to develop a design for Development Application and tender purposes. Note the procurement of architects can vary from state to state. The architect and consultant team will then be novated to the successful contractor or retained by the developer. Developers will generally not proceed with a development until they have a pre-commitment from a tenant, or tenants. This varies from developer to developer but is typically a 50–65 per cent pre-commitment. It's rare, although not unheard of, for a developer to develop a large commercial building on a speculative basis.

GREATER CHINA AND HONG KONG

Similar to other regions the commercial office development sector is primarily split into three main categories: developer base build fit-out, owner/occupier fit-out and tenant fit-out. Predominantly the developer would undertake the base build development to a Category A standard. The owner-occupier then has the option of an integrated fit-out with the developer or to develop the Category B component using a single stage traditional or design and build approach. The tenant fit-out is generally delivered either single stage traditional or design and build with dedicated and integrated design and construction teams.

INDIA

Commercial office development is split into two parts – base build and fit-out. The base build is procured through either the design and build or traditional route, with some developers managing the design and construction themselves. The consultant teams, led by an architect or individually appointed by the developer, include structural, mechanical, electrical and plumbing, quantity surveying as well as specialist consultants including traffic, lighting and green building consultants. The pre-construction approvals and permissions are led by the developer and with the post-award led by the contractor. The fit-out managed by individual tenants and predominantly procured as design and build, with loose furniture and white goods, is procured separately. Additional specialised work such as IT and communication is undertaken by separate contractors.

MIDDLE EAST

The majority of commercial office fit-out projects are procured traditionally, either on a single stage or, less commonly, two stage basis. Both design and build and construction management procurement routes are in their infancy within the region, however in the more developed countries such as the United Arab Emirates, design and build single stage is becoming more prevalent.

SOUTH EAST ASIA

Single stage traditional arrangements are typically used for fit-out works of commercial spaces to the base build provided by the developer of office buildings. The architect leads the consultant team which primarily includes the interior designer, mechanical and electrical services engineer and the quantity surveyor. The scope of fit-out works comprises all trades including built-in furniture and fittings. Occasionally, the loose furniture may be procured separately as a direct supply contract by the tenant client who may have global agreements with such suppliers.

Figure 9.1: Commercial arrangements around the world (AECOM)

USA

Tenant interior design and construction is typically design – bid – build, with design – build more common in the public sector. Smaller general contractors typically have relationships with building landlords and owners and often deliver multiple projects in a building. In these cases, architects develop complete construction documents for contractors to bid, prior to award. For larger tenants, especially those who have a national reach, the client will typically operate a master service agreement with one or two national general contractors. These national contractors either self-perform or act as construction manager at risk. For these projects, because the architect and contractor are typically commissioned together, they collaborate in the early stages of the project to streamline drawing requirements, prepare early permit and pricing packages and pre-order long lead materials, all leading to short duration and more cost effective delivery.

UK

The vast majority of commercial office development is design and build. But the development of offices is split into base build and fit-out. Developers use design and build to develop commercial space to Category A and then tenants procure a fit-out contractor. The fit-out is delivered traditionally or design and build. Owner/occupier commercial office developments are more likely to be design and build or two stages. It is rare for projects to be procured on a management contracting or construction management basis.

151

working may struggle to gain traction. So, architects should ensure that technology is a critical-path consideration during the design phase, and that this is fed into the master schedule. Getting the audiovisual (AV) installation right is also crucial to organisations, as these are the tools that facilitate collaboration. Minor technical issues in support systems such as wifi or room booking systems may lead to a loss of faith in the workplace strategy.

The office AV network is one of the largest packages in terms of the percentage of overall cost of measured works. Virtual working will continue to increase, making it essential that these support systems are robust. Design impacts include the fact that greater use of large screens requires adjustment of standard plasterboard specifications and, together with the requirement for data, power and containment, this means that the AV is a key consideration at the design coordination stage – much earlier than the equipment is ever needed on site.

INTEGRATED BUT SECURE

Many agile working schemes also deploy integrated network systems (INS), which put all IT systems on one common data network and enable data from all building systems to be viewed at the same time – the so-called 'single pane of glass'. But INS requires the building's data network to be installed and commissioned early in the fit-out programme. It also means the role of the fit-out team changes, from one that is relatively isolated and removed from the critical path to one that is fundamental to the build sequencing.

With so much IT integration involved in agile working designs, implementing good network security is paramount. But this can also cause problems. INS capital cost savings are predicated on the assumption that the building's data

network is already in place and that INS is merely making more efficient use of an existing installation. However, corporate IT networks are highly sensitive, which may lead to separate networks being installed, physically removed from the business-critical networks.

THE AGILE EXPERIENCE

An example of agile working in action can be found at AECOM's UK HQ in east London. The company used the move from its former central London premises to rethink ideas of what a head office could be. Led by in-house design and workplace specialists, the design strategy featured the key element of encouraging interaction and informal meetings by designating 50 per cent of the space for collaborative working. There are touchdown and project areas, as well as quiet working areas. As part of the design to facilitate networking, an internal open staircase links four of the floors and complements the usual lifts and escape stairs. Agile working protocols mean that groups of desks (25 per cent of which can be used for working in either a standing or sitting position) are shared by a designated team, but there are opportunities for staff to work on any floor if desired. To replace desk phones, calls can be made and received through computers, and a high proportion of staff have smartphones.

Extensive research, employee engagement and training accompanied the move, which has resulted in the highest utilisation of all AECOM's UK offices at 85 per cent occupancy. Staff demonstrated their approval of the changes, with employee turnover dropping by over 25 per cent in Central London in the year following the move. And feedback from teams throughout the building has been positive, with employees noting that the new workplace has increased productivity and collaboration.

Beyond staff perception, the in-house design team partnered with an external occupational psychology firm to undertake cognitive testing of staff before and after agile working. Industry-standard psychometric tests were used to measure levels of concentration, multi-tasking, logical reasoning and creativity. This research was carried out on 2,300 staff working in a range of disciplines.

Highlights from the results included the following: after the move, organisational culture was rated as 50 per cent more supportive of interdisciplinary working, and people were 25 per cent more likely to agree that the different departments work well together. The research showed that the office layout was almost twice as effective at supporting cross-departmental collaboration.

Some of the more technical disciplines were concerned initially about how they would be able to concentrate in a shared-desk environment. However, the results from the cognitive tests showed that concentration levels were maintained.

More interesting is the increased cognitive scores in creativity: people in the agile working environment are performing 10 per cent better. The change to agile working was achieved with no significant increase in real-estate costs, despite the fit-out providing a much higher-quality and more varied work environment.

PROCEED WITH CAUTION

Despite the popularity of agile working, and its success for some companies, organisations should still proceed with caution in some areas.

Even in environments where agile working is appropriate, employee inertia may prevent increases in productivity. Employees should be given training regarding appropriate behaviours and how to get the most benefit from agile working, and this should be backed up with clear, agreed processes and strong leadership from management. A building alone will not change anything, as outlined in Chapter 7. Preparing people for the space is just as important as preparing the space for the people.

As a result, change management and employee engagement will be critical for the successful transition to these new ways of working. An organisation's real-estate strategy may become more closely aligned with the concerns of its corporate HR functions, such is the role of the working environment in attracting and retaining staff.

Building on the theme of delivery, and having looked at energy, materiality and specification in Chapter 8 and procurement in this chapter, Chapter 10 explores the changes that developments in technology are going to bring to design professionals: what is the future of design practice?

LEARNING POINTS

1. The emergence of global programmes driven by balance sheet-conscious PMOs and FM teams has unbalanced the corporate real-estate world. Cost and quality may be nailed down in this way of working, but all too often user experience and productivity aren't part of the equation.

2. A focus on lowest-cost tendering means opportunities for streamlining costs during operation are missed. Greater involvement of architects and design teams during procurement can help address this.

3. Architects bring a consideration of users back into the process – how people actually use their workspaces – and can advise on best value for materials and professional services. As more organisations look to agile environments

to drive productivity and wellbeing, the architect's expertise will become invaluable in setting the standards for cost-effective, agile workspaces.

4. University syllabuses tend to focus on design principles at the expense of design practice and wider skills. Architects, therefore, will need more training in the dynamics of the project team and how to work effectively with client organisations.

5. Training needs to acknowledge the complementary disciplines of project, cost, change management and programme management, and take into account the increasing professionalisation of facilities management.

6. The strongest educational programmes will be those that enable cross-disciplinary

teams to work together and contribute to a collaborative approach.

7. It is time to involve client representatives as well as architects, particularly in the PMO. The benefit is synergistic, integrating corporate real estate and FM with the HR function and the employees it supports. This would make it easier to link building design and construction to recruitment, staff retention, wellbeing and productivity.

8. This approach would also give real-estate teams better insight into organisational concerns and motivations as they change over the coming years and decades. A shift from long leases in purpose-built office blocks to shorter leases and memberships is already happening in some organisations. Providers of co-working

spaces report that corporate memberships are almost as popular as those for start-ups and SMEs. These large, slow-moving companies are, perhaps, attracted by the spirit of collaboration and energised pizzazz generated when a bunch of dynamic, focused organisations get together.[2]

9. Will the future see organisations reducing their core real estate, preferring instead to buy in office space from other providers as needed? Will the real-estate function itself be outsourced to suppliers? Design, procurement and FM perspectives will all need to adjust to meet these challenges.

10. Whatever happens in the future, there will be a need to prove value while delivering workspaces that are fit for those working in them.

THE FUTURE OF DESIGN PRACTICE

Dale Sinclair

10 CHAPTER

Other chapters have succinctly explained that the future office will bear no resemblance to that of today. A host of factors are contributing to these changes: current and emerging priorities such as sustainability (Chapters 2 and 8) and employee wellbeing (Chapter 5) are affecting what organisations want and expect from their office buildings, and organisations want the benefits that recent technological developments can provide (Chapter 4). The way buildings are designed and constructed is changing, too: users are actively involved (Chapter 6); design professions need to take a leadership role in the procurement process (Chapter 9); and new technology is having a profound effect here as well, as discussed in Chapter 3. This chapter considers what the implications of these changes could be for design practice.

INTRODUCTION

The way we design the office is rapidly changing as we transition away from 2D CAD towards transformational, intelligent, 3D digital libraries linked to many data sources. Increasingly, designs are being reviewed in immersive environments that set the scene for game-changing ways to engage clients, including new tools such as the configurators leveraged by the car industry for mass customisation.[1] We are not far away from a scenario in which real-time changes can be made on projects – linked to dashboards that provide instantaneous feedback on cost, carbon, daylighting or other crucial project metrics. These dashboards will be driven by engineering and cost analysis software linked directly to the architect's model, enabling design to be undertaken in unimaginably short timeframes.[2]

More and more, smart sensors in the workplace will collect a wealth of data. It is inevitable that this digital information will enable analytics to learn how a building is being used, automatically adapting the space, with the creation of digital libraries; learning and evolving in line with real-time feedback. The people-focused nature of workplace and the desire of employers to attract the best talent, however, also create the challenge of how to make design measurable. This includes addressing what good design is, and how the subjective aspects of design can be measured, quantified by analytics and presented as data visualisations forming part of design storytelling. Taking this into account, four trends look set to change how we design offices in the future.

CRAFT AND AUTOMATE

The transition from the drawing board to CAD wasn't easy or quick, nor has it been transformational. In essence, the drawing board was digitised but the drawings produced and the processes wrapping around them – including reviewing, issuing and quality control – have remained the same. Despite drawing 'full size'

for 30 years, CAD is output to formats indistinguishable from their drawing-board predecessors.

As building information modelling (BIM) helps to drive digital transformation, many are failing to recognise its transformative benefits and the new possibilities it generates.[3] Although designers create intelligent, 3D, data-rich models, contracts and workflow are still predicated on 2D information. Crucially, although 2D information may be required for various purposes for some time – for example, to submit planning applications or to engage with suppliers at the end of the digital tail – workflow must move away from 2D to effect a transformation in the design process.

To change the way the workplace is designed, two tasks must be undertaken. First, the design review process must be altered. Already, new tools are being framed incorrectly and negatively. For example, reactive tools for clash detection, where elements of different models occupy the same space, have been created – rather than proactive tools that enable the lead designer to coordinate the design in new and smarter ways. Second, everything needs to be in 3D. Many people are modelling to create 2D outputs at 1:50 scale using 'call-outs' to overlay detail in 2D. Simply, nothing has changed. Designers will remain wedded to CAD workflow until everything is modelled and delivered in 3D.

Change for the better is happening, though. The introduction of Stage 7 (In Use) to the RIBA Plan of Work acknowledges that a building is used and maintained by a client, requiring designers to consider whole-life costs, including maintenance requirements and asset management information, as we nudge towards circular economy considerations.[4] Construction has been transformed with 4D (time) technologies, making it possible for contractors to rehearse a number of build scenarios. Specialist subcontractors are ahead of the curve in embracing

digital tools, shifting the industry towards designing for manufacturing and assembly (DfMA) and away from traditional construction methodologies. We are now seeing artificial intelligence (AI) used to enhance site safety with machine-learning tools recognising workers who are not wearing helmets or who exhibit other unsafe working practices. Cloud-point scans allow actual progress to be mapped in granular detail against the planned progress, or listed buildings to be re-designed in the same fashion as newbuild. The list goes on.[5]

Those delivering construction information are increasingly automating the way they work. Scripts ensure that mundane tasks can be undertaken automatically, enabling designers to focus on the other tasks that matter. Many aspects of technical delivery, including regulatory ones, are dictated by rules. Initially, this allows verification and validation to be automated, but aspects of design will also be automated. New tools will change the briefing process so that the client can engage more directly with the design. For example, co-design platforms or configurators aligned to user-interface tools will make it possible for clients to record decisions directly into the designer's digital library, eliminating many iterations of the design process.

At the conceptual end of the design process, there is considerable resistance to using digital tools. While millennials may be digitally savvy, workflow is often determined by those brought up using a pen or pencil, and who are wedded to architecture as art. They consider drawings and models to be as important as the completed building, not just a stepping stone on the journey of making a building. However, smaller, younger, more nimble practices are using virtual reality (VR) as part of their 'business as usual', with some already pushing their information directly to the new machines that will manufacture their buildings.[6]

There is no doubt that the challenges of conceiving and creating a building are different from those required to design a product. Sites have different shapes, ground conditions and contexts, many with historical or other stakeholder constraints. Client briefs vary from project to project. Clients continue to want buildings that are unique and differentiated from their neighbours, and generating the creative spark required to deliver such buildings is difficult. However, to extend this uniqueness argument through to every component of a building seems foolish in a product-saturated world, and many clients are wrestling with how to deal with the descriptive-to-prescriptive product journey during their projects.

Who should select the products, and when? It is inevitable that buildings will, in the future, be designed more like products. As these products become bigger, will more product-orientated design tools be used? For example, what will the impact be when an entire toilet-block module becomes available to buy, instead of being designed from scratch every time?

While the initial creative process in the future will need to be as energetic and exciting as it has always been, after the idea has been crafted it is unlikely that it will continue to be developed painstakingly through a number of stages before construction can start. The future points to the creative process engaging with new automated delivery that will eventually enable manufacturing to start the day after the concept design has been signed off: the era of craft and automate is not far away.

THE DIGITAL INTERFACE

While design remains a crucial aspect of any project, in recent years the role of the architect has become less central to project processes, as project managers have rightly placed greater emphasis on programme and cost certainty. There is now the opportunity for the lead designer

to harness digital to add value to the design process: a digital approach can create a proactive workflow that de-risks design and places less emphasis on project management techniques. This will redefine and reimagine the crucial project role of the lead designer, positioning it higher up the pecking order of the key players in the project team.[7]

To achieve this requires an understanding of the diversity of digital tools available and the development of a design workflow that efficiently and effectively connects them, creating a balance between design and delivery, and facilitating 'craft and automate'. Those doing this work need to consider what good looks like, and why one tool should be chosen over another.[8]

From a multidisciplinary perspective, the clunky workflow connecting the architect's geometry to the engineer's analysis software is nudging closer to the ideal state where real-time analysis is feasible between both. Increasingly, the design team's model is leveraged for other previously unimagined uses such as 4D (time) and 5D (cost) data, making it imperative to connect the initial design spark to the intelligent model as quickly as possible. Those adhering to sketches will find them worthless until they are converted into 3D, data-rich models that can immediately be used by all.

For those rethinking the design process, automating the flow between the sketch and the information required to make a building will be the next consideration. Construction information will soon become obsolete, and to exist in this space will require a shift towards the manufacturing information alluded to above. Designers will need to consider how to connect seamlessly from design to manufacturing, and imagine a future where the making of the workplace begins seconds after the client signs off the concept design, triggering automated procurement processes that immediately order materials, with some product suppliers commencing manufacturing immediately.

Practices will need to adapt quickly to digital working. Major innovations are just around the corner, and those failing to act fast may not be able to deal with the technology lag. It is an understatement to say that driving change is difficult when your competitors have already done so, and are selling faster, better and smarter as part of new business models.

THE ERA OF CONSTANT CHANGE

For the foreseeable future, designers will need to work concurrently with different

Figure 10.1: Collaborative, digitally-enabled spaces

design and delivery innovations, using new multidisciplinary tools on today's projects. Yet all the while, they need to be aware of the tools under development that will be adopted and rolled out next, considering the clients that will support their use, and being conscious of the direction of digital travel. This includes the trends featured in this book that will inform the next generation of work and workplaces.

Weaning one generation off CAD and simultaneously framing new digital ways of working is harder than it sounds. While buildings now contain highly complex systems, the way we design buildings hasn't changed substantially since the Colosseum was designed in Rome using 2D and isometric drawings to sell the idea to Emperor Vespasian. Nor has construction radically changed since New York's Empire State Building was completed in 1931 (Shreve, Lamb and Harmon Associates). While CAD has nudged things along, BIM has unleashed a stream of innovation, and we are on the cusp of real and substantial changes that will radically transform the way we design – moving from a steady-state environment to a world of perpetual change.[9] Perfection will become difficult as one tool is replaced by another in a cycle of perpetual innovation. Constant change will create a challenging environment for many. Those unable to embrace lifetime learning, or who resist change, will soon find themselves far behind the curve. The ability to learn new tools will become a crucial skill. Understanding how to leverage new tools to constantly redefine the design process will be invaluable.

Perhaps the most important skill in the future will be adapting to this constantly

TIME UTILISATION STUDY

LOCATION: GLOBAL

CONCEPT: AECOM

CASE STUDY 10.1

Knowledge is power in space utilisation

Measuring how we use buildings is key to making the best use of valuable office space. For example, most desks are occupied only about 45 per cent of the time during regular work hours (see Figure 10.2). To make an accurate record of space use, the Time Utilisation Study℠ (TUS) was developed as the world's first systematic methodology for measuring building occupancy. It involves objectively measuring how space is used over time, and is now a widely accepted methodology across the industry, most commonly employed to help define future space requirements.

The TUS was developed in 1991, when IBM wanted to explore the potential impact of computers on office space. In response, the TUS – initially a paper-based tool – was created to record observations of how and when buildings were being occupied. Today, trained observers use a specially developed tablet-based app, linked to a database, creating a powerful tool for recording and analysing space use.

As building use changes and evolves in response to new technology and different work patterns, the challenge in optimising space use is to understand these patterns, to anticipate the impact of potential innovations, and to plan and design for the future. The benefits of these studies include being able to build the right kind and amount of space in the future, to specify and procure furniture that will be tailored to how people work, and also to make sure that offices incorporate the right mix of spaces for the different teams and departments.

The TUS tool was designed and created by AECOM, which now has an extensive database containing information collected from over 170,000 workspaces in more than 500 buildings worldwide – with approaching 12 million 'core day' observations of workspaces. The app can be used to collect occupancy data from any environment, and has been adapted for a range of sectors from laboratories to learning environments.

Time Utilisation Studies have always taken advantage of new technology developments, with data collection being done using first paper, then various generations of palm-top, 'personal digital assistants' and, currently, tablet devices that transmit the data back instantaneously to a database in the cloud. However, there are now some exciting possibilities for measuring the use of space in office workplaces automatically and reporting on the data in real time. There are already several systems on the market that use sensors – either pressure or body heat, or a combination – to detect which desks or meeting room chairs are occupied. Other approaches, developed from applications in retail settings, use cameras to detect the flow of people in and out of particular areas in the building. All these systems have the benefit of providing data over a period of months or years rather than a few weeks as with the TUS – but, unlike the TUS, they cannot discriminate changing environment as new disruptors enter the design arena; these include companies leveraging artificial intelligence and machine learning tools that can be supervised until they contain the knowledge of many design experts.

WORKPLACE

The design process is being transformed in a profound way, and so consideration needs to be given to the spaces where design will take place. What are the environments that will spark the initial ideas core to the future of design? Will they be people-centric collaborative spaces, or monk-like cells supporting hyper-concentration? What are the spaces that will enable digital avatars to sit inside the buildings being designed as these designs are presented to clients from within?

If we automate a great deal of the design process, leveraging closed-loop systems that quickly catapult designs from the head of the designer into robotic assembly lines and/or 3D printers, then the emphasis in projects will revert to early design innovation. Will new collaborative spaces containing 3D printers and robotics (see Figure 10.1) enable us to experiment with the new materials and possibilities that will create the buildings of the future?

definitively between spaces left temporarily unoccupied (while the person using the space is elsewhere in the building), and spaces unoccupied and available for someone to use. Furthermore, they lose the valuable 'eyes on the ground' provided by the human observers in a TUS. Installation and set-up time, and the cost of the sensor or camera systems are also considerations. Different technologies offer different benefits and are best suited to answering slightly different kinds of questions.

Measuring occupancy is, though, of great value, both in terms of helping FM to provide the right mix and quantity of different types of work setting for each team, and for making sure costly workspace is used efficiently. It doesn't, however, provide any information about where teams are working. A different type of system can do this: one based on logins to the organisation's LAN and wifi infrastructure. Such systems not only allow people to locate their colleagues and to identify whether they are working alone or collaborating with others, but could potentially provide inferences about who communicates with whom, and might furnish rich data about the relationship between collaboration and productivity. This approach has the advantage that no sensors, cameras or other monitoring equipment needs to be installed.

More sophisticated systems – which incorporate data from many different types of sources as described above, and are also based on an artificial intelligence analysis engine that learns about the building inhabitants and their work patterns – can offer even greater insights into the life of an organisation. Crucially, they can feed back to building management systems to ensure that work settings are tailored to suit the preferences of the people using them and the tasks they are carrying out. A scenario that would have seemed like science fiction only a few years ago is now within our sights.

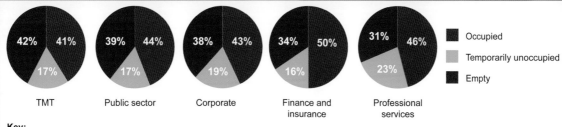

Key:
Empty: No person or signs of life present at time of observation, e.g. no computer, no cups or coats, and seat is pushed into desk.
Temporarily unoccupied: Signs of life present, but no person at time of observation, e.g. a coffee cup or laptop.
Occupied: A person was physically present at the time of observation.

Figure 10.2: Sectoral comparison of desk occupancy, 2018

161

Top 10 workspace planning principles

1 A building typology with side cores to provide contiguous floorplates. This arrangement enables interaction and knowledge sharing as:
- Large teams can be co-located and still maintain visual connection
- Circulation paths are minimised, allowing groups to reach one other easily
- It creates natural 'social and meeting' spaces close to lifts or open stairs leading to team neighbourhoods and finally quieter spaces at the perimeter away from high traffic zones

2 Vertical hubs to break down interdepartmental silos. Centrally located internal stairs allow staff to move easily between floors – helping to breakdown silos
- Wrapping social and informal meeting area around open stairs will naturally create a hub of activity to draw people up and down floors.
- A staircase has other advantages – it saves people time waiting for lifts, promotes physical movement and evens out the usage of meeting spaces across floors

3 Permeable ground plane to give back to the local community and build an accessible brand. Retail services, lobby cafés, co-working spaces and publicly shared meeting areas activate the ground plane and contribute to the public realm
- Buildings may also provide workspace for start-ups, specialist advisory and on-demand services to support the larger tenant organisations
- Exterior landscaping provided to encourage public use, open stairs leading to team neighbourhoods and spaces away from high traffic zones

4 Regular floorplate shapes and planning grids for space efficiency. Occupier requirements are different and will change over time, buildings and particularly layouts need to be able to respond
- A floorplate designed to a modular grid, with no awkward angles, pinch points
- or column placements to limit layout options or compromise usable floor area

5 Human scale: a domestic 'look and feel' to draw people in and provide a sense of belonging
- Work is becoming more informal, less bureaucratic. Rows of desks reflect a command and control culture. Workplaces today are more about people and teams
- Think human scale, fluid spatial arrangements, places to work together or be alone, domestic lighting and furniture
- Providing variety and choice is key, desks in an agile working environment

6 Sensory comfort to support wellbeing. Biophilic design elements including:
- Outdoor terraces and landscaped roofs for access to fresh air
- Building shape designed to maximise natural light and views
- Indoor planting to create optimal indoor air quality
- Office lighting that mimics people's circadian rhythms and counteracts harsh glare through the addition of indirect lighting
- Carpets with shock absorbing properties to take care of joints

7 Movement and ergonomics for health
- The focus on adjustable workspaces assumes that people sit at their desks all day
- AECOM TUS data shows that people typically sit at their desks only 40 percent of the time
- The biggest positive health impacts are achieved through movement and standing up
- Provide a mix of work settings to encourage movement

8 Sustainability
- Solar shading, solar photovoltaic panels, wind turbines, black water recycling, rainwater harvesting, landscaped roof and tri-generation plants
- Understanding work patterns and real demand so that we only build what we need or we repurpose existing buildings rather than building new

9 Digitally intelligent to respond to the changing nature of work
- Sensors to feed real time data back into the ongoing building information management systems allowing the building to learn and customise
- Mobile technology to enable mobile work patterns within and outside the building, e.g. WI-FI, VOIP, follow-me printing, laptops and thin client systems

10 User experience and research-led design
- Workplaces are for people — the most valuable asset a business has
- People need to be the unit of design rather than operational efficiencies
- New generational workspace is led by research and designed from the 'inside out', with extensive stakeholder engagement throughout the design process

Figure 10.3: Top 10 new-generational workplace planning principles

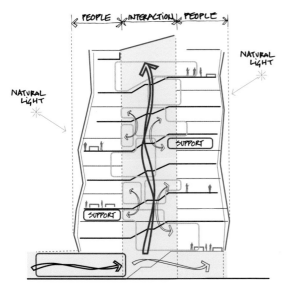

Figure 10.4: A diagram of a vertical village that draws on the planning principles

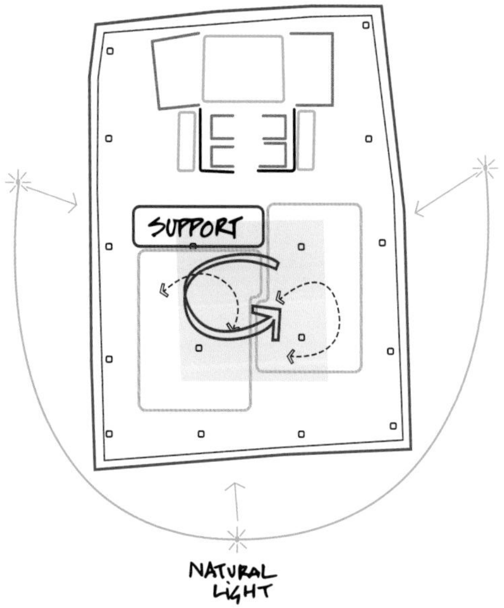

Figure 10.5: A plan showing connections and openness in a modern floorplate

CONCLUSION

There is much to be excited about, yet there is also much to be done to shift the built environment industry to become more productive, where creativity and innovation is core. More importantly, the biggest challenge to the professionals designing the future

office will be waking up to a world of perpetual change as one digital tool replaces another. As Professor Flora Samuel, Professor of Architecture in the Built Environment, Reading University, and RIBA Vice-President for Research, posits, 'There is no knowing what practice will look like by the time our undergraduates qualify. Architecture students need an armoury of research

methodologies, representation techniques, collaboration skills, consultation skills and business knowhow to enable them to respond to any eventuality with creativity and professionalism.'[10] What is clear is that those able to define, develop, use and sell the digital tools of the future will take their place at the heart of the design process in the years ahead.

LEARNING POINTS

1. **Craft and automate:** The move to a more extensive, if not exclusive, use of digital design tools is inevitable and should be seen as a positive step. The era of craft and automate is not far away.

2. **The digital interface:** There is now the

opportunity for the lead designer to use digital tools and processes to add value and regain the role of project lead by redefining and re-imagining it.

3. **The era of constant change:** Embracing and adapting to a constantly changing environment

will help some firms stay ahead of the competition. This is particularly important with new disruptors such as AI entering the design arena.

4. **Workplace:** These are dynamic times. To stay ahead and play a role in designing the offices and

other workplaces of the future will require keeping a constant watch on new developments, trends and changes such as those set out in the top ten new-generational workspace planning principles illustrated in Figures 10.3 to 10.5.

THE DEPARTMENT STORE

LOCATION: LONDON, UK

ARCHITECT: SQUIRE AND PARTNERS

COMPLETION DATE: 2017

Figure 10.6: The Department Store is an Edwardian building reborn as a mixed-use cultural hub (Brixton, London; Squire and Partners; 2017)

Changes in our shopping habits have had a major negative impact on the high street. Department stores have faced particularly challenging times. However, one handsome Edwardian example in Brixton, London has been reborn as a mixed-use 'cultural hub' combining office space with a public cafe, restaurant, coffee roastery, community post office, vinyl record store and rooftop bar and restaurant. The vision came from London architecture and design practice Squire and Partners, which owns and occupies the building.

In masterminding the structure's adaptive reuse, the architect stripped away a century of layered additions to reveal original features and structure. Together with celebrating the decayed grandeur of the place, the practice added sensitive contemporary interventions to repurpose the building as an inspiring modern workspace.

On the exterior, layers of paint were removed to reveal original brickwork, stone, marble and terracotta (see Figure 10.6). A new rooftop level was added, comprising a series of oak-framed pavilions with copper shingle roofs, and a crafted glass dome to replace a dilapidated existing cupola.

Inside, at ground level, a striking reception area and active model shop animate the street, while a triple-height void and central landscaped courtyard provide resting space. Generous social and event spaces are on the lower ground and fourth floors, with workspaces on the first to third floors supported by a series of meeting and breakout areas.

Figure 10.7: Original features mix with the new to provide a creative and collaborative workspace (Brixton, London; Squire and Partners; 2017)

Spectacular original features that have been retained and refurbished include the mahogany and teak parquet flooring, a grand tiled central staircase, a series of cast-iron radiators, and evidence of some of the historic wall colours (as shown in Figure 10.7). A series of voids were cut through the building to create dramatic volumes, opening up vistas between levels.

The office floors offered the opportunity to reveal facets of the architectural design process, with plenty of space for displaying models and drawings. Staff facilities include secure cycle spaces with high-quality showers, and drying and changing areas. A 280m² event space hosts twice-weekly yoga classes, and office-wide presentations as well as outside events.

A new fourth floor provides 465m² of social space, with table football, ping-pong and a large outside terrace. Freshly cooked lunch is served daily, subsidised by the practice, and a restaurant and bar operates into the evening and on weekends.

FAST FORWARD TO THE FUTURE

Nicola Gillen

11

This book has argued that the world around us is reshaping the ways in which we live and work every day. This chapter will outline and assess some of the biggest trends that are emerging. It offers a picture of what our future professional lives could be, and emphasises the core elements of the workplace that will endure.

Imagine a future where the office workforce is half of what it is today. The remaining workforce operates in the next-generation leisure and welfare industries, providing entertainment, health management and care for young and old. The universal wage supports those who are not in higher-paid professions (see Figure 11.1). 'Office' workers will primarily connect virtually with colleagues, working in local community hubs and from home. Going to the office will be a rare and prized experience.

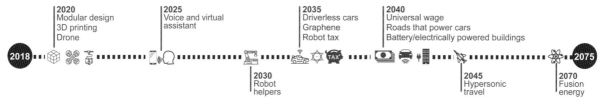

Figure 11.1: Some of the develoments that could help shape the future office

ARE WE THERE YET?

This is a pivotal moment for the office. As explored earlier, this most familiar of spaces is undergoing significant and extensive change as we enter another chapter in its history. This change is having an impact on architects and architecture that cannot be overstated, and will continue to be felt for decades to come.

Distilled to its essence, the core cause of this shift is our new new digital age and the emergence of an incredible suite of new tools at our disposal. The effect of this digital evolution is being seen in the ripples spreading outwards and into every corner of the work we do, how we do it, and where and when we do it. Along the way, we are seeing fascinating changes taking place in approaches, processes and relationships both to work itself and in design teams.

It is early days. The key impacts already being experienced are on the types of work being undertaken, swiftly followed by how and where that work is done. New types of office workplace are already finding favour with users and being rolled out in cities worldwide. The impact of the digital revolution on creating and using those spaces is huge, from design, specification and procurement to construction, fit-out, operation and maintenance, and then reuse and recycling beyond that.

PEOPLE MATTER

While there are those who foresee a future filled with robots and automation, we see the role of people, specifically the workforce, becoming ever more important. While the size of the workforce may reduce, those remaining will be highly valued by their employers. In fact, we envisage a time in the not-too-distant future when the office user becomes the client; their wellbeing, comfort, creativity, productivity and job satisfaction all being supported by the workplace. The office offer will be a key part of the benefits package.

The emphasis on putting people at the centre of design and decision making is a very clear thread through this book. It is a truism to say that being human is our differentiator, but it is specifically our creativity, innovative capabilities, empathy, imagination and glorious, messy unpredictability that marks people out from the processors. Place plays an important part in this human experience.

Rooted in the reality of what's happening now, here are some of key pointers to the office of the future.

PLUG AND PLAY

The impacts of technology on the changing workscape

In the near future:

- **Digitisation of work:** Work is mobile and flexible. It can be done any time and anywhere. The only barriers to true flexibility are old-fashioned management attitudes.

- **Loud and clear:** Voice will be used to control and interact with technology. Noise management in the workplace will be a key consideration. As people collaborate more and are increasingly mobile, we will first see the inclusion of more soundproofed pods, and then noise-cancelling wearable tech.

- **Craft and automate:** Drawing new practices from the automotive sector and others, offices will incorporate more modular design elements. Expect product books filled with ready-to-go kitchens, toilets, meeting rooms, laboratories, staircases and more. Order today and it will be 3D printed and delivered tomorrow.

And beyond:

- **Our robot helpers:** It is still a matter for debate, but many pieces of research indicate that more than half of today's jobs will not exist in coming decades. According to McKinsey Global Institute, 40 to 75 million jobs worldwide could be affected by robots and AI by 2025.[1] Machines will certainly take the slog out of much routine work. The implications for the construction industry are clear and present through the entire office-building life cycle, from design and build to operate and maintain.

- **Enter the new:** New types of jobs and new forms of organisation will emerge. One new type of job already in view is the emergence of the professional line manager. A specialist HR professional will act as a coach, mentor, manager and career-development guide. A key reason for workers to come to the office will be to interact with these specialists.

BE MORE HUMAN

Celebrating and supporting our unique and distinctive qualities

In the near future:

- **Work and the workplace:** The office will retain a role as a place for collaboration and exchange, also providing many people with a place where they can belong.

- **Create and relate:** Creativity, communication, empathy and interpretation of data – all things we humans are great at. We will continue to meet and innovate with like-minded communities of people. Already work is a thing we do, not a place we go to.[2]

- **The centennial way:** Multitasking is the trademark mode of working for centennials, also known as Generation Z, the demographic born between 1995 and 2010, for whom the internet has always been a part of their lives.[3] Offices being designed now need to factor this in.

And beyond:

- **The generation game:** How to accommodate four generations at work together? The future office will need flexibility and accessibility for all. Expect more flexi-hours working, for example. The role of the experienced mentor will become more prominent and valued (see Figure 11.2).

- **Whole-life learning:** To keep up with the pace of change, we will all need to top up knowledge and skills at regular intervals. Those who survive will be adapters. Workplaces will become places for learning as much as production or innovation.

- **The robot tax:** Coming soon, a new tax to generate revenues to support those jobs that robots are really no

Four generations at work, with centennials just entering the job market

CHANGING NATURE OF WORK →

	Baby boomers	Generation X	Millennials/ Generation Y	Centennials/ Generation Z
Economic context	Post-war boom, fall of communism	Invention of the internet	Two recessions	Social media, war on terror, WikiLeaks
	b. 1946–1964	b. 1965–1984	b. 1985–1996	b. 1997–
Work style	Process-driven	Results-driven	Outputs-driven	Autonomous and opportunity-driven
Management approach	Taylorist	Lean	Agile/scrum	Mentoring
Motivation	Meaning in life from work	Work/life balance	Work/life blend, team collectiveness	Fulfilment, choice
Health and wellbeing	Not prioritised	Managed around work	Priority, work isn't everything	Tech driven, always monitoring
Collaboration	Independence	Self-reliance	Group motivated, team working	Open-source
Work location	Office	Network of places, office, client home	Anywhere, anytime work follows me	Anywhere, virtual, always connected

Figure 11.2: The generation game

good at – particularly related to caring and service. Expect the arrival of the universal wage, and with that perhaps a universal dwelling.

FROM THE HQ TO YOU

Evolving office designs to support new ways of working and new concepts for the corporate place

In the near future:

- **Free to roam:** Coming soon, expect the widespread adoption of agile working. Presenteeism and desk ownership will be dead.

- **Virtuality and reality:** Work will become almost completely digitised and we will communicate virtually most of the time. Face-to-face interaction will be highly valued, even precious.

- **Pride of place:** The future office must act as the catalyst for meaningful experiences, helping people develop a shared sense of culture, fostering the brand and encouraging serendipitous interaction.

And beyond:

- **Less is more:** Organisations will occupy less space, but it will be of higher quality and better used. With mobility comes choice and variety. Space standards will no longer exist. Instead, we will see the office as an extension of brand expression; not a place for process work, but a place for innovation. It will be a pleasure to go there.

- **The global corporate communities:** Expect the rise and rise of the mega-corporation. They will be at the centre of entirely new campus-style city districts employing huge numbers of people from all over the world. These places will provide constant learning, exemplary wellbeing, stimulating environments, and high levels of service, curated career paths and enviable benefits packages.

- **The free spirits:** For those not seduced by the new corporate lifestyle, there will be ultimate freedom as a sought-after, specialist supplier/consultant. They will fill the spaces that robots and large organisations cannot. They will be nimble, move faster than large organisations, and react more quickly to change. They will work in a smaller, more personalised way. Their career paths will be highly changeable, with four or five different careers over their lifetime. These individuals will look after themselves in terms of benefits and pensions, but they will be part of bigger networks of common practice, and join others to achieve economies of scale for purchasing and access to resources.

MAKING IT HAPPEN

Delivering the perfect environment to optimise creativity, innovation and productivity

In the near future:

- **Control your environment:** The future is wearable and controllable. Clothing will be programmed to the perfect temperature, and intelligent materials incorporating substances such as graphene will be applied to

walls to radiate heat and light. Building services, plant and boiler rooms will be a thing of the past.

- **Product lifecycle management:** Traditional construction will be replaced by modular assembly. The cost of materials should reduce as products become more reusable and recyclable. The principles of circular economy will be commonplace.

- **Just in time:** We will design and build in months rather than years. This presents a greater opportunity to test and learn how spaces work. It may make post-occupancy evaluations cheaper and more commonly accepted, which would allow this valuable insight to be fed back into the client organisation and architectural practice/education – something rarely done today.

And beyond:

- **The future architect:** Production drawings, specifications and cost models will all be completed by machines. The architect will take the role of directing the design process, interpreting and assessing scenarios produced by computer, or becoming the software designer.

- **Back to school:** There needs to be a substantial change in the architect's education, away from construction, production and aesthetics and towards psychology, sociology, product design, post-occupancy evaluation, software development and data science.

- **People, people, people:** People remain at the very centre of the future office and will be the focus of design as occupiers and clients.

GLOSSARY

This glossary is an update of the publication: Workplace Consulting Organisation (WCO), *The WCO Guide to: A Glossary of Workplace Terms (Occasional Paper OP2, v1.0)*, ed. N. Gillen, WCO, UK, January 2013. The WCO, established in 2009, is a professional body of workplace consultants aimed at: 'raising the profile of workplace consulting and improving the understanding of the value of workplace consulting within the property and design industry, client organisations and the research community'.

Activity-based working (ABW)
A term coined by Veldhoen, which describes the alignment of work activities with work settings or spaces. It can, but doesn't have to, imply desk sharing.

Activity-based work settings (also known as alternative work settings)
These are collaborative and individual work settings within which work takes place, e.g. a quiet room for concentrated work, or a soft-seating area for informal collaboration. Adapted from an idea by Robert Luchetti in 1983.

Agile working
Originally a North American concept, and now used more widely elsewhere, to describe how people work across a variety of spaces. Usually, it involves using **desk sharing** to allow a building to rapidly respond to organisational (headcount) change.

Agile methodology (Scrum)
Scrum is a project management model, usually found on software development projects. It adopts an iterative evidence-based approach to product development, as opposed to traditional sequential approaches. Team work is broken into a series of actions called sprints that are scheduled in less than 30 days each, while daily progress is tracked through 15-minute-long scrums (stand-up meetings).[1]

Alternative work strategies
A term used to describe three concepts: **remote working**, **non-dedicated space** or **desk sharing** in office buildings, and 'flexible working' arrangements.

Amenity space
This relates to spaces other than desking, e.g. coffee areas, meeting rooms, restaurants, conferencing, and social and sports facilities.

Ancillary space
A usable area provided to accommodate locally shared spaces, e.g. vending, printing and local meeting spaces.

BIM
Building information modelling (BIM) is a 3D model-based process for creating and managing information on a construction project during its life cycle. It brings together all the information about every component of a building and makes it accessible to engineering and construction professionals involved in the planning, design, construction and management process.[2]

Biophilic design
A design strategy that aims to create strong connections between people and the natural environment. It integrates natural elements, forms, materials and processes into architecture and interiors.[3]

Breakout space (also referred to as 'soft-seating area')
These are settings in open-plan areas that support social interaction and informal meetings for small groups.

Building supply
Workplace consultants may refer to the building supply as the total area, quality and quantity of space in a given building. Engineers may use the term to refer to the air flow provided by the building services or to the power distribution.

Bürolandschaft (office landscape)
An open-plan office typology developed by the Schnelle brothers, which broke up the rows of desks that had previously dominated office planning into smaller, more open sections using curved screens, potted plants and other space definers.

Centennials (also known as Generation Z)
This is the demographic born between 1995 and 2010, for whom the internet has always been a part of their lives.[4]

Circular economy model
Driving a shift from current extractive industrial models, this concept is a regenerative system that works to 'design out waste and pollution, promote the use of recyclable solutions and materials, and regenerate natural systems'.[5]

Core area
The area of a building containing lifts, stairs, common lobbies, plant and service areas, ducts, WCs and vertical structures.

Co-working
A concept first attributed to Brad Neuberg in 2005, co-working refers to a group of people working in a shared, communal and often membership-based working setting. The co-working movement has typically comprised freelancers, remote workers, those who travel frequently, independent contractors, and professionals working for start-ups and smaller enterprises. These spaces aim to promote creativity, innovation and collaboration, not just between colleagues, but also across member organisations.

Cradle to Cradle® design
Cradle to Cradle® is a biomimetic design approach which describes the safe and potentially infinite use of materials in cycles. It is inspired by nature's processes and follows the principles of circular economy.

Current capacity
Workplace consultants use this term to refer to the staff/desk population that may be accommodated in a building or on a site, within the constraints of the existing fit-out.

Desk sharing
This involves a team area where people share desks between them, e.g. 12 people sharing ten desks. The team may 'own' their area and always work from that area when in the building.

Digital twin
This refers to a virtual model - of physical assets, processes, systems or services - that enables the building to be monitored and analysed. This allows actions to be taken to prevent issues, to identify and implement improvements, and to support planning.[6]

Dynamic density
This is a measure of space efficiency used in a desk-sharing environment, where more than one individual is allocated to a single desk. The dynamic density of an area is calculated by dividing the total **net internal area** by the total headcount that use it. This figure will give a lower density per person than **static density**, i.e. less space per person.

Fit factor
This relates to the allowance of space in a **space budget** to take account of the fact that fitting into actual buildings inevitably means some inefficiencies in space use will occur.

This can be due to:

- natural obstructions (columns and awkward angles, etc.)
- floor sizes (if they do not fit the size of divisions/units precisely)
- the configuration and shape of floorplates, and
- the building's planning grid (office sizes may be dictated by window mullion locations).

Flexible working
This usually refers to a contractual arrangement where an individual will work an agreed minimum number of hours over a non-standard working week or month, e.g. a compressed week or four-day week, etc. The phrase is also used to express a workplace strategy that encompasses flexible hours, **desk sharing** and **mobility**.

Free address
This refers to the ability of a worker to choose any empty desk or workspace when in the office.

Gross internal area (GIA)
Floor area of building(s) measured to the internal face of external walls or atrium walls, including internal structure and core. The GIA includes the **core area**, **primary circulation** and **net internal area**. It excludes roof plant and any totally unlit areas.

Hot desking
A system in which people use an unassigned desk. Typically, hot desking is associated with either 100 per cent shared work environments, often seen in large consultancies, or a small number of unassigned desks within a department that are used by visitors dropping in. Also known in some organisations as **hotelling**, especially where a formal desk booking system is in place.

Home working
Initially referred to as 'teleworking' or 'telecommuting', generally this involves working from home at least one day a week in an IT-supported 'home office'. With the migration from desktops to laptops and the advent of wireless technology, the term is now associated with a much broader context of 'working from home' practices. It should be noted, however, that there are still regulations relating to a company's responsibilities for those who are contracted to work from home permanently.

Hotelling
This describes a **hot desking** environment or a 100 per cent shared work environment or building. It can also refer to the additional services that may be provided to support desk sharing, such as a formal desk booking system or a concierge.

Industry 4.0
Also known as the fourth industrial revolution, the Industry 4.0 concept originated in Germany over the last decade. It describes the increasing digital connectivity of clients, product, process, and factory through the use of emerging and disruptive technologies, such as mobile internet and 3D printing, the Internet of Things (IoT), cloud storage and automation, in manufacturing.

Integrated network systems (INS)
INS put all IT systems on one common data network and enable data from all building systems to be viewed at the same time.

Millennials (also known as Generation Y)
These are individuals born in the 1980s and 1990s.[7]

Mobile officing, mobility or move to mobility
These terms refer to unassigned workplaces in office buildings. They are often used in North America in place of **flexible working**.

Net internal area (NIA) (sometimes referred to as 'net lettable' by property agents/brokers in the UK)
This is the remaining internal floor area of a building after the **core area** and any structural elements, e.g. columns on the floorplate, have been subtracted.

Net usable area (NUA)
The usable area that remains after the **net internal area** and **primary circulation** have been subtracted.

GLOSSARY

New ways of working
A term developed by DEGW in the 1990s, this refers to aligning workspace to work activities. New ways of working challenges the assumption that people only work at a desk. Work is actually carried out across a number of spaces over the course of a day, and 'new ways of working' looks to understand work patterns and match the space provided to those activities.

Nomadic working or nomadism
This covers working in non-purpose-built office spaces or 'third places', such as hotels, cars, trains, home or planes. It is closest to the concept of 'work anywhere/anytime'.

Non-dedicated space
Space not owned by an individual.

Occupancy (also refer to 'utilisation')[8]
As there is no industry-standard terminology, caution is required when interpreting occupancy or utilisation study results. The Workplace Consulting Organisation (WCO) recommends that, for workplaces other than learning environments. The following definitions be applied:

Occupancy level
Usually refers to the average amount of time a building as a whole is occupied by staff, and provides one overall figure of building occupancy, averaging departments and time, etc. This figure is often calculated using swipe-card entry data, PC login data or observation studies.

Occupied
Measurement or observation of the time a person is present in the space, regardless of their activity.

Polycentric city
A city model where the spatial organisation of economic activities occurs in multiple centres.

Post-occupancy evaluation (POE)
This process evaluates buildings in a systematic and rigorous manner, after they have been built and occupied for some time. A POE provides feedback on how successful the workplace is in supporting the occupying organisation and individual end-user requirements. Industry advice is to wait at least three months after move-in before conducting a POE, to allow for an initial settle-in period.

Potential capacity
This is the population that could be accommodated in a building or on site.

Primary circulation
The area required to maintain routes for life safety, linking access and egress points, lifts and stairwells. Size and area occupied will be established with reference to local statutory codes of practice.

Procurement
In the context of a construction project, procurement is the process of allocating design and construction responsibility. Examples of procurement routes are the traditional contract, custom build, design and build, etc.

Quiet booths/pods/study rooms
Fixed, enclosed study rooms that provide spaces for either single occupancy, e.g. telephone use, or small groups of two or three people to work collaboratively. Acoustic privacy is important.

Remote working
This refers to people working from a location other than their primary office location.

RIBA Plan of Work
The RIBA Plan of Work organises the process of briefing, designing, constructing, maintaining, operating and using building projects into eight stages, detailing the tasks and outputs each stage requires. Stages include: Strategic Definition, Preparation and Brief, Concept Design, Developed Design, Technical Design, Construction, Handover and Close Out, and In Use.

Robot tax
This is the concept of a potential new tax to generate revenues from the use of robots in industry. This may be required where robots cause redundancies, resulting in increased unemployment and other social costs.

Satellite offices or locations
These sites tend to be around the outskirts of large cities, and are different from suburban branches, often because of the provision of flexible/non-assigned space.

Seat count
This is the total number of occupiable seats in the 'office area', including formal and informal workspaces. In contrast, the 'desk count' is the number of desks provided.

Serviced offices
A range of solutions, from use of non-occupied space in other companies' office buildings, to serviced office suites with shared meeting rooms and public spaces.

Sharing ratio
The ratio of desks to people being used for space-budgeting purposes (e.g. 100 desks for 120 people = 1.20 or 120 per cent or 10:12). This is often expressed in reverse, i.e. a ratio of 12 staff to 10 desks, or 83.3 per cent.

Society 5.0
Just as Industry 4.0 represents the transformation of manufacturing through the use of big data and emerging and disruptive digital technologies, Society 5.0 focuses on the tackling of social challenges, such as supporting

an ageing population or redesigning the communication channels between citizens and their governments, through the use of smart technologies and digitalisation across all levels of society. The concept emerged from the Japanese Government's 5th Science and Technology Basic Plan.

Soft-seating area (often referred to as 'breakout space')
These are settings in the open-plan areas to support social interaction and informal meetings for small groups.

Space budget
A tool (usually spreadsheet-based) used to calculate total space requirements, by summing up the space needed for all relevant space components, work settings, meeting spaces, circulation and **fit factor**, etc. A **space budget** will often include formulae to calculate the most appropriate proportion of support spaces. This can be used to model scenarios of space use.

Space demand/requirement
This relates to a numeric description of an organisation's total demand for space. The **space demand** is built up from summing the 'forecast' of individual workstations into workspace area and adding **ancillary space**, **amenity space** and **fit factor**.

Static density (also referred to as 'occupational density')
The static density of an area is calculated by dividing the total area by the total desks based in that area. This figure is based on 1:1 desk allocation. Building regulations are based on static densities.

Third places
These cover non-traditional work locations – excluding the office or home – and are part of the new mix of physical settings. Examples are libraries or coffee shops, but there is also a concept emerging for buildings designed specifically for mixed use.

Touchdown area
This covers a range of work settings supporting short, intermittent work, such as checking emails between meetings.

Utilisation[9] (also refer to 'occupancy')
As there is no industry-standard terminology, caution is required when interpreting occupancy or utilisation study results. 'The WCO recommends that for workplaces other than learning environments. The following definitions be applied:

Utilisation level
Usually refers to the average amount of time that different types of spaces or floors are in use, by different departments/grades. This figure is often calculated using a Time Utilisation Study (sometimes referred to as a 'space observation survey' or similar). Typically, it involves a trained observer following a set route and recording how spaces are being used over a period of time, usually recommended to be two weeks. The data can also be gathered via a sensor-based system. The data can generally be broken down by departments/space types/days/time, etc. The utilisation level gives a finer grain of data than an occupancy level, which typically refers to an entire building.

Utilised
Observation of when a person is present, or when there are signs of occupancy but no one is physically present.

Video-conference room
An enclosed, technology-enabled room to support collaborative work sessions and provide enhanced connectivity with remote groups.

Virtual office
The idea is that your office is wherever you access your technology.

Workspace area
This is the configuration of space and furniture within an 'office area' that enables a person to work. This includes secondary circulation.

Workstation
Area occupied by the individual office worker and accompanying furniture.

Foreword

1. The Telegraph, 'Smartphones and tablets add two hours to the working day', *The Daily Telegraph*, <https://www.telegraph.co.uk/technology/mobile-phones/9646349/Smartphones-and-tablets-add-two-hours-to-the-working-day.html>, 31 October 2012, (accessed 19 October 2018).

2. Dan Witters and Diana Liu, 'Using mobile technology for work linked to higher stress', *Gallup News*, <http://news.gallup.com/poll/168815/using-mobile-technology-work-linked-higher-stress.aspx>, 2 May 2014, (accessed 19 October 2018).

3. Christian Jarrett, 'Open-plan offices drive down face-to-face interactions and increase the use of email', *The British Psychological Society Research Digest*, <https://digest.bps.org.uk/2018/07/05/open-plan-offices-drive-down-face-to-face-interactions-and-increase-use-of-email/>, 5 July 2018, (accessed 19 October 2018).

4. Jo Carnegie, 'The rising epidemic of workplace loneliness and why we have no office friends', *The Telegraph*, <https://www.telegraph.co.uk/women/work/rising-epidemic-workplace-loneliness-have-no-office-friends/>, 18 June 2018, (accessed 19 October 2018).

Introduction

1. Barry P. Haynes, 'Office productivity: a shift from cost reduction to human contribution', *Facilities*, Vol. 25, issue 11/12, August 2007, pp. 452–462.

2. Aime Williams, 'WeWork becomes central London's biggest office occupier', *Financial Times*, <https://www.ft.com/content/40a87044-ff97-11e7-9650-9c0ad2d7c5b5>, 23 January 2018, (accessed 9 April 2018).

3. Department for Business, Energy & Industrial Strategy, '2016 UK greenhouse gas emissions', *UK Government*, <https://assets.publishing.service.gov.uk/government/uploads/system/uploads/attachment_data/file/679334/2016_Final_Emissions_Statistics_one_page_summary.pdf>, March 2018, (accessed 17 April 2018).

Chapter 1

1. Nick Robins, *The Corporation That Changed the World: How the East India Company Shaped the Modern Multinational*, Second edition, Pluto Press, London, 2012, p. 32.

2. Walter Thornbury, *Old and New London: Volume 2*, Cassell, Petter & Galpin, London, 1878, pp. 183–194. Thornbury's description relates to architect Theodore Jacobson's extensive redesign of the old Craven House, into which the company had moved in 1648. It was renamed East India House in 1661, with Jacobson's rebuild taking place between 1726 and 1729. Company surveyor Richard Jupp oversaw a major extension between 1796 and 1799. The East India Company remained there until the mid-19th century, vacating the building as part of its absorption into the British government. East India House was demolished in 1861. See William Foster, *The East India House: Its History and Associations*, John Lane, London, 1924, pp. 131–144.

3. Nick Robins, *The Corporation That Changed the World*, 2013, p. xii. Also Lucy Kellaway, 'How the office was invented', *BBC News*, <http://www.bbc.co.uk/news/magazine-23372401>, 22 July 2013,

(accessed 1 February 2018). And Amanda Ruggeri, 'The World's Most Powerful Corporation', *BBC News*, <http://www.bbc.com/capital/story/20160330-the-worlds-most-powerful-corporation>, 30 March 2016, (accessed 1 February 2018).

4. John Brewer, *The Pleasures of the Imagination: English Culture in the Eighteenth Century*, HarperCollins, London, 1997, p. 37.

5. John Brewer, *The Pleasures of the Imagination*, 1997, p. 38.

6. G.J. Marcus, *Heart of Oak: A Survey of British Sea Power in the Georgian Era*, Oxford University Press, London, 1975, p. 192.

7. This idea is explored in more detail in Toni Weller and David Bawden, 'The social and technological origins of the information society: an analysis of the crisis of control in England, 1830–1900', *Journal of Documentation*, Vol. 61, issue 6, 2005, pp. 777–802.

8. New Lanark Conservation Trust, *The Story of New Lanark*, Lanark, 1997. See also: Thomas A Markus, *Buildings and Power: Freedom and Control in the Origin of Modern Building Types*, Routledge, London, 1993, p. 288.

9. More about Cadbury's approach and legacy can be found in an overview from the Royal Institution of Chartered Surveyors (RICS), 'George Cadbury: leaving a quality of life legacy', <http://www.rics.org/uk/news/rics150/george-cadbury-leaving-a-quality-of-life-legacy/>, 13 May 2016, (accessed 1 March 2018).

10. Ebenezer Howard, *Garden Cities of To-morrow: (Second edition of 'To-morrow: A Peaceful Path to Real Reform')*, Swan Sonnenschein & Co, London, 1902.

11. Kenneth Frampton, *Modern Architecture: A Critical History*, Fourth edition, Thames & Hudson Ltd, USA, 2007.

12. Frederick Winslow Taylor, *The Principles of Scientific Management*, Harper & Brothers, New York, 1911.

13. For more about the distinction between Art Moderne and Art Deco (or lack thereof), see: Troy Segal, 'Art Deco vs. Art Moderne: the difference between two often confused styles', *The Spruce*, <https://www.thespruce.com/art-deco-vs-art-moderne-148869>, 30 December 2017, (accessed 1 March 2018).

14. Jonathan Lipman, *Frank Lloyd Wright and the Johnson Wax Buildings*, Dover Publications, New York, 2003, pp. 17–42.

15. Carl W. Condit, *The Chicago School of Architecture: A History of Commercial and Public Building in the Chicago Area, 1875–1925*, University of Chicago Press, London, 1973.

16. David Bennett and James R.Steinkamp, *Skyscrapers: Form & Function*, Simon & Schuster, New York, 1995.

17. Dirk Stichweh, *New York Skyscrapers*, Prestel Publishing, Munich, 2009.

18. Francis Duffy and Kenneth Powell, *The New Office*, Conran Octopus, London, 1997.

19. Francis Duffy, Andrew Laing, Vic Crisp and DEGW London Limited, *The Responsible Workplace: The Redesign of Work and Offices*, Butterworth Architecture in association with Estates Gazette, Oxford, 1993.

20. A good overview of this project is available here: Herman Hertzberger, 'The Future of the Building "Centraal Beheer"', <http://

www.hertzberger.nl/images/nieuws/TheFutureOfTheBuildingCentraalBeheer2016.pdf>, July 2016, (accessed 1 March 2016).

21. Herman Hertzberger, 'The Future of the Building "Centraal Beheer"', July 2016, pp. 7–8.

22. William Hollingsworth Whyte Jr., *The Organization Man*, Simon & Schuster, New York, 1956.

23. Andrew Shanahan, 'The office cubicle: from commercial flop to best-selling design classic', *Dezeen*, <https://www.dezeen.com/2015/02/01/office-cubicle-50th-birthday-herman-miller-robert-propst/>, 1 February 2015, (accessed 1 March 2018).

24. Nikil Saval, 'The cubicle you call Hell was designed to set you free', *Wired*, <https://www.wired.com/2014/04/how-offices-accidentally-became-hellish-cubicle-farms/>, 23 April 2014, (accessed on 1 March 2018).

25. Sarah Jacobs, 'A look inside The Boston Consulting Group's stunning New York office, which has an in-house café and workout rooms', *Business Insider*, <http://uk.businessinsider.com/inside-boston-consulting-group-office-2017-1/#the-underlying-idea-was-to-unlock-the-culture-which-was-always-there-people-join-bcg-because-they-like-the-people-and-the-one-thing-we-werent-able-to-do-in-the-old-office-was-give-expression-to-that-in-the-work-place-love-said-26>, 18 January 2017, (accessed 16 March 2018).

26. Hudson Yards New York, 'The Story', <http://www.hudsonyardsnewyork.com/about/the-story/>, 2018, (accessed 16 March 2018).

27. Enjoy-Work, 'Chiswick Park #Enjoy-Work', <https://enjoy-work.com/>, 2018, (accessed 1 March 2018).

Chapter 2

1. European Commission, *Communication from the Commission to the European Parliament, the Council, the European Economic and Social Committee and the Committee of the Regions, Roadmap to a Resource-Efficient Europe*, COM(2011) 571 final, European Commission, Brussels, 2011.

2. Ellen MacArthur Foundation, *Towards the Circular Economy: Economic and Business Rationale for an Accelerated Transition*, Ellen MacArthur Foundation, Cowes, UK, 2013.

3. Ellen MacArthur Foundation, *Towards the Circular Economy: Economic and Business Rationale for an Accelerated Transition*, 2013.

4. 'For many metals, this means that about three times as much material needs to be moved for the same quantity of metal extraction as a century ago.' 'The tendency to process lower grades of ore to meet increasing demand is leading to a higher energy requirement per kilogram of metals, and consequentially to increased production costs.' UNEP International Resource Panel, *Decoupling 2: Technologies, Opportunities and Policy Options*, UNEP, Nairobi, 2014, pp. 30–31.

5. 'The extraction and use of material resources is closely linked to negative impacts on aspects of the environment'. UNEP International Resource Panel, *Decoupling 2: Technologies, Opportunities and Policy Options*, 2013, p. 27.

6. Stewart Brand, *How Buildings Learn: What Happens After They're Built*, Phoenix, London, 1994, p. 12.

7. Stewart Brand, *How Buildings Learn: What Happens After They're Built*, 1994, p. 12.

REFERENCES

Chapter 3

1. For more on the role of architects in promoting innovation, see Professor Flora Samuel's latest work, *Why Architects Matter: Evidencing and Communicating the Value of Architects*, Routledge (Taylor & Francis Group), Abingdon, UK, 2018.

2. HM Government, 'Digital Built Britain: Level 3 building information modelling – strategic plan', <https://assets.publishing.service.gov.uk/government/uploads/system/uploads/attachment_data/file/410096/bis-15-155-digital-built-britain-level-3-strategy.pdf >, February 2015, (accessed 20 March 2018).

3. HM Government, 'Creating a Digital Built Britain: what you need to know', <https://www.gov.uk/guidance/creating-a-digital-built-britain-what-you-need-to-know>, 2 August 2017, (accessed 20 March 2018).

4. BSI, 'Introduction' in BSI's Guide to BIM Level 2, BSI, UK, 2016, pp. 1–14. Please note that BSI is currently in the process of updating its BIM Level 2 guidance. Updates are available at: <http://bim-level2.org/en/guidance/>.

5. BSI, Introduction' in BSI's Guide to BIM Level 2, 2016, pp. 1–14.

6. BSI, Introduction' in BSI's Guide to BIM Level 2, 2016, pp. 1–14.

7. HM Government, 'Construction 2025', <https://assets.publishing.service.gov.uk/government/uploads/system/uploads/attachment_data/file/210099/bis-13-955-construction-2025-industrial-strategy.pdf>, July 2013, (accessed 20 March 2018).

8. BSI, 'Introduction' in BSI's Guide to BIM Level 2, 2016, pp. 1–14.

9. BSI, 'Introduction' in BSI's Guide to BIM Level 2, 2016, pp. 1–14.

10. BSI, 'Introduction' in BSI's Guide to BIM Level 2, 2016, pp. 1–14.

11. BSI, Introduction' in BSI's Guide to BIM Level 2, 2016, pp. 1–14.

12. Microsoft and Royal Institute of British Architects (RIBA), *Digital Transformation in Architecture*, RIBA and Microsoft, UK, 2018, p 7.

Chapter 4

1. BBC News, 'BBC interview with Robert Kelly interrupted by children live on air', *BBC News*, <http://www.bbc.com/news/av/world-39232538/bbc-interview-with-robert-kelly-interrupted-by-children-live-on-air>, 10 March 2017, (accessed 17 April 2018).

2. Dennis Finn and Anne Donovan, *PwC's NextGen: A Global Generational Study – Evolving Talent Strategy to Match the New Workforce Reality (Summary and Compendium of Findings)*, PwC, USA, 2013, p. 8.

3. Carter Jonas Research Team, *London Office Market Trends Q1 2018*, Carter Jonas Publications, UK, 16 April 2018, p. 2.

4. Camille Roth, Soong Moon Kang, Michael Batty and Marc Barthélemy, 'Structure of urban movements: polycentric activity and entangled hierarchical flows', *PLoS ONE*, Vol. 6, issue 1 (e15923), 7 January 2011.

5. Chris Ham and Anna Brown, 'The future is now: the innovations of today that point to better health care tomorrow', The Kings Fund, UK, 2015.

6. Carl Baker, *NHS Staff from Overseas: Statistics (Briefing Paper, number 7783)*, House of Commons Library, UK, 7 February 2018, p. 5.

7. Richard Susskind and Daniel Susskind, *The Future of The Professions: How Technology Will Transform the Work of Human Experts*, Oxford University Press, Oxford, 2015.

8. Michael Pooler, 'Amazon robots bring a brave new world to the warehouse', *Financial Times*, <https://www.ft.com/content/916b93fc-8716-11e7-8bb1-5ba57d47eff7>, 24 August 2017, (accessed 19 June 2018).

9. Christopher Calisi and Justin Stout, 'Stop noise from ruining your open office', *Harvard Business Review*, <https://hbr.org/2015/03/stop-noise-from-ruining-your-open-office>, 16 March 2015, (accessed 19 June 2018).

10. Charlie Fink, 'The trillion dollar 3D telepresence gold mine', *Forbes*, <https://www.forbes.com/sites/charliefink/2017/11/20/the-trillion-dollar-3d-telepresence-gold-mine/#7fa4362a2a72>, 20 November 2017, (accessed 19 June 2018).

11. Tim Bradshaw, 'Smart speaker surge set to peak in 2019: CES organisers', *Financial Times*, <https://www.ft.com/content/7579b8d6-f43f-11e7-88f7-5465a6ce1a00>, 8 January 2018, (accessed 19 June 2018).

12. Nilofer Merchant, 'Got a meeting? Take a walk', *TED*, <https://www.ted.com/talks/nilofer_merchant_got_a_meeting_take_a_walk>, February 2013, (accessed 19 June 2018).

13. Marily Oppezzo and Daniel L. Schwartz, 'Give your ideas some legs: the positive effect of walking on creative thinking', *Journal of Experimental Psychology: Learning, Memory and Cognition*, Vol. 40, issue 4, pp. 1142–1152.

14. Cabinet Office and BSI, PAS3000:2015 Smart Working – Code of Practice, BSI, UK, 30 November 2015.

Chapter 5

1. John Michael Zelenski, Steven A. Murphy and David A. Jenkins, 'Productive worker thesis revisited', *Journal of Happiness Studies*, Vol. 9, 2008, pp. 521–537.

2. Isabel Rothe, Lars Adolph, Beate Beermann, Martin Schütte, Armin Windel, Anne Grewer, Uwe Lenhardt, Jorg Michel, Birgit Thomson and Maren Formazin, 'Psychische Gesundheit in der Arbeitswelt – Wissenschaftliche Standortbestimmung', *Bundesanstalt für Arbeitsschutz und Arbeitsmedizin (BAuA)*, Dortmund, Germany, 2017.

3. Rachel Dodge, Annette P. Daly, Jan Huyton and Lalage D. Sanders, 'The challenge of defining wellbeing', *International Journal of Wellbeing*, Vol. 2, issue 3, 2012, pp. 222–235.

4. AECOM, Key Predictors of Wellbeing and Performance in the Workplace (working title) – study in progress.

5. AECOM, Key Predictors of Wellbeing and Performance in the Workplace.

6. AECOM, Key Predictors of Wellbeing and Performance in the Workplace.

7. AECOM, Key Predictors of Wellbeing and Performance in the Workplace.

8. AECOM, Key Predictors of Wellbeing and Performance in the Workplace.

9. AECOM, Key Predictors of Wellbeing and Performance in the Workplace.

10. This was a live drawing created during the presentation of the initial findings of AECOM's study on key predictors of wellbeing in March 2016.

11. AECOM, 'Health and wellbeing: the next frontier for the built environment', *edie.net*, <https://www.edie.net/blog/Health-and-wellbeing-the-next-frontier-for-the-built-environment/6098400>, 8 November 2017, (accessed 26 April 2018).

12. AECOM, Key Predictors of Wellbeing and Performance in the Workplace.

13. AECOM, Key Predictors of Wellbeing and Performance in the Workplace.

14. Natalie Slessor, 'Leesman ranks Lendlease headquarters in top six percent of high performing workplaces', *Lendlease*, <https://www.lendlease.com/articles/2017/06/07/00/38/20170607-leesman-index-high-performing-workplace/>, 7 June 2017, (accessed 4 April 2018).

15. Leonard L. Berry, Ann M. Mirabito and William B. Baun, 'What's the hard return on employee wellness programs?', *Harvard Business Review*, Vol. 88, issue 12, December 2010, pp. 104–112, <https://hbr.org/2010/12/whats-the-hard-return-on-employee-wellness-programs>.

Chapter 6

1. For example, the WELL Building Standard™ was launched in 2014 (with WELLv2™ piloted in 2018); Fitwel® was launched over 2016/17; and RESET™ launched v2.0 of its Air Standard (replacing a pre-release version) early in 2018. An exception is the BREEAM accreditation scheme, which has included health and wellbeing credits since at least 2008 (and had a section on 'impacts on human beings' prior to that). On the other hand, the US-based LEED scheme, at the time of writing (second quarter of 2018), does not identify health and wellbeing as a specific topic, although it does have sections on thermal comfort, acoustic performance, lighting, views and indoor air quality.

2. Jacqueline C. Vischer, 'Towards an environmental psychology of workspace: how people are affected by environments for work', *Architectural Science Review*, Vol. 51, issue 2, 2008, pp. 97–108.

3. Marlon Nieuwenhuis, Craig Knight, Tom Postmes and S. Alexander Haslam, 'The relative benefits of green versus lean office space: three field experiments', *Journal of Experimental Psychology: Applied*, Vol. 20, issue 3, July 2014, pp. 1–16.

4. RIBA, RIBA Plan of Work 2013, <https://www.ribaplanofwork.com/PlanOfWork.aspx#>, 2013, (accessed 3 April 2018).

5. Ramidus and AECOM, 'Office Occupancy: Density and Utilisation', *BCO*, <http://www.bco.org.uk/Research/Publications/Office_Occupancy_Density_and_Utilisation.aspx>, 2018, (accessed 23 March 2018).

6. Ramidus and AECOM, 'Office Occupancy: Density and Utilisation', *BCO*, <http://www.bco.org.uk/Research/Publications/Office_Occupancy_Density_and_Utilisation.aspx>, 2018, (accessed 23 March 2018).

7. Wolfgang F.E. Preiser, 'Towards a performance-based conceptual framework for systematic POEs' in

Building Evaluation, ed. W.F.E. Preiser, Plenum Press, New York, 1989, pp. 1–7.

8. Bill Bordass, Robert Cohen, Mark Stavenden and Adrian Leaman, 'Assessing building performance in use 3: energy performance of the Probe buildings', *Building Research & Information*, Vol. 29, issue 2, 2001, pp. 114–128.

9. CIBSE, 'PROBE – post occupancy studies', <https://www.cibse.org/knowledge/building-services-case-studies/probe-post-occupancy-studies>, 1995–2002, (accessed 20 March 2018).

10. Carbon Trust, 'Low carbon buildings', <https://www.carbontrust.com/resources/guides/energy-efficiency/low-carbon-buildings-design-and-construction/>, 2018, (accessed 20 March 2018).

11. Technology Strategy Board, 'Building performance evaluation: competition for funding, May 2010–2012', <http://webarchive.nationalarchives.gov.uk/20130102183826/http://www.innovateuk.org/_assets/live%20from%20proofing%20300311/tsb_buildingperformanceevaluationcomp%20t11_024_final.pdf>, 2011, (accessed 4 July 2018).

12. For more on the importance of research-led, ethical architects in promoting wellbeing, sustainability and innovation, see Professor Flora Samuel's latest work, *Why Architects Matter: Evidencing and Communicating the Value of Architects*, Routledge (Taylor & Francis Group), Abingdon, UK, 2018.

13. Barry P. Haynes, 'Office productivity: a shift from cost reduction to human contribution', *Facilities*, Vol. 25, issue 11/12, 2007, pp. 452–462.

14. Herschone Mahone Group, 'Daylighting and productivity – CEC PIER', *Herschone Mahone Group*, <http://h-m-g.com/projects/daylighting/summaries%20on%20daylighting.htm>, 2003, (accessed 20 March 2018).

15. Kerstin Sailer, Ros Pomeroy and Rosie Haslem, 'Data-driven design – using data on human behaviour and spatial configuration to inform better workplace design', *Corporate Real Estate Journal*, Vol. 4, issue 3, 2015, pp. 249–262.

16. RIBA and Rowena Hay, Simon Bradbury, Dylan Dixon, Kat Martindale, Professor Flora Samuel and Alex Tait, *Pathways to POE, Value of Architects*, University of Reading, RIBA, March 2017, <https://www.architecture.com/-/media/gathercontent/post-occupancy-evaluation/additional-documents/buildingknowledgepathwaystopoepdf.pdf>.

17. Evidence-Based Design (EBD), 'The knowledge problem: As architects and designers, what do we know about people?', *EBD Journal*, <http://ebdjournal.com/blog/general-design/the-knowledge-problem>, 2014, (accessed 20 February 2018).

18. Peter Buchanan, 'The big rethink part 9: rethinking architectural education', *The Architectural Review*, <https://www.architectural-review.com/rethink/campaigns/the-big-rethink/the-big-rethink-part-9-rethinking-architectural-education/8636035.article>, 28 September 2012, (accessed 20 March 2018).

19. Andy Pearson, 'Building by the book – UEL's award-winning Stratford Library', *CIBSE Journal*, <https://www.cibsejournal.com/general/building-by-the-book/>, October 2015, (accessed 20 March 2018).

20. CIBSE, 'PROBE – post occupancy studies', <https://www.cibse.org/knowledge/building-services-case-studies/probe-post-occupancy-studies>, 1995–2002, (accessed 20 March 2018).

21. Michelle Agha-Hossein, 'Soft Landings Framework 2018: Six Phases for Better Buildings' (BSRIA BG 54/2018), BSRIA, UK, 2018, p. 3.

22. Barry P. Haynes, 'Office productivity: a shift from cost reduction to human contribution', *Facilities*, Vol. 25, issue 11/12, 2007, pp. 452–462.

23. Simon Carter and Hilary Jeffery, 'National Grid: how workplace design has boosted productivity', *Personnel Today*, <https://www.personneltoday.com/hr/national-grid-workplace-design-boosted-productivity/>, 29 September 2015, (accessed 20 March 2018).

24. Simon Carter and Hilary Jeffery, 'National Grid: how workplace design has boosted productivity', 29 September 2015.

25. Simon Carter and Hilary Jeffery, 'National Grid: how workplace design has boosted productivity', 29 September 2015.

Chapter 7

1. John P. Kotter, *A Sense of Urgency*, Harvard Business School Press, Boston, 2008.

2. Booz & Company, 'Why culture matters and how it makes change stick', *strategy&*, <www.strategyand.pwc.com/reports/cultures-and-change-infographic>, November 2013, (accessed 16 March 2018).

3. Jennifer A. LaClair and Ravi P. Rao, 'Helping employees embrace change', *McKinsey Quarterly*, <www.mckinsey.com/business-functions/organization/our-insights/helping-employees-embrace-change>, November 2002, (accessed 16 March 2018).

4. Center for Creative Leadership, '3 key skills for successful change', <https://www.ccl.org/articles/leading-effectively-articles/3-key-competencies-for-successful-change/>, 2016, (accessed 16 March 2018).

5. Center for Creative Leadership, '3 key skills for successful change', 2016.

6. Center for Creative Leadership, '3 key skills for successful change', 2016.

7. Esther Cameron and Mike Green, *Making Sense of Change Management: A Complete Guide to the Models, Tools and Techniques of Organizational Change*, Fourth edition, Kogan Page, Philadelphia, 2015, pp. 150–152.

8. Mary Beth A. O'Neill, *Executive Coaching with Backbone and Heart: A Systems Approach to Engaging Leaders with Their Challenges*, John Wiley & Sons, San Francisco, 2007, Chapter 4.

9. Esther Cameron and Mike Green, *Making Sense of Change Management: A Complete Guide to the Models, Tools and Techniques of Organizational Change*, Fourth edition, 2015.

Chapter 8

1. United Nations, 'Background on the UNFCCC: the international response to climate change', United Nations Framework Convention on Climate Change, <http://unfccc.int/essential_background/items/6031.php>, 2014, (accessed 1 March 2018).

2. Department for Business, Energy & Industrial Strategy, '2016 UK greenhouse gas emissions', UK Government, <https://assets.publishing.service.gov.uk/government/uploads/system/uploads/attachment_data/file/679334/2016_Final_Emissions_Statistics_one_page_summary.pdf >, March 2018, (accessed 17 April 2018) and Department for Business, Energy & Industrial Strategy, 'Annual Statement of Emissions', UK Government, <https://assets.publishing.service.gov.uk/government/uploads/system/uploads/attachment_data/file/694859/Annual_Statement_of_Emmisions_for_2016.pdf> , March 2018, (accessed 17 April 2018).

3. Department for Business, Energy & Industrial Strategy, '2016 UK greenhouse gas emissions', March 2018.

4. European Commission, 'Buildings', <https://ec.europa.eu/energy/en/topics/energy-efficiency/buildings>, 2018, (accessed 1 March 2018).

5. European Commission, 'Buildings', 2018.

6. European Commission, 'Buildings', 2018.

7. European Commission, 'Buildings', 2018.

8. European Commission, 'Buildings', 2018.

9. European Commission, 'Buildings', 2018.

10. European Commission, 'Buildings', 2018.

11. European Commission, 'Buildings', 2018.

12. Matt McGrath, 'Paris climate pullout: the worst is yet to come', *BBC News*, <https://www.bbc.com/news/science-environment-44330709>, 1 June 2018, (accessed : 28 June 2018).

13. The University of Manchester, 'Graphene', <http://www.graphene.manchester.ac.uk/explore/what-can-graphene-do/>, 2018, (accessed 10 March 2018).

Chapter 9

1. Martin Kellett and Nicola Gillen, 'Cost model: office fit-out', *Building*, <https://www.building.co.uk/cost-models/cost-model-office-fit-out/5090488.article>, 8 November 2017, (accessed 23 March 2018).

2. WeWork Team, 'WeWork 2016 Year in Review', <https://www.wework.com/blog/posts/wework-2016-year-in-review>, 19 December 2016, (accessed 23 March, 2018). See also Aime Williams, 'WeWork becomes central London's biggest office occupier', *Financial Times*, <https://www.ft.com/content/40a87044-ff97-11e7-9650-9c0ad2d7c5b5>, 23 January 2018, (accessed 9 April 2018).

Chapter 10

1. Philipp Gerbert, Santiago Castagnino, Christoph Rothballer, Andreas Renz and Rainer Filitz, *Digital in Engineering and Construction: The Transformative Power of Building Information Modeling*, The Boston Consulting Group, USA, March 2016.

2. Institution of Civil Engineers, 'Digital transformation', <https://www.ice.org.uk/knowledge-and-resources/digital-engineering-and-the-built-environment>, 2018, (accessed 20 June 2018).

3. Denise Chevin, 'BIM Level 2 uptake still slow, but AR and automation up', *BIM+*, <http://www.bimplus.co.uk/news/bim-level-2-uptake-still-slow-ar-and-automation/>, 4 April 2018, (accessed 20 June 2018).

4. RIBA, RIBA Plan of Work 2013, <https://www.ribaplanofwork.com/PlanOfWork.aspx#>, 2013, (accessed 3 April 2018).

5. Philipp Gerbert, Santiago Castagnino, Christoph Rothballer, Andreas Renz and Rainer Filitz, *Digital in*

REFERENCES

Engineering and Construction: The Transformative Power of Building Information Modeling, The Boston Consulting Group, USA, March 2016.

6. Microsoft and Royal Institute of British Architects (RIBA), *Digital Transformation in Architecture*, RIBA and Microsoft, UK, 2018, p. 8.

7. Jane Duncan, 'Time to take a lead', *RIBA Journal*, <https://www.ribaj.com/culture/time-to-take-a-lead>, 25 Februrary 2016, (accessed 20 June 2018).

8. Microsoft and Royal Institute of British Architects (RIBA), *Digital Transformation in Architecture*, RIBA and Microsoft, UK, 2018, pp. 22–26.

9. Tom Cheshire, 'BIM's "Google Docs for buildings" is transforming architecture – but could it kill creativity?', *WIRED*, <http://www.wired.co.uk/article/architecture-software-creativity>, 10 January 2017, (accessed 20 June 2018).

10. For more on this, see Professor Flora Samuel, *Why Architects Matter: Evidencing and Communicating the Value of Architects*, Routledge (Taylor & Francis Group), Abingdon, UK, 2018.

Chapter 11

1. Killian Fox and Joanne O'Connor, 'Five ways work will change in the future', *The Guardian*, <https://www.theguardian.com/society/2015/nov/29/five-ways-work-will-change-future-of-workplace-ai-cloud-retirement-remote>, 29 November 2015, (accessed 12 April 2017).

2. Bridget Hardy, Richard Graham, Paul Stansall, Alison White, Andrew Harrison, Adryan Bell and Les Hutton, *Working Beyond Walls: The Government Workplace as an Agent of Change*, DEGW/Office of Government Commerce, UK, 2008.

3. Amy Gibbs, 'Creative, authentic, mobile: the characteristics of Generation Z', *Digital Pulse*, <https://www.digitalpulse.pwc.com.au/creative-authentic-mobile-gen-z/>, 24 July 2017, (accessed 12 April 2017).

Glossary

1. Ken. W. Collier, *Agile Analytics: A Value-Driven Approach to Business Intelligence and Data Warehousing*, Pearson Education, Inc., USA, 2011.

2. Microsoft and Royal Institute of British Architects (RIBA), *Digital Transformation in Architecture*, RIBA and Microsoft, UK, 2018.

3. Stephen R. Kellert, Judith Heerwagen and Martin Mador, *Biophilic Design: The Theory, Science and Practice of Bringing Buildings to Life*, John Wiley & Sons, Inc., Hoboken, New Jersey, 2008.

4. Amy Gibbs, 'Creative, authentic, mobile: the characteristics of Generation Z', *Digital Pulse*, <https://www.digitalpulse.pwc.com.au/creative-authentic-mobile-gen-z/>, 24 July 2017, (accessed 12 April 2017).

5. Ellen MacArthur Foundation, 'Circular Economy Overview', <https://www.ellenmacarthurfoundation.org/circular-economy/overview/concept>, 2017, (accessed 24 May 2018).

6. Bernard Marr, 'What is digital twin technology – and why is it so important?', *Forbes*, <https://www.forbes.com/sites/bernardmarr/2017/03/06/what-is-digital-twin-technology-and-why-is-it-so-important/#62e842eb2e2a>, 6 March 2017, (accessed 24 May 2018).

7. Merriam-Webster, 'Millennial', <https://www.merriam-webster.com/dictionary/millennial>, 2018, (accessed 26 April 2018).

8. WCO, *The WCO Guide To: A Glossary of Workplace Terms (Occasional Paper OP2, v1.0)*, ed. N. Gillen, WCO, UK, January 2013.

9. WCO, *The WCO Guide To: A Glossary of Workplace Terms (Occasional Paper OP2, v1.0)*, ed. N. Gillen, WCO, UK, January 2013.

REFERENCES

All websites accessed between February and July 2018.

Introduction

Department for Business, Energy & Industrial Strategy, '2016 UK greenhouse gas emissions', UK Government, <https://assets.publishing.service.gov.uk/government/uploads/system/uploads/attachment_data/file/679334/2016_Final_Emissions_Statistics_one_page_summary.pdf>, March 2018.

Haynes, B.P., 'Office productivity: a shift from cost reduction to human contribution', *Facilities*, Vol. 25, issue 11/12, August 2007.

Williams, A., 'WeWork becomes central London's biggest office occupier', *Financial Times*, <https://www.ft.com/content/40a87044-ff97-11e7-9650-9c0ad2d7c5b5>, 23 January 2018.

Chapter 1

Bennett, D. and Steinkamp, J.R., *Skyscrapers: Form & Function*, Simon & Schuster, New York, 1995.

Brewer, J., *The Pleasures of the Imagination: English Culture in the Eighteenth Century*, HarperCollins, London, 1997.

Condit, C.W., *The Chicago School of Architecture: A History of Commercial and Public Building in the Chicago Area, 1875–1925*, University of Chicago Press, London, 1973.

Duffy, F. and Powell, K., *The New Office*, Conran Octopus, London, 1997.

Duffy, F., Laing, A., Crisp, V. and DEGW London Limited, *The Responsible Workplace: The Redesign of Work and Offices*, Butterworth Architecture in association with Estates Gazette, Oxford, 1993.

Enjoy-Work, 'Chiswick Park #Enjoy-Work', <https://enjoy-work.com/>, 2018.

Foster, W., *The East India House: Its History and Associations*, John Lane, London, 1924.

Frampton, K., *Modern Architecture: A Critical History*, Fourth edition, Thames & Hudson Ltd, USA, 2007.

Hertzberger, H., 'The Future of the Building "Centraal Beheer"', <http://www.hertzberger.nl/images/nieuws/TheFutureOfTheBuildingCentraalBeheer2016.pdf>, July 2016.

Howard, E., *Garden Cities of To-morrow (Second edition of 'To-morrow: A Peaceful Path to Real Reform')*, Swan Sonnenschein & Co., London, 1902.

Hudson Yards New York, 'The Story', <http://www.hudsonyardsnewyork.com/about/the-story/>, 2018.

Jacobs, S., 'A look inside The Boston Consulting Group's stunning New York office, which has an in-house café and workout rooms', *Business Insider*, <http://uk.businessinsider.com/inside-boston-consulting-group-office-2017-1/#the-underlying-idea-was-to-unlock-the-culture-which-was-always-there-people-join-bcg-because-they-like-the-people-and-the-one-thing-we-werent-able-to-do-in-the-old-office-was-give-expression-to-that-in-the-work-place-love-said-26>, 18 January 2017.

Kellaway, L., 'How the office was invented', *BBC News*, <http://www.bbc.co.uk/news/magazine-23372401>, 22 July 2013.

Lipman, J., *Frank Lloyd Wright and the Johnson Wax Buildings*, Dover Publications, New York, 2003.

Marcus, G.J., *Heart of Oak: A Survey of British Sea Power in the Georgian Era*, Oxford University Press, London, 1975.

Markus, T.A., *Buildings and Power: Freedom and Control in the Origin of Modern Building Types*, Routledge, London, 1993.

New Lanark Conservation Trust, *The Story of New Lanark*, Lanark, 1997.

Robins, N., *The Corporation That Changed the World: How the East India Company Shaped the Modern Multinational, Second edition*, Pluto Press, London, 2012.

Royal Institution of Chartered Surveyors (RICS), 'George Cadbury: Leaving a quality of life legacy', RICS, <http://www.rics.org/uk/news/rics150/george-cadbury-leaving-a-quality-of-life-legacy/>, 13 May 2016.

Ruggeri, A., 'The world's most powerful corporation', *BBC News*, <http://www.bbc.com/capital/story/20160330-the-worlds-most-powerful-corporation>, 30 March 2016.

Saval, N., 'The cubicle you call Hell was designed to set you free', *Wired*, <https://www.wired.com/2014/04/how-offices-accidentally-became-hellish-cubicle-farms/>, 23 April 2014.

Segal, T., 'Art Deco vs. Art Moderne: the difference between two often confused styles', *The Spruce*, <https://www.thespruce.com/art-deco-vs-art-moderne-148869>, 30 December 2017.

Shanahan, A., 'The office cubicle: from commercial flop to best-selling design classic', *Dezeen*, <https://www.dezeen.com/2015/02/01/office-cubicle-50th-birthday-herman-miller-robert-propst/>, 1 February 2015.

Stichweh, D., *New York Skyscrapers*, Prestel Publishing, Munich, 2009.

Taylor, F.W., *The Principles of Scientific Management*, Harper & Brothers, New York, 1911.

Thornbury, W., *Old and New London: Volume 2*, Cassell, Petter & Galpin, London, 1878.

Weller T. and Bawden D., 'The social and technological origins of the information society: an analysis of the crisis of control in England, 1830–1900', *Journal of Documentation*, Vol. 61, issue 6, 2005, pp. 777–802.

Whyte Jr., W.H., *The Organization Man*, Simon & Schuster, New York, 1956.

Chapter 2

Brand, S., *How Buildings Learn: What Happens After They're Built*, Phoenix, London, 1994.

European Commission, *Communication from the Commission to the European Parliament, the Council, the European Economic and Social Committee and the Committee of the Regions, Roadmap to a Resource-Efficient Europe, COM(2011) 571 final*, European Commission, Brussels, 2011.

Ellen MacArthur Foundation, *Towards the Circular Economy: Economic and Business Rationale for an Accelerated Transition*, Ellen MacArthur Foundation, Cowes, UK, 2013.

UNEP International Resource Panel, *Decoupling 2: Technologies, Opportunities and Policy Options*, UNEP, Nairobi, 2014, pp. 30–31.

Chapter 3

BSI, 'Introduction' in *BSI's Guide to BIM Level 2*, BSI, UK, 2016.

HM Government, 'Construction 2025', <https://assets.publishing.service.gov.uk/government/uploads/system/uploads/attachment_data/file/210099/bis-13-955-construction-2025-industrial-strategy.pdf>, July 2013.

HM Government, 'Creating a Digital Built Britain: what you need to know', <https://www.gov.uk/guidance/creating-a-digital-built-britain-what-you-need-to-know>, 2 August 2017.

HM Government, 'Digital Built Britain: Level 3 building information modelling – strategic plan', HM Government, <https://assets.publishing.service.gov.uk/government/uploads/system/uploads/attachment_data/file/410096/bis-15-155-digital-built-britain-level-3-strategy.pdf>, February 2015.

Microsoft and Royal Institute of British Architects (RIBA), *Digital Transformation in Architecture*, RIBA and Microsoft, UK, 2018.

Samuel, F., *Why Architects Matter: Evidencing and Communicating the Value of Architects*, Routledge (Taylor & Francis Group), Abingdon, UK, 2018.

Chapter 4

Baker, C., *NHS Staff from Overseas: Statistics (Briefing Paper, number 7783)*, House of Commons Library, UK, 7 February 2018.

BBC News, 'BBC interview with Robert Kelly interrupted by children live on air', *BBC News*, <http://www.bbc.com/news/av/world-39232538/bbc-interview-with-robert-kelly-interrupted-by-children-live-on-air>, 10 March 2017.

Bradshaw, T., 'Smart speaker surge set to peak in 2019: CES organisers', *Financial Times*, <https://www.ft.com/content/7579b8d6-f43f-11e7-88f7-5465a6ce1a00>, 8 January 2018.

Cabinet Office and BSI, *PAS3000:2015 Smart Working – Code of Practice*, BSI, UK, 30 November 2015.

Calisi, C. and Stout, J., 'Stop noise from ruining your open office', *Harvard Business Review*, <https://hbr.org/2015/03/stop-noise-from-ruining-your-open-office>, 16 March 2015.

Carter Jonas Research Team, *London Office Market Trends Q1 2018*, Carter Jonas Publications, UK, 16 April 2018, p. 2.

Fink, C., 'The trillion dollar 3D telepresence gold mine', *Forbes*, <https://www.forbes.com/sites/charliefink/2017/11/20/the-trillion-dollar-3d-telepresence-gold-mine/#7fa4362a2a72>, 20 November 2017.

Finn, D. and Donovan, A., *PwC's NextGen: A Global Generational Study – Evolving Talent Strategy to Match the New Workforce Reality (Summary and Compendium of Findings)*, PwC, USA, 2013.

Ham, C. and Brown, A., 'The future is now: the innovations of today that point to better health care tomorrow', The Kings Fund, UK, 2015.

Merchant, N., 'Got a meeting? Take a walk', TED, <https://www.ted.com/talks/nilofer_merchant_got_a_meeting_take_a_walk>, February 2013.

Oppezzo, M. and Schwartz, D.L., 'Give your ideas some legs: the positive effect of walking on creative thinking', *Journal of Experimental Psychology: Learning, Memory and Cognition*, Vol. 40, issue 4, pp. 1142–1152.

Pooler, M., 'Amazon robots bring a brave new world to the warehouse', *Financial Times*, <https://www.ft.com/content/916b93fc-8716-11e7-8bb1-5ba57d47eff7>, 24 August 2017.

BIBLIOGRAPHY

Roth, C., Kang, S.M., Batty, M. and Barthélemy, M., 'Structure of urban movements: polycentric activity and entangled hierarchical flows', *PLoS ONE*, Vol. 6, issue 1 (e15923), 7 January 2011.

Susskind, R. and Susskind, D., *The Future of the Professions: How Technology Will Transform the Work of Human Experts*, Oxford University Press, Oxford, 2015.

Chapter 5

AECOM, 'Health and wellbeing: the next frontier for the built environment', edie.net, <https://www.edie.net/blog/Health-and-wellbeing-the-next-frontier-for-the-built-environment/6098400>, 8 November 2017.

AECOM, *Key Predictors of Wellbeing and Performance in the Workplace* (working title) – study in progress.

Berry, L.L., Mirabito, A.M. and Baun, W.B., 'What's the hard return on employee wellness programs?', *Harvard Business Review*, Vol. 88, issue 12, December 2010, pp. 104–112., <https://hbr.org/2010/12/whats-the-hard-return-on-employee-wellness-programs>.

Dodge, R., Daly, A.P., Huyton, J. and Sanders, L.D., 'The challenge of defining wellbeing', *International Journal of Wellbeing*, Vol. 2, issue 3, 2012, pp. 222–235.

Rothe, I., Adolph, L., Beermann, B., Schütte, M., Windel, A., Grewer, A., Lenhardt, U., Michel, J., Thompson, A. and Formazin, M., 'Psychische Gesundheit in der Arbeitswelt – Wissenschaftliche Standortbestimmung', *Bundesanstalt für Arbeitsschutz und Arbeitsmedizin (BAuA)*, Dortmund, Germany, 2017.

Slessor, N., 'Leesman ranks Lendlease headquarters in top six per cent of high performing workplaces', *Lendlease*, <https://www.lendlease.com/articles/2017/06/07/00/38/20170607-leesman-index-high-performing-workplace/>, 7 June 2017.

Zelenski, J.M., Murphy S.A. and Jenkins, D.A., 'Productive worker thesis revisited, *Journal of Happiness Studies*, Vol. 9, 2008, pp. 521–537.

Chapter 6

Agha-Hossein, M., 'Soft Landings Framework 2018: Six Phases for Better Buildings' (BSRIA BG 54/2018), BSRIA, UK, 2018

Bordass, B., Cohen, R., Stavenden, M. and Leaman, A., 'Assessing building performance in use 3: energy performance of the Probe buildings', *Building Research & Information*, Vol. 29, issue 2, 2001, pp. 114–128.

Buchanan, P., 'The big rethink part 9: rethinking architectural education', *The Architectural Review*, <https://www.architectural-review.com/rethink/campaigns/the-big-rethink/the-big-rethink-part-9-rethinking-architectural-education/8636035.article>, 28 September 2012.

Carbon Trust, 'Low carbon buildings', <https://www.carbontrust.com/resources/guides/energy-efficiency/low-carbon-buildings-design-and-construction/>, 2018.

Carter, S. and Jeffery, H., 'National Grid: how workplace design has boosted productivity', *Personnel Today*, <https://www.personneltoday.com/hr/national-grid-workplace-design-boosted-productivity/>, 29 September 2015.

CIBSE, 'PROBE – post occupancy studies', <https://www.cibse.org/knowledge/building-services-case-studies/probe-post-occupancy-studies>, 1995–2002.

Evidence-Based Design (EBD), 'The knowledge problem. As architects and designers what do we know about people?', *EBD Journal*, <http://ebdjournal.com/blog/general-design/the-knowledge-problem>, 2014.

Haynes, B.P., 'Office productivity: a shift from cost reduction to human contribution', *Facilities*, Vol. 25, issue 11/12, 2007, pp. 452–462.

Herschone Mahone Group, 'Daylighting and Productivity – CEC PIER', Herschone Mahone Group, <http://h-m-g.com/projects/daylighting/summaries%20on%20daylighting.htm>, 2003.

Nieuwenhuis M., Knight, C., Postmes, T. and Haslam, S.A., 'The relative benefits of green versus lean office space: three field experiments', *Journal of Experimental Psychology: Applied*, Vol. 20, issue 3, July 2014, pp. 1–16.

Pearson, A., 'Building by the book – UEL's award-winning Stratford Library', *CIBSE Journal*, <https://www.cibsejournal.com/general/building-by-the-book/>, October 2015.

Preiser, W.F.E., 'Towards a performance-based conceptual framework for systematic POEs' in *Building Evaluation*, ed. W.F.E. Preiser, Plenum Press, New York, 1989, pp. 1–7.

Ramidus and AECOM, 'Office occupancy: density and utilisation', BCO, <http://www.bco.org.uk/Research/Publications/Office_Occupancy_Density_and_Utilisation.aspx>, 2018.

RIBA, 'RIBA Plan of Work 2013', <https://www.ribaplanofwork.com/PlanOfWork.aspx#>, 2018.

RIBA and Hay, R., Bradbury, S., Dixon, D., Martindale, K., Samuel F. and Tait, A., 'Pathways to POE, value of architects', University of Reading, RIBA, March 2017, <https://www.architecture.com/-/media/gathercontent/post-occupancy-evaluation/additional-documents/buildingknowledgepathwaystopoepdf.pdf>.

Sailer K., Pomeroy, R. and Haslem, R., 'Data-driven design – using data on human behaviour and spatial configuration to inform better workplace design', *Corporate Real Estate Journal*, Vol. 4, issue 3, 2015, pp. 249–262.

Samuel, F., *Why Architects Matter: Evidencing and Communicating the Value of Architects*, Routledge (Taylor & Francis Group), Abingdon, UK, 2018.

Technology Strategy Board, 'Building performance evaluation: competition for funding, May 2010–2012', <http://webarchive.nationalarchives.gov.uk/20130102183826/http://www.innovateuk.org/_assets/live%20from%20proofing%20300311/tsb_buildingperformanceevaluationcomp%20t11_024_final.pdf>, 2011.

Vischer, J.C., 'Towards an environmental psychology of workspace: how people are affected by environments for work', *Architectural Science Review*, Vol. 51, issue 2, 2008, pp. 97–108.

Usable Buildings Trust, Way, M. and Bunn, R., *The Soft Landings Framework for Better Briefing, Design, Handover and Building Performance-In-Use (BSRIA BG 54/2014)*, BSRIA and Usable Buildings Trust, UK, 2014.

Chapter 7

Booz & Company, 'Why culture matters and how it makes change stick', strategy&, <www.strategyand.pwc.com/reports/cultures-and-change-infographic>, November 2013.

Cameron, E. and Green, M., *Making Sense of Change Management: A Complete Guide to the Models, Tools and Techniques of Organizational Change, Fourth edition*, Kogan Page, Philadelphia, 2015.

Center for Creative Leadership, '3 key skills for successful change', <https://www.ccl.org/articles/leading-effectively-articles/3-key-competencies-for-successful-change/>, 2016.

Kotter, J.P., *A Sense of Urgency*, Harvard Business School Press, Boston, 2008.

LaClair, J.A. and Rao, R.P., 'Helping employees embrace change', *McKinsey Quarterly*, <www.mckinsey.com/business-functions/organization/our-insights/helping-employees-embrace-change>, November 2002.

O'Neill, M.B.A., *Executive Coaching with Backbone and Heart: A Systems Approach to Engaging Leaders with Their Challenges*, John Wiley & Sons, San Francisco, 2007.

Chapter 8

Department for Business, Energy & Industrial Strategy, '2016 UK greenhouse gas emissions', UK Government, <https://assets.publishing.service.gov.uk/government/uploads/system/uploads/attachment_data/file/679334/2016_Final_Emissions_Statistics_one_page_summary.pdf>, March 2018.

Department for Business, Energy & Industrial Strategy, 'Annual Statement of Emissions', UK Government, <https://assets.publishing.service.gov.uk/government/uploads/system/uploads/attachment_data/file/694859/Annual_Statement_of_Emmisions_for_2016.pdf>, March 2018.

European Commission, 'Buildings', <https://ec.europa.eu/energy/en/topics/energy-efficiency/buildings>, 2018.

McGrath, M., 'Paris climate pullout: the worst is yet to come', *BBC News*, <https://www.bbc.com/news/science-environment-44330709>, 1 June 2018.

The University of Manchester, 'Graphene', <http://www.graphene.manchester.ac.uk/explore/what-can-graphene-do/>, 2018.

United Nations, 'Background on the UNFCCC: the international response to climate change', United Nations Framework Convention on Climate Change, <http://unfccc.int/essential_background/items/6031.php>, 2014.

Chapter 9

Kellett, M. and Gillen, N., 'Cost model: office fit-out', *Building*, <https://www.building.co.uk/cost-models/cost-model-office-fit-out/5090488.article>, 8 November 2017.

WeWork Team, 'WeWork 2016 Year in Review', <https://www.wework.com/blog/posts/wework-2016-year-in-review>, 19 December 2016.

Williams, A., 'WeWork becomes central London's biggest office occupier', Financial Times, <https://www.ft.com/content/40a87044-ff97-11e7-9650-9c0ad2d7c5b5>, 23 January 2018.

Chapter 10

Cheshire, T., 'BIM's "Google Docs for buildings" is transforming architecture – but could it kill creativity?', *Wired*, <http://www.wired.co.uk/article/architecture-software-creativity>, 10 January 2017.

Chevin, D., 'BIM Level 2 uptake still slow, but AR and Automation up', *BIM+*, <http://www.bimplus.co.uk/news/bim-level-2-uptake-still-slow-ar-and-automation/>, 4 April 2018.

Duncan, J., 'Time to take a lead', *RIBA Journal*, <https://www.ribaj.com/culture/time-to-take-a-lead>, UK, 25 Februrary 2016.

Gerbert, P., Castagnino, S., Rothballer, C., Renz, A. and Filitz, R., *Digital in Engineering and Construction: The Transformative Power of Building Information Modeling*, The Boston Consulting Group, USA, March 2016.

Institution of Civil Engineers, 'Digital transformation', <https://www.ice.org.uk/knowledge-and-resources/digital-engineering-and-the-built-environment>, 2018.

Microsoft and Royal Institute of British Architects (RIBA), *Digital Transformation in Architecture*, RIBA and Microsoft, UK, 2018.

RIBA, 'RIBA Plan of Work 2013', <https://www.ribaplanofwork.com/PlanOfWork.aspx#>, 2018.

Samuel, F., *Why Architects Matter: Evidencing and Communicating the Value of Architects*, Routledge (Taylor & Francis Group), Abingdon, UK, 2018.

Chapter 11

Fox, K. and O'Connor, J., 'Five ways work will change in the future', *The Guardian*, https://www.theguardian.com/society/2015/nov/29/five-ways-work-will-change-future-of-workplace-ai-cloud-retirement-remote>, 29 November 2015.

Gibbs, A., 'Creative, authentic, mobile: the characteristics of Generation Z', *Digital Plus*, https://www.digitalpulse.pwc.com.au/creative-authentic-mobile-gen-z/, 24 July 2017.

Hardy, B., Graham, R., Stansall, P., White, A., Harrison, A., Bell, A. and Hutton, L., 'Working beyond walls: the government workplace as an agent of change', DEGW/Office of Government Commerce, UK, 2008.

Glossary

Collier, K.W., *Agile Analytics: A Value-Driven Approach to Business Intelligence and Data Warehousing*, Pearson Education, Inc., USA, 2011.

Ellen MacArthur Foundation, 'Circular Economy Overview', <https://www.ellenmacarthurfoundation.org/circular-economy/overview/concept>, 2017.

Gibbs, A., 'Creative, authentic, mobile: the characteristics of Generation Z', *Digital Plus*, https://www.digitalpulse.pwc.com.au/creative-authentic-mobile-gen-z/, 24 July 2017.

Kellert, S.R., Heerwagen, J. and Mador, M., *Biophilic Design: The Theory, Science and Practice of Bringing Buildings to Life*, John Wiley & Sons, Inc., Hoboken, New Jersey, 2008.

Marr, B., 'What is digital twin technology – and why is it so important?', *Forbes*, <https://www.forbes.com/sites/bernardmarr/2017/03/06/what-is-digital-twin-technology-and-why-is-it-so-important/#62e842eb2e2a>, 6 March 2017.

Merriam-Webster, 'Millennial', <https://www.merriam-webster.com/dictionary/millennial>, 2018.

Microsoft and Royal Institute of British Architects (RIBA), *Digital Transformation in Architecture*, RIBA and Microsoft, UK, 2018.

Workplace Consulting Organisation (WCO), *The WCO Guide To: A Glossary of Workplace Terms (Occasional Paper OP2, v1.0)*, ed. N. Gillen, WCO, UK, January 2013.

BIBLIOGRAPHY

Page numbers in *italic* indicate figures.

INDEX

INDEX

187

Adobe Stock Photography: 10.1

AECOM: Part I opener, Part II opener, 1.8, 1.14, 3.1, 4.1, 4.3, 4.6, 4.7, 4.8, 5.1, 5.2, 5.4, 6.1, 6.2, 8.9, 8.10, 9.1, 10.2, 10.3, 10.4, 10.5, 11.1, 11.2

AECOM / Accenture: 3.3, 3.4, 3.5, 10.0

AECOM / Hufton + Crow: Part III opener

AHMM / Derwent London: 2.5

Anthony Collins Photography: 1.11, 1.12, 11.0

Architectural Press Archive / RIBA Collections: 1.0, 1.2, 1.9

Ascendas-Singbridge: Acknows iv, 1.15

Brannan: 7.0, 7.1

Charly Boyer: 4.2

Dave Cheshire / AECOM: 2.1, 2.2

Dave Parker Photography: 2.6

Delta Development Group: 2.9

Dirk Lindner: 8.0, 8.13

DIRTT: 2.10, 2.11

Doug Shaw: 5.3

Estée Lauder Companies: 7.2

Grigoriou Interiors: 2.3

Hufton + Crow: 4.0, 4.4, 4.5, 5.11, 6.0, 6.7, 8.1, 8.2, 8.3

James Jones photography: 9.0, 10.6, 10.7

Janet Hall / RIBA Collections: 1.10

Leesman: 6.4, 6.5, 6.6

Lendlease: 5.0, 5.5, 5.6, 5.7, 5.8

Lendlease / HASSELL: 5.10

Lendlease / Rogers Stirk Harbour + Partners: 5.9

Matt Chisnall: 2.0, 2.4

Ocubis: 5.13, 5.14

Peter Bennetts: 5.12

Ralph Deakin / RIBA Collections: 1.6

RIBA Collections: 1.1, 1.3, 1.4, 1.5, 1.7

Ronald Tilleman Photography: 3.0, 3.2

Sharon Risedorph: 8.4, 8.5, 8.6, 8.7, 8.8

Timothy Soar: 2.7, 2.8, 6.3

Uniqlo: Intro viii, 1.13

Werner Huthmacher: 1.17, 1.18

WeWork: Part IV opener, 1.16

WWF: 8.11, 8.12

IMAGE CREDITS